D1367037

Copyright©1992, by John C. Harrington

Published by John Wiley & Sons, Inc.

Library of Congress Cataloging-in-Publication Data

Harrington, John C., 1945–
    Investing with your conscience : how to achieve high returns using
    socially responsible investing / by John C. Harrington.
        p.   cm.
    Includes index.
    ISBN 0-471-55072-8 (cloth)
    1. Investments—Moral and ethical aspects.   I. Title.
HG4528.H37   1992
332.6—dc20   91–48005

Printed in the United States of America
10 9 8 7 6 5 4 3 2 1
Printed and bound by Courier Companies, Inc.

ACKNOWLEDGMENTS

In late 1987 Jane Cutler of the Linda Allen Agency in San Francisco read about my work, called me, and asked me to write a book about my 20-year career in the responsible investing community. It took me over a year to get my act together and meet with Linda Allen to seriously consider writing this book. Thanks, Jane—for "kick-starting" me. I am also very grateful to Linda for patiently bearing with me as I put a book proposal together in July 1990. Next, a big thank-you to John Lowry for his literary skills in helping me write the book proposal and introduction for Linda to carry to the publishing world.

How can I not thank Peter Wiley for referring me not only to John Wiley and Sons (who else?), but for his constructive criticism of the first book proposal and outline. Within John Wiley and Sons I must thank my editor, Wendy Grau, for her assistance, good humor, enthusiasm, youth, and Eastern wit. Without her I would surely have taken myself much too seriously.

My development editor, Mary Humboldt, is without equal. Thirteen years ago Mary served as an intern for the California State Senate Select Committee on Investment Priorities and Objectives, helping me draft investment studies and write corporate responsibility legislation. Her ability to edit my well-intentioned rhetoric into readable English has been a godsend, and her progressive, enlightened view of the world has been an inspiration. Thank you, Mary.

My colleagues and friends in the responsible investment movement deserve more credit than I can ever give them for their patience, guidance, and leadership in a world crying out for it. My clients, those named and unnamed in the book, deserve a great deal of credit for the respect and trust they've given me in our professional relationship as well as in my role as an author.

All of the help given me by my office staff of Dodi Bueno, Susan Bogar, Madelon Martinovich, Jane Dunlap, and Gatian Cunningham was terrific. Thank you, Dodi, for wading through volumes of paper!

A special thanks also goes to Jessica Tuteur, a University of California intern, Napa born and raised, whose abilities and resourcefulness far exceed her age.

Last, and certainly not least, I thank my wife, Diana, my daughters, Brenna and Brianna, my mother-in-law, Louise Hook, and my mother, Jean Harrington, for their support and patience with grumpy Dad throughout the summer and fall of 1991.

CONTENTS

INTRODUCTION: THE MYTH AND POWER OF MONEY

There is nothing in the world so powerful as an idea whose time has come, and the idea of responsible investing has come of age. In the aftermath of Earth Day 1990, American corporations are competing over who is more "environmentally correct." Large brokerage firms now offer "green" and "socially responsible" investment products, and there is even the First Environmental Bank. In recent years, large mutual funds and investment organizations have been built on this theme, to the point where they are now significant players in the investment field, managing over $625 billion in assets. At long last, "doing good" is no longer automatically seen as diametrically opposed to "doing well."

Socially responsible investing has been doing well. Calvert Social Investment Funds, with over a billion dollars in assets, represents over 55 percent of socially screened mutual fund assets. Both its stock and bond portfolios have consistently earned higher returns than a portfolio consisting of stock indexes such as the S&P 500 by an average annual return ranging from 2 to 11 percent since their inception. Other major social funds and professional portfolio managers such as Pax World, Parnassus, U.S. Trust, the Eco-Logical Trust, and Dreyfus Third Century continue to outperform the indexes as well as nonsocial funds as of this writing.

Responsible investing is building a better grade of economics. Instead of an economy that produces toxic wastes, junk food, junk products, and junk bonds and that squanders the wealth of our resources for the benefit of corporate management and to the detriment of stakeholders, responsible investing works to build a safe and sane world. It promotes the production of real goods, of environmentally sustainable manufacturing and agriculture, and of institutions more structurally responsible to the real needs of the world.

If the 1980s was the decade of greed, it was also a decade in which socially responsible investing grew by leaps and bounds, thanks primarily to the issue of apartheid in South Africa and the resulting divestiture movement. For investors the decade of the 1990s is shaping up to be one to save the world's environment. Already mutual funds and portfolio managers are offering clients environmental screening. Large institutional pension funds are being asked to vote affirmatively on resolutions to require corporate management to adopt comprehensive environmental codes of conduct to guide their worldwide corporate activities.

It's never too late to change the world. Money is the tool, and responsible investing is the strategy.

This book will give you the knowledge, resources, and tools to manage your money responsibly to not only increase your net worth, but to make the world a better place to live. It will explore responsible investing in the United States and its short history, as well as identify key players that have helped define it over the last 25 years. It will discuss the experience of some people who have used their investments to make an imprint on society. It will also talk about the debate inside the responsible investment community and find out where this social and economic "movement" is going.

In this book there will be a discussion of building a portfolio and selecting a responsible investment professional. It will also discuss setting social goals and evaluate socially and environmentally responsible mutual funds available.

The last chapter in the book will discuss how the South African investment issue has already lost its popularity to the "issue of the 90s"—the global environment. This book will also reveal the findings of a survey of national environmental organizations and outline environmental criteria now being developed by investment professionals. Other investment and social issues will be reviewed, including corporate governance, women, family issues, and economic development. A socially responsible investment strategy for the future will be outlined.

Before we begin, it is important to understand the political, economic, and social ramifications of the uses of money and investment dollars. Socially responsible investing (SRI) is much more than a successful investment strategy—it is, in every sense, a movement. SRI can and will change the world, and there are many compelling reasons behind its philosophy. Let's look at our government, our representatives on Wall Street and in the boardrooms, and our own past behavior.

Government is becoming less a force for positive social change and more a negative intrusion—usually socially harmful and regressive, not progressive. By the same token, government services will in no way keep pace with demand, and taxes levied by politicians to support declining services are extremely regressive. From California to New York, taxes raised include liquor, tobacco, sales, license, fuel, transportation, and other user taxes. This all hurts working people who have been pushed out of the cities because of high housing costs, forcing them to commute and thereby bear a disproportionately higher share of the increased taxes. The working poor are getting poorer, but so are the middle class. Politicians are still not believed, political parties are becoming even more irrelevant, and the public sector is on the decline. Increasingly, the public will have to rely on the private sector to promote social change and economic and social justice.

The expertise of Wall Street is used not to create new and innovative investment vehicles to ensure that every segment of American society has access to capital, but to "spin money from money" in the secondary market through the misuse of options, indexes, and futures. For example, many pension funds rushed into leveraged buyouts, and now many of the investments are in serious financial trouble. The very investment banking firms that sold high-yield junk bonds to pension funds, insurance companies, and savings and loans to keep poorly managed and highly leveraged companies afloat are now reorganizing the debt of the same companies so that they can get out of bankruptcy. The investment bankers are being paid enormous fees to save the very firms that paid them handsomely to get into trouble in the first place.

The old rules governing investment for the benefit of others are written by bankers and insurance company executives, who remain the primary trustees of pooled money. They collaborate with their favorite (and financed) legislators for the purpose of solidifying their power and raising their notions of finance to the level of law. Many of them are well intentioned. They believe that risk can be calculated without the exercise of subjective human judgment. However, investing is human and it is subjective. The careful husbanding of all our resources is the complex process that results in the creation of wealth. What careful husbanding means in day-to-day practice depends on specific objectives and is always the product of subjective human judgment. Synthesizing all those varied purposes and strategies into the single goal of making the most money possible makes financial managers' jobs easier, but it also causes them to lose sight of the details that generate real value.

Money managers are more comfortable with their mathematical models than with the details of real value. Their lives are made easier when they follow established investment dogma; thinking about what would really be to the advantage of the beneficiaries and society is much more difficult. These managers have convinced the general public that they alone, without interference, hold the key to financial and economic success. Instead, investment bankers and Wall Street should be concentrating on putting together investment opportunities that create jobs, economic opportunity, housing, and innovative health care programs.

This being said, what influence will the public have, if not through its investing dollars in the private sector?

For middle-aged children of the 1960s, the unique "triple squeeze" is on. We've got to plan for retirement, help with elderly parents, and set aside enough money for our children's education. We have not planned for the future. Our savings rate is too low and our consumer debt is too high. This puts us in a financial bind and limits our options. The sad fact is that money and investing are mysterious stuff to most people. It's only paper and ink, yet it holds the power to make us sad or happy, to provide or deny the things that make for a successful life, to make us feel like somebody or nobody. In America, and increasingly in the rest of the world, it measures our worth as human beings. Whether we like it or not, money rules our lives and defines us, our future, and our children's future.

Money is only a symbol of value—not the real thing. This fact that money is just an abstract symbol of value and wealth makes talking about money very difficult. Most of us sense when we are being dealt with honestly and fairly, and when we are being hoodwinked. Yet we do not often complain when we sense financial trouble because we do not have the time or stamina to navigate the murky terrain of obtuse economic argument. Even though our future is at stake, we give up trying to comprehend how "they" say money works and submit to conventional wisdom, even as we resent it. This invites those "experts" to consolidate their power and serve their own career and financial interests rather than their true fiduciary responsibility. We may have overthrown the king, but we continue to pay homage to lords of the land.

But times are changing; we are waking up to the realities we face. Values of the American family are changing, giving rise to issues of single parents, child care, health care, and parental leave, all of which face the corporation and eventually corporate shareholders. Traditional health and safety advocates are challenging pension funds and other investors to sell off tobacco stocks. Environmental groups are confronting corporate management, demanding that companies nominate environmentalists to their boards of directors and provide annual environmental audits and policy statements. If the environment does become the major issue of the nineties, then women, family, health and safety issues, and other issues of social and economic justice will not be far behind.

As the traditional economy struggles with environmental concerns, with decreasing need for defense expenditures, and with a growing need for improved competitiveness and wider distribution of economic benefits, a new economy is rising to answer those concerns—an economy created by socially responsible investing. It isn't that the principles of sound and profitable investing are new or different; in the complexity of things today, the old rules of investing simply no longer represent reality or principles.

As the "junk bond" era fades from the scene and we see that deregulation has turned the market into a jungle, socially responsible investments have begun to outperform traditional investments. Because they are based on real goods and true value and because they harken to mutual benefit as the true meaning of profit (rather than the prevailing interpretation of profit as simply one-sided "gain" or "advantage"), socially responsible investing now represents the best hope for applying our intelligence and good judgment to the task of building a sane and prosperous future.

Today socially responsible investing has developed ways to identify firms that improve the general prosperity and those that detract from it. We can identify managers who understand that the value of the dollar begins with the will to benefit society and depends on honest dealing in the market. We know that firms whose mission is to foster economic development through environmentally sustainable manufacturing and agriculture, or through the construction of affordable housing, are more likely to be profitable in the long run, as they are doing things that are truly useful and rebound to the general benefit of society. Indeed, when stodgy institutional investors have been forced to broaden their selection formula to include social criteria, as was the case when South African divestment was mandated, financial performance improved, as it forced those money managers to become more diversified and innovative.

Money represents authority. The recipient of an investment of money gets permission to engage in an economic activity. The giver of the investment money expects value in return. The investment would not be made if it did not seem sound, if the giver did not believe that the activity would produce recognized value for the intended market and return even more money. But few of us feel prepared to make those kinds of judgments. Most of us are keenly aware of our fallibility, and we leave "money matters" to the "specialists" and "experts." We don't need to do this. We can take charge of our own financial lives, set our social and economic goals, and manage our assets in a socially responsible manner. If we retain "experts" we can learn to evaluate, choose, and supervise them. Money and investing is mysterious because we've made it so.

Many wage earners and people of inherited wealth would prefer to do some good for the world with their money, but are advised by their brokers and financial managers that this is not wise, as it would "dissipate capital" and everyone would be poorer. They assuage their clients' social concerns by saying that if the monetary return from investment is maximized, even more money will then be available for "worthy causes." The financiers, however, are focused on the abstractions of the bottom line, and have lost sight of the details of real life situations that generate value. If they invest in a company that pollutes, and if a portion of the profit goes to an environmental group cleaning it up, the job will never get done.

True reform will not occur until more people wake up from the hypnotic trance imposed by the way we handle money. If there is the possibility of hope in this cynical time, it lies within ourselves. Through personal responsibility, careful shopping, and responsible investing to promote a thought-out set of values, we can truly change the world.

PART I

The History
and Major Players

CHAPTER ONE

What Is Socially Responsible Investing?

Socially responsible investing is truly a unique American invention. It is only now gaining momentum in Europe. It is fundamentally a process; an art, not a science; a positive approach to linking your money constructively to life, to society, to the environment, and to the world. Responsible investing is based on the recognition that all investing has a social, economic, and often a political impact. You cannot escape the interdependence between your money and what goes on in your community and your world from day to day.

Responsible investing has evolved from the mere avoidance of socially harmful corporate activities, such as the production of cigarettes and weapons, to the pursuing of positive economic and social goals, such as the creation of low-income housing, support for economic development, and the provision of affordable health care. This form of responsible investing is sometimes defined as "targeted investing" since it tries to specifically target investment capital to areas of the economy that are in the greatest need.

The importance of social responsibility in investing is far from self-evident. In fact, many deny that "social responsibility" has any role in investing. Milton Friedman, one of the world's best known economists has said, "Maximization of profits is the corporate purpose, and infusion of social objects will destroy the free enterprise system."[1] Friedman adds, "A corporate executive's responsibility is to make as much money for the stockholders as possible, as long as he operates within the rules of the game. When an executive decides to take action for reasons of social responsibility, he is taking money from someone else—from the stockholders, in the form of lower dividends; from the employees, in the form of lower wages; or the customer, in the form of higher prices."[2]

Friedman softens this otherwise rigid stand when he writes that the corporate goal of maximum profits must be conditioned by ethical and legal considerations.[3] Friedman's position has been supported by many commentators addressing specific investment controversies.

When the investment community was debating whether or not retirement funds should be divested from companies operating within South Africa's hated system of apartheid, some pension administrators accused the divestment advocates of acting as "social engineers." In the critic's view "social investing" is really irresponsible investing—at best a form of charity, or simply a way to lose other people's money. Many argue that instead of investing in a socially responsible manner, investors should seek to maximize their profits and then, in the words of one critic, "If they desire, each such investor should make contributions and gifts from their gains to aid causes that they . . . consider socially responsible."[4]

This argument is deeply flawed. It ignores the fact that the investment decision in itself may have created or contributed to the social problem in the first place. Suppose that I am an environmentalist. Should I invest in and provide capital for a company that is expanding its production of CFCs, which destroy the stratospheric ozone layer that protects the earth from harmful ultraviolet rays, and then turn around and give the money I earn from my investments to the Natural Resources Defense Council (NRDC)? This would make no sense! I'd be donating money to clean up a problem I helped create by providing the capital to produce the harmful substance.

Examples like this one abound. If I were an American steel worker, I certainly wouldn't want my pension fund investing in the Japanese steel industry, a competitor whose success could ultimately cost me my job and my pension. Should the pension fund of the American Medical Association invest in Philip Morris, whose cigarettes cause a major health problem?[5] Such an action would defy logic!

Sometimes the connections between our investments and their social consequences are complicated. Take one real-life example. In 1984 Chicago steelworkers discovered that steel beams being used to construct a new state building in their city were imported from South Africa. Around the same time, U.S. Steel's Southworks plant in Chicago, which makes the same kind of steel beams, was laying off steelworkers by the thousands. Upon further investigation, the steelworkers found that Continental Illinois Bank was lending money to South Africa's ISCOR, which made the beams for the new state building. Steelworkers with their savings in Continental Illinois began questioning why they were putting their hard-earned money in a bank that was helping the South African government eliminate their jobs.[6]

The concept of socially responsible investing means that all of us have a duty to recognize how our investments affect society in general and our communities specifically. No longer can investors ignore the realities of the worldwide flow of capital and its effects on our society. If we blind ourselves to these truths, our own jobs, our own families, and our own futures may be the next to suffer.

Corporations do have a responsibility to society. Until this century, new businesses needed permission to operate by legislative incorporation or by royal charter. Many states' original incorporation laws required business enterprises to conduct business with stated obligations to society. Now businesses are allowed to incorporate with little, if any, formal state review other than minimal filing requirements.

Many corporations now recognize their social responsibilities. Some spend vast amounts of corporate funds on charitable giving, economic development, community service, and public relations. Businesses have formalized their political role by creating political action committees (PACs), which donate millions of dollars to state, federal, and local government lobbying efforts, pay for junkets for elected officials, finance candidates for both partisan and non-partisan races, and try to influence votes on referendums and other measures. Corporations join forces to pursue their political, economic, and social agendas, forming organizations such as the American Chamber of Commerce and the California Manufacturers Association. Make no mistake about it—corporations are very political, and they know how to play hardball. If individual investors today are scrutinizing the social impact of their investment decisions, they are not "politicizing" an otherwise neutral economic process; they are simply making their voices heard in an arena where corporate clout has always been important.

Investing responsibly is no longer a chore. Opportunities abound for the investor—from safe money market funds, community banks, and mutual funds to investing in higher-risk loan funds and social venture funds. Responsible investing in America has been defined in its short 25 year history by its products, but even more by its participants. Responsible investing is humanistic and powerful.

The Early Years

The birthplace of socially responsible investing was the American church. In the 1800s many churches found investing in alcohol and tobacco morally repugnant and prohibited church funds from being invested in such businesses. As early as 1928, the Boston-based Pioneer Fund screened out investments in companies whose primary activities involved liquor, tobacco, and gambling.

In the early 1960s the National Committee on Tithing in Investments, comprising many leading churchmen, proposed that churches and foundations invest 10 percent of their investment assets in integrated and open housing. Although it received a great deal of publicity, this idea made little headway. Churches didn't raise social investment issues again until 1966, when students from Union Theological Seminary in New York petitioned New York banks not to renew South African loans.[7]

American churches became more active in the issue of responsible investing during the sixties. In 1966 a coalition of black activists calling their organization FIGHT (Freedom-Integration-God-Honor-Today) began pressuring Eastman Kodak to provide 600 jobs to minorities in Rochester, New York. A confrontation ensued when the company reneged on a pledge, and FIGHT took it to the 1967 shareholders' meeting.

The United Church of Christ, the Unitarian-Universalists, and the Methodists attended the Eastman Kodak shareholders' meeting, along with the Teachers Investment Annuity Association/College Retirement Fund (TIAA/CREF). The churches' outspoken concern and the accompanying publicity made a big difference. Eventually the Rochester minority community won several hundred additional jobs and a job training program.

In 1967 the General Synod of the United Church of Christ adopted resolutions linking the churches' financial management to social concerns. In 1968 the General Assembly of the United Presbyterian Church mandated all of the boards under its jurisdiction to set aside 30 percent of its unrestricted funds for "higher-risk, lower-return" community investments.[8]

In 1968 New York stockbroker Bob Schwartz began working with investors wishing to avoid investing their money in companies and banks operating in South Africa and in companies that supported America's war effort in Vietnam. Dow Chemical Company's production of napalm and Honeywell's manufacture of antipersonnel weapons were being criticized more and more by the public, following the release of the Council on Economic Priorities' (CEP) report detailing the war and weapons business of over one hundred U.S. companies.

In 1969 and 1970 Clergy and Laity Concerned (CALC) and the Medical Committee for Human Rights were organized to introduce corporate shareholder resolutions in an effort to halt the production of these weapons. CALC demonstrations were held at Honeywell's 1969 and 1970 shareholder meetings, and the city of Ann Arbor, Michigan adopted a resolution banning the purchase of all Honeywell products. Honeywell was selected as a target because, in the words of the CALC National Steering Committee, "We believe that Honeywell, Inc. symbolizes the heinousness of the entire Southeast Asia affair because it produces 70 percent of all antipersonnel weapons used in the war."[9]

People began to figure out that, just as war could not be waged without tax dollars, the weapons of war could not be produced without investment dollars. The small investor learned what the large institutional investor had known all along: Money is power. Thousands of small investors banding together with a cause could significantly reduce the flow of investment capital into corporations producing the death machinery of the Vietnam War. People felt that they made a political and moral statement by removing their money from war-related corporations.

Mutual Funds

In 1968 Luther Tyson was in charge of the economics department of the Board of Church and Society of the United Methodist Church in Washington, D.C. He received a letter from a United Methodist Church member in Ohio who wanted to know if he could recommend a mutual fund where she could invest some money without investing in the military. He made inquiries with the Quakers, the Brethren, and the Mennonites and discovered that the lack of a military-free investment vehicle was a frequent topic of conversation within the religious community.

The seed had been sown. Pax World Fund was registered in 1970 and opened to public investors in 1971. Thanks to Luther Tyson, Jack Corbett, and Anthony and Paul Brown, funds were raised to capitalize the management company of Pax World. Luther and Jack were the officials of the United Methodist Church's Board of Church and Society who were responsible for drafting the social criteria. Luther Tyson recalled, "We wanted to develop positive criteria around the question of life-supporting goods and services while avoiding what detracts from life, such as military expenditures and pollution."

On the heels of the creation of Pax World came the Dreyfus Third Century Fund. It was founded by Howard Stein, who was a backer of Senator Eugene McCarthy in his bid for the Democratic Party's presidential nomination in 1968. Third Century's social criterion was not to avoid certain companies per se, but to invest in companies that

"contributed to the enhancement of the quality of life in America."
Dreyfus considered a company's record in the areas of protection and
improvement of the environment and the proper use of natural resources; occupational health and safety; consumer protection and product purity; and equal employment opportunity.

Campaign GM

It wasn't until 1970 that a full-fledged SRI movement got off the
ground. The Project on Corporate Responsibility, founded by four
attorneys and endorsed by consumer activist Ralph Nader introduced
two shareholder issues at General Motors Corporation and thereby
launched Campaign GM. The shareholder resolutions called for management to expand the board of directors to include women, blacks,
consumers, and environmentalists and for GM to create a committee
for corporate responsibility.

The resolutions were defeated, but many institutional shareholders supported one or both resolutions.[10] The next year, the Project
introduced three new shareholder proposals to allow nomination of
directors by employees, dealers, and consumers; to require GM to disclose information on minority employment and on pollution control
and safety measures; and to require GM to include shareholder nomina-
tions of directors in management's proxy materials. All the resolutions
were defeated, and some of the colleges and universities that had voted
for the resolutions in 1970 succumbed to a political and media blitz by
GM and abstained or voted against the resolutions in 1971.

ICCR

In 1971 the Interfaith Committee on Corporate Responsibility and Investments and the Corporate Information Center were created by ecumenical Protestants and the National Council of Churches. These two
merged and later became the Interfaith Center on Corporate Responsibility (ICCR), which organizes and coordinates corporate shareholder
resolutions introduced at annual meetings by concerned institutional
and individual investors.

Shareholder campaigns similar to Campaign GM were waged in
1971 by shareholders of Gulf Oil, Honeywell, Fidelity Trend Fund,
AT&T, and Potomac Electric Power. The proposal made at the Fidelity Trend Fund annual meeting demanding that the Fund review
the pollution and civil rights records of companies being considered
for investment received more than 12 percent of the shareholder vote.[11]

Although 12 percent was not a majority vote, it was significant in that many institutions with substantial capital voted against management, and the vote exceeded the 3 percent required by the SEC to bring the issue back to shareholders the next year.

In the early 1970s more resolutions were proposed by socially conscious shareholders. For example, in 1973 resolutions were introduced at Ford Motor Company to broaden the composition of the board of directors to include employees, consumers, women, and minorities; at General Motors to nominate a woman to the Board of Directors; and at Exxon to produce a report on the company's military production and research.

Bank of America

Corporate management had yet to prepare for the increasing amount of negative publicity. In March 1974 I attended a Bank of America shareholders' meeting in San Francisco to question management about the bank's $40 million loan to the South African government. Bank of America refused to reveal the details to shareholders of this loan after church researchers had uncovered the information when investigating other bank loans to South Africa. Even though corporate management was cordial to me and to other shareholders, it was clear that they were uncomfortable with being questioned about bank lending practices.

At the annual shareholders' meeting in April 1978, Irwin L. Gubman, Bank of America's Secretary, disclosed that approximately one-half of the bank's $188 million loan portfolio in South Africa was to the South African government and public and private corporations.[12] The bank's President, A. J. Clausen, told shareholders and bank employees that the bank should not ally itself with any racial group; but, on the other hand, Bank of America would do business anywhere in the world regardless of the political system.[13]

California Responsible Investing

Antiwar Protests

In the 1960s and 1970s, California's institutions of higher education were being rocked by antiwar protests. University of California students publicly raised the issues of University of California (UC) investments and individual UC Regents' personal investments in war and weapon-related industries in 1969. The UC Davis student newspaper, The *California Aggie,* disclosed that UC was investing in Dow Chemical, Lockheed, Boeing, and Ling-Temco-Vought (LTV).[14]

Student activists were outraged when they read what their university was investing in. They felt that the university was hypocritical. It was supposedly an institution dedicated to exploring the higher pursuits of humanity, not earning money from the weapons of war. Later in the year, students at UC Santa Barbara (UCSB) adopted a resolution requesting that the UCSB placement center prohibit the use of the center in recruiting graduates by firms having subsidiaries in South Africa.[15]

Shareholder Voting

In 1970, after UC Regents William Roth and Bill Coblentz had raised the issue of the university voting its shares at annual corporate shareholders' meetings, the Board of Regents adopted a formal proxy voting policy of automatically voting with management unless an issue was raised by an individual regent. The same year, UC voted against the Campaign GM resolutions. Although no formal shareholder voting records were kept by the University of California Regents, the UC Treasurer, Owsley B. Hammond, proclaimed that UC had never voted in favor of a shareholder proposal.[16]

In the early and mid-1970s public investing institutions were extremely hostile to the idea of public disclosure of shareholder voting. Secrecy reigned. The University of California and California's two largest retirement systems, the Public Employees Retirement System (CALPERS) and the State Teachers Retirement System (CALSTRS), successfully defeated legislation in Sacramento to open Regents' and Trustees' meetings to the public when they discussed and voted shareholder proxies. As late as 1979, when I was a trustee on the Sacramento City Investment board, I couldn't even get a second to my motion to change the meeting schedule from mid-afternoon on a weekday to evenings so that public employees and other beneficiaries could attend meetings.

South African Divestment

Until the early seventies I was an observer and not a participant in the responsible investment movement. Like many other Americans concerned about social and economic change, I focused almost entirely on electoral politics. Until now I have given a history in which I had only a passing interest. Apartheid in South Africa had a global impact on responsible investing, and I became convinced that California's economic involvement with companies benefiting from racial injustice was wrong.

In early 1972, while I was an analyst for the Assembly Office of Research (AOR) in the California legislature, I discussed my research on U.S. corporate activity in South Africa with Assembly member John Burton, Chair of the Assembly Rules Committee, which ran AOR. He formally asked me to conduct a study of California's economic involvement with companies operating in South Africa. In June of that year the AOR sent my report to Burton. In July he released the study at a press conference in Sacramento, announcing that over $1 billion in state funds were invested in U.S. companies operating in South Africa.[17] Burton went on to say,

> The study shows that these State agencies are doing business with over 200 corporations having Southern African operations. Many, perhaps most, of these firms use black slave labor to reap huge profits from their investments. Their activities contribute to the suppression of black majorities in South Africa, Namibia, Angola, Mozambique and Rhodesia.
>
> For instance, investments in IBM amount to more than $68 million. This is the same company which computerizes the data necessary for the "pass system" employed to enforce apartheid in South Africa. Polaroid last year produced passbook photographs. The "pass system" controls the movement of black labor and prohibits any black worker from staying in an urban area for more than 72 hours at a time.
>
> American Motors produces military vehicles used to keep the black majority under domination. Chrysler employs blacks on its assembly lines at wages lower than the established poverty level. Such examples are numerous.[18]

The report received a great deal of statewide publicity. The *Sacramento Bee* on July 22, 1972, proclaimed, "Burton: State Invests $1 Billion in Nations That Oppress Blacks," while the July 23, 1972, Sunday *San Francisco Examiner and Chronicle* headlines read "State Link to 'Racist' Lands Told." The report was immediately attacked by a conservative pro–South African group calling itself the U.S. League of Men Voters. The League wrote every member of the legislature, praising South Africa, Portugal, and Rhodesia, while claiming that I was "connected with organizations allied with the terrorist gangs engaged in murderous operations against those territories and . . . makes no effort to conceal this."[19] This came as quite a shock to me, since the closest I had ever come to a gang was in the third grade in Greenville, Texas, and I ran the other way.

The South African divestment campaign got under way later in 1972, when the World Council of Churches voted to divest its $3.5 million in stocks invested in companies operating in South Africa.[20]

Shortly thereafter, in San Francisco, Supervisor Quentin Kopp (now a California State Senator) unsuccessfully attempted to divest San Francisco city and county retirement funds from companies operating in South Africa.[21]

If history teaches us nothing else, it does teach us tenacity. Those of us who have worked in the field of socially responsible investing over the past 20 years are hardened to rejection. When defeated we just come back again and again. Tom Friery, the Sacramento City Treasurer and an opponent of South African divestment and responsible investing in the early eighties, told me once that even if he didn't agree with me, he respected my tenacity and consistency. I'm not alone in that regard.

Congressman Ron Dellums first introduced divestment legislation in 1971. The Legislative Black Caucus in Sacramento, California, introduced divestment legislation in 1973. Both pieces of legislation were soundly defeated. Divestment has been a long, slow, and hard-fought battle. It took over 10 years for the city and county of San Francisco to divest. It took 15 years for Congress to override President Reagan's veto of Dellum's call for comprehensive economic sanctions against South Africa. It was 13 years before Assemblywoman Maxine Waters, now a member of Congress, was successful with California divestment legislation, which was enacted in 1986.[22]

In March 1973, a Napa, California legislator, Assemblyman John Dunlap, released a report that I wrote for him entitled, "University of California Investments: Racist or Responsible?" which disclosed that the University of California had invested over $312 million in companies operating in South Africa. Later in the month Dunlap was joined by Assemblymen John Burton and John Miller (representing the Legislative Black Caucus), and the three introduced a legislative package to divest all California public and pension funds from companies operating in South Africa.

Following the release of the UC report, I was contacted by an attorney, John Sink, representing a wealthy Santa Barbara woman named Kit Tremaine. He informed me that after reading the report Ms. Tremaine had changed her mind and decided to withdraw a gift of 100 acres of prime coastal property, which was to be given as an endowment to the University of California. I immediately called a reporter I knew on the San Francisco Examiner, Carl Irving, and said that if he would promise me the front page of the Sunday edition of the *Chronicle/Examiner* I'd give him an exclusive story. On June 10, 1973, the Sunday *San Francisco Chronicle/Examiner* ran the story about Ms. Tremaine withholding the property from UC. Tremaine said that UC had 32 percent of its investments in firms operating in South Africa and that the university almost invariably cast proxy votes on behalf of management "...in essence endorsing apartheid."[23]

The University of California

Finding out how large institutions voted their stock continued to be a major challenge in those days. No one was forthcoming with information. California pension funds and UC continued to refuse to disclose how they voted. It was only after quite a bit of wrangling that I was able to get the staff of the Assembly Ways and Means Committee to insert control language in the California State Budget to require the University of California to report its corporate shareholder votes. Because of the new disclosure requirements I was able to discover that the UC Regents, in 1973, had specifically voted *against* shareholder resolutions to nominate a woman to the board of directors, allow IBM shareholders to submit nominees for the board of directors, and require General Electric to report on its South African operations.[24] Corporate America was locked up tight as a drum and the University of California was doing its best to keep it that way.

My first meeting with Owsley Hammond in mid-1973 was an eye-opener. We met to discuss UC's activity as a corporate shareholder. We were talking about sources of information, and I mentioned that it might be helpful for him to subscribe to the Investor Responsibility Research Center (IRRC) and receive its publications on corporate shareholder issues. He said that if he couldn't read it in the *Wall Street Journal* or *Barron's,* he wasn't interested.

I was dumbfounded. Owsley Hammond, a very formal-looking bureaucrat, was in charge of UC's billion-dollar portfolio. He was a well-paid, highly educated civil servant of one of the most advanced systems of education in the world. The fact that he relied on only two publications for shareholder information was chilling to say the least. This was the American old boy network operating at its best. Hammond simply voted UC's stock portfolio based exclusively on information he received from *The Wall Street Journal* and *Barron's.*

Public Pension Funds

I shouldn't have been so shocked. Earlier in the year I had my first encounter with Mel Peterson, the chief investment officer for the California Public Employees Retirement System (CALPERS) and the California State Teachers Retirement System (CALSTRS). As a legislative staff member, I was attempting to document the state's shareholder voting record on social and economic issues. I went to meet with Mel to see how the process worked.

As I was talking to Mel I spotted stacks of annual shareholder reports and proxy statements on the floor spread out in the different corners of the room. Mel told me those were corporate proxy statements that he hadn't been able to get to yet.[25] One of his jobs was to vote the proxies for the multibillion dollar CALPERS and CALSTRS systems. He did eventually vote. He signed and blindly voted every proxy over to management. He voted against dozens of important social and economic issues.

As a reaction to CALPERS voting with corporate management on literally every shareholder issue, the California Legislature blasted Mel Petersen and the CALPERS Board of Administration. In 1974 CALPERS, because of the legislative criticism, voted in *favor* of a shareholder resolution to "deplore" Phillips Petroleum's illegal campaign contribution to President Nixon's reelection campaign committee and voted in favor of a resolution at Exxon to request management to report to shareholders the company's present and future plans relating to strip mining in the northern plains of the United States. CALPERS did, however, vote *against* resolutions at Celanese Corporation to require management not to discriminate on the basis of sex when nominating a member of the Board of Directors, at Ford Motor Company to request reports to shareholders disclosing corporate political contributions and equal employment information, and at Union Carbide to request a report to shareholders relating to the corporation's South African operations.[26]

In January 1975 I wrote a legislative report entitled, "California State and Local Investments: A Guide for Responsible Ownership," which recommended the creation of a California State Investment Responsibility Advisory Commission to advise and make recommendations to the state retirement systems and the UC on voting of shareholder proxies. This was in response to the fact that in the previous year over 90 shareholder resolutions were introduced before 60 corporate shareholders' meetings throughout the United States. Legislation to create an Advisory Commission was subsequently introduced in February by Assemblyman John Dunlap, who said that stock was owned in many of these companies by the State of California and its local public agencies and "with very few exceptions, most publicly owned stock has been voted against various corporate reforms and socially beneficial measures." He went on to say that "not only have the votes by public agencies been contrary to the public interests but have at times been inconsistent with the policy of state law."[27]

The Advisory Commission legislation was supported by State Treasurer Jesse Unruh and church and student organizations but was opposed by state retirement systems and UC. Even though the commission that would have been created was only advisory, the bill was soundly defeated in the first policy committee. The old Financial Guard was still at the helm in California.

The "Browning" of California

In 1975 the 36-year-old Edmund G. (Jerry) Brown, Jr., governor of California and son of former governor Edmund G. Brown, Sr., was still on a "honeymoon" with the legislature after being swept into office after his cry for political campaign financing and disclosure reform when he was Secretary of State in 1974. He brought with him an intellectual "avant garde" of reformers who shared his distaste for the old-style politics of his father and legislative politicians. A great deal of corporate responsibility legislation that I wrote was adopted by the legislature and signed into law by Governor Brown. Legislation was enacted to require California government agencies to vote for cumulative voting (to protect minority shareholders' rights) and to allow state shareholders to "abstain" in their voting of proxies, and to request city and county governments to set up local advisory committees to advise them on shareholder voting. Considering the conservative nature of California's public pension funds, these small democratizing reforms were actually quite revolutionary.

In 1975 California state government was under intense pressure by Jerry Brown to "open government to public inspection." Big changes occurred in the California political arena when committee voting and campaign financing were finally publicly disclosed. I wrote legislation to require that the meetings of state retirement systems and the University of California, because they voted hundreds of thousands of shares of stock in publicly owned corporations, be open to the public. The legislation was opposed by state pension fund administrators and UC Regents and was defeated. So, too, was an amendment to another bill to require UC Regents to meet in public when they voted on shareholder issues.[28] Public pension funds and the UC Regents were at that time paranoid about public disclosure.

I didn't give up. In 1976 I wrote legislation to require state and local retirement systems and UC to annually report their voting on shareholder resolutions. This legislation was also opposed by the state retirement systems and UC Regents, and the bill was defeated. It's ironic that the disclosure legislation was so adamantly opposed in 1975 and 1976; yet a few years later and to date, the state's two large retirement systems publicly disclose their shareholder votes. New ideas are often opposed vigorously in California, despite the state's reputation for being on the cutting edge of reform.

Shareholder Resolutions

IRRC

The shareholder resolutions at Gulf Oil and increasing controversy at many Ivy League Schools caused Derek Bok, former president of Harvard University, to ask several other schools for assistance in setting up a research center to evaluate shareholder resolutions and other issues being raised at the university level. This was the genesis of the Investor Responsibility Research Center (IRRC), which was founded by Harvard, Carnegie, Boston, Cornell, Princeton, Stanford, and Wellesley Universities; Dartmouth, Oberlin, and Smith Colleges; the Ford and Rockefeller Foundations; and a half dozen other institutions. The University of California was asked to join, but it declined.

The IRRC was initially funded by grants from Ivy League schools and foundations. It raised $25,000 from the Ford and Rockefeller Foundations, and Carnegie Corporation put up another $20,000.[29] It now has revenues of over $3 million, primarily from annual subscription fees paid by more than 400 institutions. Subscribers are overwhelmingly investment management firms, banks, insurance companies, pension funds, and educational organizations.

At first, corporate management reacted quite antagonistically toward shareholder activists. They even turned off microphones at annual meetings so that shareholders could not ask embarrassing questions. Management would also stack shareholder meetings with employees who booed dissident shareholders when they spoke. Consultants were hired to educate corporate management on how to "stage manage" the annual shareholders' meeting to generate favorable publicity.

Chevron

Shareholder issues continued to have great media visibility, and resolutions were numerous. I attended the Standard Oil of California (Chevron) shareholders meeting in San Francisco in 1974, 1975, and 1976, when nine shareholder resolutions were introduced, including one relating to requesting the company not to expand operations in South Africa. The meetings inside were civil, but street demonstrations by church organizations were loud. Chevron management stacked the meetings with employees who occasionally booed church speakers. In 1975, after I spoke in favor of a church resolution at Chevron's meeting, I was "accidentally" pushed by several Chevron employees going down the stairs to leave the building.

Del Monte

In 1977 I introduced a shareholder resolution at Del Monte Corporation, requesting information on Del Monte's South African operations. In 1978 I introduced another resolution at Del Monte, this time to prohibit corporate expansion in South Africa. Del Monte's management offered to meet with me in San Francisco to discuss the resolution. I took a South African friend with me to the meeting, and the Del Monte representatives were visibly upset. Management representatives were polite and cordial, but their only interest was in having me withdraw the resolution, not in negotiating the contents. It was at that meeting these representatives admitted that Del Monte could easily have released information requested in my 1977 resolution, but the company simply didn't want to because it believed that such information would be used by activists to further attack Del Monte's South African operations. The 1978 Del Monte resolution was cosponsored by Kit Tremaine. Both the 1977 and 1978 resolutions were defeated. Corporate management must have viewed responsible investment activists as gadflies who simply wouldn't go away—vote them down and they just came back again!

Owing to the shareholder success of the Interfaith Center on Corporate Responsibility (ICCR), starting in 1974 many corporations, unlike Del Monte, began to provide all or most of the corporate disclosure information requested by shareholders on such topics as equal employment opportunity data, operations in South Africa, and strip mining operations in Appalachia.

Institutionalizing Shareholder Activism

By the early eighties it had become apparent that shareholder issues and resolutions at annual meetings were not going to go away. Resolutions were receiving the required percentage of votes to be reintroduced, and resolutions on South Africa, employment discrimination, corporate governance, and military production were constantly being introduced. Each year corporate management around the country was bombarded with a new round of shareholder resolutions. The ICCR has in many ways defined a large part of the socially responsible investment movement ever since the Episcopal Church filed the first church shareholder resolution over 20 years ago.

Recently, companies have been asked to disclose limited environmental information and to promise to work with shareholders in the future to protect the environment. Both Westinghouse Electric Corporation and Philip Morris Company were hit with resolutions introduced by my clients and church organizations requesting environmental disclosure. These companies agreed to provide this information if my clients and their church cosponsors would agree to withdraw the resolutions. It's certain that environmental shareholders will return to the boardrooms and annual shareholders' meetings to keep the pressure on.

Shareholder resolutions are not just being introduced by ICCR, church organizations, and individual investors. Portfolio managers such as Franklin Research and Development (FRDC) and mutual funds like the Calvert SIF Managed Growth Fund have also introduced resolutions.

In 1991 FRDC introduced shareholder resolutions at DuPont, Exxon, and Procter and Gamble. In 1992 FRDC plans to return to shareholder meetings and to expand the number of resolutions introduced to put pressure on companies to sign the Valdez Principles, an environmental code of conduct. Other filers of shareholder resolutions include large pension funds such as the New York State Common Retirement Fund, Minnesota State Board of Investors, State of Wisconsin Investment Board, State of Connecticut Retirement Trust Funds, Los Angeles Unified School District (LAUSD), the city of New York, State of Florida Board of Administration, and TIAA/CREF.

For almost 15 years large investors have institutionalized proxy voting policies and procedures to introduce shareholder resolutions. This trend will continue, and large institutional investors will increasingly be drawn into major social, economic, and political issues confronting corporations and American society. It is inevitable that dramas will be played out both behind the scenes in closed corporate boardrooms and at annual shareholders' meetings. Trustees of these large institutions will find it in their beneficiaries' interest to take an active role as an owner. In the future, *not* voting stock or introducing shareholder resolutions to protect the beneficiaries' interest may be seen as a violation of an institution's fiduciary duties and a direct conflict with the best interests of beneficiaries.

The Prudent Expert Rule

In 1975 trustees of many large institutional investors, such as pension funds, began to reevaluate their role in managing large amounts of capital. A year earlier the Employee Retirement Income Security Act (ERISA) was enacted; it set fiduciary standards for privately held pension assets and established individual trustee liability for violations of ERISA. The U.S. Department of Labor was authorized to administer the act. A fiduciary was defined as a person responsible for managing the assets of an employee benefit plan (pension plan), and a fiduciary was to "discharge his duties with respect to a plan solely in the interest of the participants and beneficiaries... with the care, skill, prudence, and diligence under the circumstances then prevailing that a prudent man acting in a like capacity and familiar with such matters would use in the conduct of an enterprise of a like character and with like aims, by diversifying the investments of the plan so as to minimize risk of large losses, unless under the circumstances it is clearly prudent not to do so."[30]

Prior to ERISA there were questions over conflicts of interest in fund transactions, the degree of responsibility required of fund fiduciaries (trustees or investment managers), and the standards of accountability required in the management of pension fund assets. ERISA was designed to ameliorate these problems. As a very lengthy, complicated, and technical law, ERISA established a variety of standards that private pension plans must meet, including vesting standards and fiduciary requirements. The legislation also created the Pension Benefit Guaranty Corporation (PBGC) to ensure the payment of pension benefits in instances where a plan is terminated without sufficient assets to pay promised benefits.

ERISA has been both condemned and applauded by labor and corporate management and has often been the excuse for conservative fund management by banks, insurance companies, and portfolio managers creating the "herd instinct" and a lack of innovation. I believe that it leads many fiduciaries to invest in a similar, if not identical, manner with other portfolio managers or advisors. It has been described as the "prudent expert" law. If everyone manages money in the same way no one can get into trouble for extremely poor performance. On the other hand, no one can excel either.

ERISA also created a controversy that continues to this day. Is it a violation of ERISA to consider "social" objectives? When this issue first reared its head, Ian Lanoff was the administrator of the Pension and Welfare Benefit Programs within the U.S. Department of Labor, which was responsible for administering ERISA. Lanoff was quoted thus:

> While fiduciary considerations, such as investment performance, may not properly be sacrificed in order to advance the social welfare of a group or region, an investment is not impermissible under ERISA solely because it has social utility. If a socially beneficial investment meets objective investment criteria which are appropriate to the goals of the portfolio, it may be considered in the same manner as other investments which meet these criteria.[31]

Lanoff's comments were directed to an issue the authors of ERISA never envisioned. Was pension capital being invested against the interest of pension beneficiaries even if the fiduciaries didn't technically violate ERISA? Could fiduciaries redirect capital and invest to protect the pension plan's economic health?

Targeted Investing

A fire that continues to burn to this day was set off by Randy Barber and Jeremy Rifkin when they wrote the book *The North Will Rise Again* (Beacon Press) in 1978. The book explained that pension fund assets concentrated in the older, industrialized Northeast and Midwest were being channeled increasingly to companies in the South and overseas. This investment trend could only exacerbate the economic deterioration of the beneficiaries' regional economy and would eventually destroy the beneficiaries' pension funds. By exporting pension fund money out of the area, the workers' jobs were undermined and the viability of pension plans weakened.

Many industrial unions, the AFL–CIO, and building and construction trade unions launched efforts to make sure that assets were not only invested to meet strict financial standards, but also to ensure that trustees were investing to strengthen local, regional, and national economies. State legislatures and many local government pension fund trustees started to explore investment strategies that would reinforce community investing.

Wisconsin

In late 1976 Don Smart, a trust officer with a local bank in Madison, Wisconsin, was asked by a friend who ran a nonprofit foundation to help write a grant proposal to the American Federation of State,

County and Municipal Employees Union (AFSCME). AFSCME wanted to know whether the State of Wisconsin Investment Board (SWIB) could increase investments in the state and thus increase local economic development and create additional jobs.

Don was hired by the Wisconsin Center for Public Policy to hold a conference and conduct a detailed analysis of the SWIB's investment policy and evaluate in-state investment targeting. The study was released in 1979, and it found that the viability of public pension funds depended upon a healthy state economy and that "to ignore the social and economic ramifications of its investment policy on certain participants within a certain geographic region, when those participants and that region are the contributors of its investment funds, is poor public policy and perhaps imprudent investment policy as well. Investment targeting does not cast aside the financial wisdom of investment managers. It does not have to involve additional risk."[32]

Thanks in large part to Smart's study, the Wisconsin Investment Board is required by law to report on the state's in-state investment every two years, and the Wisconsin Department of Development must recommend investments that would benefit the state's economy. Of the SWIB's $23 billion investment portfolio, over $5.4 billion is in Wisconsin-related investments.[33]

I asked Don, president of Charing Company, Inc., a retirement plan consultant, administrator, and actuary, what was the major problem he encountered while conducting his study.

> Most investment managers followed a herd mentality and tended to create artificial barriers as a part of their investment research process which eliminated important considerations. For example, the State of Wisconsin Investment Board (SWIB) did not consider investments of less than $5 million, so small companies were effectively tossed out. Also, managers would not look at any benefit to the investor (beneficiaries) other than the direct return. Coupling an investment's merit to job stability or the economic health of the region was completely verboten. Additionally, trying to make the connection to an investment being good if it was good in other ways—environmental, social, etc.—was simply too remote for SWIB to pursue. Still, all these connections seemed quite valid to me if you took a long-term perspective.

By 1991, 25 states required public employee pension funds to reserve part of their assets for in-state investing. From California to Pennsylvania to New York, state and local government pension funds have invested in real estate and small business within their communities to foster state and local economic development and create jobs.

Linked Deposits

Linked deposit programs also became important programs to "link" sources of capital to specific community economic and social goals. By the late 1970s such programs were successfully being run by Missouri, Massachusetts, Colorado, and Illinois. These states required banks and other financial institutions to compete for state deposits not only on the basis of yield, but also on the number of housing, small business, and agricultural loans they made within the boundaries of the state.

The California Bankers' Association convinced State Treasurer Jesse Unruh to oppose Senator John Dunlap's 1978 legislation authorizing Unruh to establish a linked deposit program in the State. It was in Unruh's interest to oppose the legislation because he was building a campaign war chest and could use CBA's considerable financial resources. Other opponents included the California Savings and Loan League, the County Treasurers' Association, and the California Municipal Treasurers' Association. The legislation was easily defeated in the State Senate, and Dunlap was defeated a year later in his reelection bid. The financial and corporate community spent well over $300,000 in the successful effort against him.

Even though linked deposit legislation and Senator Dunlap were defeated in California, it remains to this day a popular concept. The state of Louisiana, which is implementing a linked deposit program similar to one in Ohio, hopes to increase deposits under the plan nearly 10-fold. Louisiana plans on placing $40 million at 3 percent below the rate of return it would otherwise receive, passing on the savings to borrowers. The program would deposit money in state banks, which would in turn lend funds to benefit small business, agriculture, and aquaculture.[34]

The Cry for Housing and Jobs

In December 1978 the U.S. Department of Labor exempted the "J for Jobs" program of Union Labor Life Insurance Company (ULLICO) from prohibited transactions under ERISA, to allow Union Labor Life to accept pension fund capital for investments made in union-only construction programs.[35] About the same time, the AFL-CIO Building and Construction Trades Councils and trustees of pension funds were setting up informal regional union pension trustee groups, or "superfunds," to permit pension funds to invest in union-built real estate in many communities across the country. Superfunds were being created in a half-dozen cities, including Houston, Los Angeles, Denver, and Boston.[36]

Investing pension fund capital to promote jobs and employ union members is not an altogether new concept. Twenty-five years ago, in the mid-1960s, the AFL-CIO had created the AFL-CIO Mortgage Investment Trust, providing an opportunity for pension funds to invest in safe, income-producing real estate that generates employment, housing, and economic development. The AFL-CIO program created two trusts: the housing investment trust and the building investment trust.

The housing investment trust invests in residential projects, including single- and multifamily housing, nursing homes, and retirement facilities throughout the country. The trust invests primarily in construction loans and mortgages or mortgage-backed securities that are federally insured or guaranteed by the U.S. government or federal agencies. All of the trust's investments are limited to completely union-built projects. The trust has financed over $800 million in new construction nationwide.

The building investment trust invests in construction loans, mortgages, and participating mortgages and will take equity positions in real property. According to Jeff Greendorfer, the west coast representative of the AFL-CIO Mortgage Investment Trust, the building investment trust has $122 million in assets, and the housing investment trust has $438 million in assets.

The Industrial Union Department of the AFL-CIO released a report in June 1980 that found that professional portfolio managers in charge of many benefit plans were performing poorly. The department also found a tremendous concentration of financial power in few hands (banks, insurance companies, and large portfolio managers) and an almost universal absence of consideration of the economic and social interests of fund beneficiaries in setting investment policies. In addition to recommending that unions exert leadership in gaining control of pension funds for workers, the report cited several strategies to be considered by investment managers, including "investment in residential mortgages and other investments that promote development of communities where beneficiaries live and investments that generally tend to promote the ready availability of food, shelter and energy for fund beneficiaries."[37]

Employee Home Loans

At the same time as this examination of investment strategies, state and public agencies were developing programs to recruit qualified employees to their states and keep their current employees by making it easier for them to buy homes. The University of California, in early 1979, adopted a faculty home loan program to provide funds to allow faculty members to obtain below-market-rate interest and reduced-down-payment home loans in California.

In 1960 the State of Hawaii Public Employees Retirement System initiated a member home loan program that provided below-market home loans to Hawaiian public employees. The program was immediately successful and combined an investment program that invested funds for future beneficiaries in an investment program to benefit existing employees.

In March 1979 I wrote legislation that was enacted in 1980 to create a similar program in California. The program has made 131,000 loans to California public employees of over $1.3 billion. Other states have been active over the last decade in utilizing pension fund capital to make prudent in-state residential real estate investments in the form of mortgage loans to pension beneficiaries. Recently the $9 billion State of Connecticut Trust Funds launched a $100 million program to provide below-market residential mortgages to first-time home buyers in Connecticut; half of these funds are reserved for pension fund beneficiaries, and half are given through a lottery-style selection process.

California Pension Controversy

Senator Dunlap was rewarded for his leadership on pension fund investment issues. In 1977 a Select Committee on Investment Priorities and Objectives was created and Dunlap was appointed chair.

The Senate Select Committee was very controversial in its two years of operation, and it incurred the wrath of just about every major financial special interest in the state. The committee, and Senator Dunlap in particular, provided leadership on controversial investment issues such as the public use of public capital regarding linked deposits, greatly influencing public pension funds and the University of California to vote their proxies more responsibly and redirect or target the flow of capital into investment programs to generate jobs and economic wealth within the state. The committee had also become the catalyst for South African divestment throughout the state. As consultant to the committee, I worked with several local government commissions established to recommend reinvestment strategies for city government funds. Much to the chagrin of powerful California financial special interests, the defeat of Dunlap and the termination of the committee in early 1979 did not slow down the pace or the momentum of responsible investing throughout the state.

In June 1979, following several months of discussion, the State and Consumer Services Agency, which administers CALPERS and CAL-STRS, signed a contract with the New York-based CEP to prepare a report on the desirability of incorporating criteria on South Africa and corporate equal opportunity into the state retirement system's investment decision making process. The CEP report, released in 1980, recommended that California's state retirement boards reevaluate corporate investment in South Africa and consider divestment of securities in firms operating in South Africa. With regard to equal employment opportunity (EEO), the CEP study recommended that state retirement systems implement a comprehensive and proative EEO policy.

Jerry Brown always had an interest in South Africa, foreign policy, and pension fund investments. He repeatedly met with students and others to gain a greater understanding of all of the issues. He often referred to himself as a student of history and new ideas. Even though he signed into law all of the corporate responsibility legislation authored by Senator Dunlap that got to his desk, it took him a great deal of time to figure out how to implement a statewide plan. He was particularly interested in the concept of pension fund power following the publication of *The North Will Rise Again*. In the fall of 1978, when Randy Barber was in Sacramento, we were invited to one of Brown's cabinet meetings for a discussion of Barber's book.

In every private meeting with Brown, I was amazed at his ability to grasp not only concepts, but a whole array of factual information. The cabinet session lasted several hours, and the governor constantly interrupted to ask questions before his previous question was even answered. The meeting, like many with the governor, ended with no real conclusion or strategy for future action. It was later that Tom Hayden, political activist and now a member of the California State Assembly, convinced Brown to develop a statewide pension fund strategy.

The Governor's Public Investment Task Force

Tom Hayden, in the late 1970s and early 1980s, created an ambitious and successful statewide political organization, the Campaign for Economic Democracy (CED), that increasingly became associated with the governor's national political ambitions. Hayden had success at the local government level by organizing professional grassroots political campaigns for local activists. Many of these local activists were elected to city councils and school boards, and CED was wielding some influence in the legislature and within the California Democratic Party. He clearly had the ear of Governor Brown.

Hayden's and CED's political platform of economic democracy was philosophically consistent with many of the investment issues raised by Senator Dunlap's Select Committee. Hayden had earlier testified at Select Committee public hearings and convinced Governor Brown to take a more active leadership role on South Africa. When Jerry Brown came to Sacramento in 1975, and until 1980, I had unsuccessfully tried to get the governor to pay attention to social investment issues within the state, nationally, and internationally. I found his cabinet officers and many of his staff receptive, but I was repeatedly frustrated in my attempts to have the Governor develop and implement an overall statewide strategy to evaluate the power of pension capital and promote a model for action. Tom Hayden succeeded where I had failed.

On March 3, 1980, Governor Brown called for the trustees of public investment funds to act as "the conscience of California" and vote their stock against apartheid in South Africa and against further development of nuclear power. He said that investment funds should sell stock in companies with "unacceptable" records on either issue.

Governor Brown created a statewide public investment task force to develop specific proposals for new investments that were prudent and responsive to the needs of the state in the areas of affordable housing, small business development, alternative energy development and job creation. He also asked the task force to develop guidelines to ensure that public investment practices met social responsibility criteria and public interest goals and to recommend necessary changes in California tax and pension laws and regulations to aid such new investment alternatives. I was appointed chair of the statewide task force.

The governor's task force was the first of its kind in the nation. On many issues California is either 10 years ahead or 10 years behind the rest of the nation. In this case I believe the task force recommendations were 10 years ahead. In 1978 CALSTRS, thanks to the efforts of Ray Leonardini and Leonard Grimes with the State and Consumer Services Agency and Sid McCausland with the State Department of Finance, adopted a Shareholders' Rights and Proxy Voting Guideline, including socially responsible investment criteria regarding CALSTRS investments. The task force recommended that the policy be expanded to all public retirement systems. The CALSTRS guidelines defined "social injury" thus:

"Social injury will be said to exist when the activities of a corporation serve to undermine basic human rights or dignities. Social injury may also be said to exist when the Board perceives that it is the prevailing belief of the members of the Retirement System that the practices of a corporation result in undesirable side effects for others, and that the side effects are grave in nature. A company should not be held responsible for the infliction of social injury merely by virtue of its agreements or relationships with other (independent) entities engaged in socially injurious activities.

The extent of the responsibility of the System to engage in activity for the prevention, reduction, and elimination of social injury should be determined by the number of shares held in the corporation and the gravity of the social injury."[38]

The task force also recommended that all investments be consistent with social responsibility and in-state guidelines and that the Funds actively seek investments that benefited the California economy, its taxpayers, and its citizens, particularly the fund beneficiaries. This was in reference to investments that generated new economic wealth in the state and were consistent with sound investment policy. Investments that caused social injury should be avoided. In voting their stock, the governing boards were asked to establish their own issue priorities. The task force also recommended that CALPERS and CALSTRS do the following:

- Pursue a more active proxy strategy, including electing members to the boards of directors of companies where they were major stockholders
- Coordinate votes with other institutional investors where appropriate
- Write proactive letters to portfolio companies as outlined in the CALSTRS guidelines
- Establish an advisory committee with representation by plan participants to discuss questions and develop criteria of social responsibility, advise the boards on in-state investments in areas of capital need within the California economy, and coordinate alternative investment strategies with local governments to avoid economic and demographic dislocations
- Consider commissioning studies (similar to the CEP study) if a shareholder issues arises on which the boards seek expert advice
- Establish a liaison with other appropriate government agencies, directly or through the Pension Investment Unit, which is to operate in part as a clearinghouse for coordination of information

Much of the work of the task force was continued by the Pension Investment Unit, which was set up within the governor's office. More importantly, many of the recommendations for pension funds targeting in-state investment opportunities, social criteria relative to corporate shareholder proxy voting, and housing investment recommendations were institutionalized by the state pension funds and legislation that followed. The California state constitution was even changed by voters to provide for a more flexible investment policy for state pension funds based upon the task force's recommendations. Much that was opposed and ridiculed in the seventies was accepted in the eighties and institutionalized in the nineties. The California state retirement systems have become the largest and most active institutional shareholders in the country.

The Politics of Pension Funds

When the statewide task force was created, I was working as a legislative advocate for the California Council of Service Employees (SEIU) and had just been appointed by the Sacramento mayor and city council to the Sacramento Board of Administration, Investment and Fiscal Management, the entity responsible for overseeing the $96 million city employees' pension fund.

In August 1979 I and a colleague on the Sacramento Regional Transit District Board of Directors, Grantland Johnson (now a Sacramento County Supervisor), introduced South African divestment resolutions at our respective retirement and investment boards. The resolutions were not going anywhere because of strong political opposition from the financial community, the Sacramento Treasurer, the South African government, and the local newspaper, the *Sacramento Union*, which was purchased by John McGoff using illegal South African slush funds.[39]

Looking back on my experience in the period from 1979 to 1980, I find it very interesting that my brief tenure on the Sacramento Investment Board created so much controversy. It was then that I discovered that the control of pension funds and other capital is the key to having a positive social and economic impact on our society. In the case of my South African divestment proposal, the South African government successfully lobbied the city treasurer and other board members. Clearly, keeping U.S. pension funds invested in companies operating in South Africa was important to the South African government.

In 1979 Sacramento Mayor Phil Isenberg (now in the California State Assembly) and the city council appointed me to the investment

board knowing full well that I was going to raise responsible investment issues at the city investment board level. They were not prepared
for the political heat they received from the financial community, the
Sacramento Union, and the South African government when I started
raising corporate responsibility, shareholder voting, and South African
issues. Feeling the political heat, Isenberg called me into his office to
attempt to convince me to stop raising these controversial investment
issues. His lack of political commitment on these issues instead inspired
me to continue.

Tom Friery, the Sacramento City Treasurer, after being lobbied by
the South African government, announced that my divestment proposal could have a house-of-cards effect on the economy and that Sacramento's divestment from American companies that had operations in
South Africa could start a major national divestment movement, which
"could start a run on the bank, producing total economic chaos resulting in the destruction of the U.S. securities market."[40] Friery's ex-
aggerated claim was typical of the opponents of divestiture in those
days. Not only did the U.S. securities market survive South African
divestiture, but those investors investing in South Africa–free portfolios outperformed those investing in South African companies.

In 1979 demystifying the investment process was frightening to
California's local government treasurers and pension fund administrators. Led by arch-conservative and friend of South Africa's white
minority government, former California State Senator H.L. Richardson, the California Municipal Treasurers' Association and the California County Treasurers' Association were able to lobby successfully
to kill a federal funding proposal to study California local government investment practices by the California Alternative Investment
Task Force (CAITF). The task force had been created as a nonprofit
educational organization, initially funded by the Tides Foundation,
a San Francisco–based community foundation, to educate pension
fund managers and public administrators about alternative investment
options. (The Ford Foundation funded such a study in 1991.) I was
the executive director of the task force and the target of Richardson
and his conservative supporters. Not only did pension bureaucrats
and treasurers not want to be educated about alternatives to traditional and nonscreened stock and bond investing, but they also were
incensed that the California State Senate Select Committee on Investments, of which I was the consultant, had published a report
in December 1978 finding that many local government treasurers
were not obtaining "the highest rate of interest" and technically were

violating state law. They were following the advice of their friends in the old boy network and depositing much of their public funds in low interest–bearing bank and savings and loan passbook savings accounts.

There was even an unsuccessful move by the Sacramento financial community, represented by seasoned city career bureaucrats, to oust me from the board when I was traveling in Africa and had missed several board meetings. When I did resign from the board in early 1980, McGoff's *Sacramento Union* ran a Sunday front-page story alleging that I had moved out of Sacramento before I resigned from the Board of Investment, therefore technically violating the City Charter.[41] The fact that the *Sacramento Union* did such a "hit piece" convinced me of the tremendous economic and political importance of the South African issue and of the power of capital. It actually inspired me to work harder to demystify investing and focus on the control of capital.

The 1980s: South Africa

Greed became the high priest of the American financial community during the Reagan years. At the same time, responsible investing matured into a potent financial and economic force. While Michael Milken was making hundreds of millions of dollars taking Drexel Burnham Lambert's corporate clients into "adventure land" with junk debt, billions of dollars were being divested by institutions and individuals from companies operating in South Africa. The American socially responsible investment movement has been the only national economic and political counterforce against a steady drift toward a more conservative domestic and foreign policy since the Vietnam war. Activists at the church, community, and shareholder levels have applied pressure on corporations regarding their South African operations.

For over 20 years, shareholders, led by major religious and secular organizations, have introduced shareholder resolutions addressing South African issues. The white minority government of the Republic of South Africa has maintained the most sophisticated and highly technological and industrial police state since Nazi Germany. It has carried out its constitutional policy of racial segregation through torture, mass arrests, bannings, and detentions.

South Africa's reliance on Western multinational corporate capital still provides much of the underpinning for its unique blend of national socialism and controlled capitalism. U.S.-based multinational corporations, many of which have been in South Africa since the early

1900s, provide strategic materials, capital, technology, and other vital resources to strengthen the apartheid government.

At one time the United States was South Africa's largest trading partner (it's now number four), and banks couldn't lend South Africa enough money. I recall questioning Bank of America's management at a 1974 shareholder's meeting about the bank's loan to the South African government. The management of the bank at that time said that they would lend to *any* creditworthy bank customer in the world. There was absolutely no sense of social responsibility at the highest levels of corporate America.

While U.S. banks provided South Africa easy access to capital, American corporations controlled over 70 percent of the computer market, including such companies as IBM, Burroughs, NCR, Control Data, Hewlett Packard, Wang Labs, Mohawk Data Science, Sperry Rand, Computer Sciences Corporation, 3M, Kodak, and Tron Systems.[42]

The IBM computer used by the Department of the Interior facilitated the very system of racial classification that underlies apartheid. It also provided the most efficient method of tracking the movements of black South Africans for security purposes.[43] U.S.-supplied computer technology was utilized for internal security, the nuclear industry, transportation, and defense and police, and to support security forces that occupied Namibia. U.S. computers provided the answer for one of the great bottlenecks in the South African economy—the lack of skilled white labor.

Another great bottleneck in the South African economy was and is energy. South Africa has no petroleum resources. Here again, U.S. firms are still the key to white rule. Almost two-thirds of South Africa's oil is refined by Mobil and Caltex (Chevron and Texaco). Nuclear power has been supplied by Westinghouse Electric and Allis Chalmers. IT&T has provided the telecommunications network, and General Electric, the electrical machinery and diesel engines. The automotive industry was also dominated by General Motors and Ford. Bechtel and Fluor Corporations helped South Africa develop the synthetic fuels industry.

Churches, student activists, community leaders, and shareholders became increasingly disgusted with the behavior of U.S. corporations and bank lending in South Africa while witnessing corporate greed at home. The black community, in particular, believes that there is a direct correlation between black poverty in America and oppression against black South Africans by a white minority government supported by America's top corporations.

U.S. corporations were supplying badly needed tax revenue to South Africa for defense and internal security, and those taxes paid in South Africa by American corporations were deducted from their state and federal tax liability. In essence, U.S. taxpayers were subsidizing U.S. corporate involvement in South Africa.

Governor Jerry Brown of California was so outraged by California's financial support of apartheid before he left office he fired off another volley at South Africa through shareholder action.

In 1982 his administration was successful in convincing both state retirement systems to cosponsor a resolution at the Xerox Corporation annual shareholders' meeting held in New York on May 20. Alice Lytle, an articulate and politically savvy black woman, was head of Brown's State and Consumer Services Agency. (In January 1983 she was appointed to the Sacramento Municipal Court by Brown.) She represented the state retirement systems' 1.2 million shares at the Xerox shareholder meetings. She told shareholders,

> The choice you have before you today is whether to continue to ally yourself with what is perhaps the most vicious regime on the face of the earth or, instead, to begin to move in a direction which is not only the most ethical but also the most economically sound and politically astute one open to you.[44]

The shareholder proposal, which received 10 percent of the vote, called for Xerox to cut off sales to the military and police in South Africa. It was opposed by Xerox's only black director, Vernon E. Jordan, Jr., formerly president of the National Urban League, saying he had "great sympathy" for ending police and military sales in South Africa but that the resolution as a whole would reduce jobs for blacks.[45]

In June 1987 Xerox sold its South African subsidiary to Allied Technologies LTD but continued to license the South African company for sales and servicing.[46] In 1990 Xerox was one of 15 companies identified by IRRC that announced that the company would severe its nonequity link to South Africa.[47]

Beginning in the early eighties, U.S. corporations were under constant domestic pressure to withdraw from South Africa. Corporate risk analysts such as Business Environment Risk Information (BERI), a Geneva-based firm, warned corporate management of the business risk in South Africa. In late 1982 BERI recommended to the management of firms operating in South Africa that they should do the following:

- Deemphasize South Africa and prepare to shift production elsewhere, if possible
- Protect industrial sites and personnel against violence
- Consider the costs of exclusion from other African markets because of the South African operations, and the costs of management difficulties in handling stockholders' initiatives and adverse publicity from anti-apartheid advocacy groups
- Examine the possibility of an orderly withdrawal early in the decade to avoid financial losses[48]

In addition, in mid-June 1985, Frost and Sullivan, another risk analyst, concluded that "South Africa is showing a deteriorating risk picture, in both the short and long term."[49]

Between 1980 and 1985, 30 U.S. corporations withdrew from South Africa. Opportunity abounding, some firms actually opened new offices in South Africa to take advantage of U.S. corporate concerns over South African instability. As *The Wall Street Journal* reported on March 11, 1985,

> Given the current mood, few U.S. firms are beginning new enterprises there these days. There are exceptions, like Alexander and Alexander Services, Inc., an insurance brokerage firm. "Our clients have greater need for our services in South Africa now," says Peter Reid, Senior Vice President, describing his firm's ability to put together protection packages against fires, revolutions, and other calamities. "They're concerned about getting wiped out," he explains.

At the same time, in March 1985, the American Chamber of Commerce in South Africa asked the South African government for "visible expression" of reforms in order to diffuse the disinvestment campaign in the United States.[50]

Many of the companies belonging to the American Chamber of Commerce had signed the Sullivan Code of Conduct, a voluntary corporate code that pledged that they would move toward desegregating restrooms and dining facilities, provide equal pay for equal work, and financially support African education, housing, and other reforms within the context of apartheid. The architect of the Code of Conduct was General Motors director Rev. Leon Sullivan. Although Sullivan was sincere in his belief that internal pressure by U.S. companies could lead South Africa to abandon or reform apartheid, most of us in the responsible investment community believed that it was too little, too late. As early as 1977, the South African government supported the objective of Sullivan's original code of conduct and never attempted to discourage U.S. corporate compliance with it.[51]

Sullivan abandoned his code on June 3, 1987, 10 years after he had developed it. He called for complete divestment, a total embargo, and a break in diplomatic relations with South Africa. Sullivan clearly had changed his mind about his code:

> It was clear from the beginning that these principles alone would not, and could not, be the total solution to the South African problem. It was clear to me that a greater corporate force must be used. Greater than the corporate force of the Sullivan Principles. Greater than those things that were being done by businesses. Greater than those things that were being espoused in Washington. Something had to be done with greater corporate force because the crying need in South Africa was not just equal employment or jobs or better housing, but freedom and justice.[52]

By the mid-1980s seven states, 28 cities, and the Virgin Islands had enacted divestment proposals.[53] Forty-three educational institutions had fully or partially divested,[54] and as many as 20 California State University and Colleges (CSUC) auxiliary organizations had enacted socially responsible guidelines.[55]

On April 23, 1985 I gave a speech to the Anti-Apartheid Convocation in Harmon Gym on the UC Berkeley campus. Over 5,000 students attended, as well as several U.C. Regents and the Treasurer, and the President of the University. I will never forget the noise, the excitement, and the anger expressed over UC's investments in firms operating in South Africa. It is no wonder that the force for divestment across America could not be stopped.

By May 1991, according to the IRRC, some form of South Africa–related economic action had been taken by 28 states, 24 counties, 92 cities, and the Virgin Islands. Between 1984 and May 1990, 206 U.S. companies had completely or partially withdrawn from South Africa. In addition, in at least 49 states, some level of state or local government (or both) had enacted selective purchasing or contracting laws, which restricted or prohibited a public agency from buying products or services from companies operating in South Africa. This represented a national "corporate campaign" that had the effect of exerting tremendous economic leverage on South Africa's domestic economy. This economic pressure eventually helped bring the white minority government to the negotiating table to discuss sharing power with the nonwhite majority. It obviously also led to the release of political prisoners, the lifting of the ban on the African National

Congress, and major legislative changes that cracked the apartheid legal structure.

Within the financial community much of the success of the South African divestment movement was due to a series of investment studies that compared the investment performance of portfolios that were South Africa free (SAF) and South Africa invested (SAI). Over a dozen major studies on the financial effect of divestiture on equity portfolios concluded that with a slight increase in risk and volatility, SAF outperformed SAI portfolios. Studies have now been supplemented by actual results, proving that divestment has not had a negative impact, and in many cases has had a positive effect upon portfolio performance.

The progressive financial community and the major church institutions in America combined forces and unleashed a powerful "corporate campaign" that continues to have significant international political repercussions. Even after President Bush had lifted sanctions in 1991, most corporations that had withdrawn from South Africa were not willing to immediately return. Most cite "economic" reasons, as many are reluctant to return because of economic and political repercussions from state and local governments, investors, and consumers who continue to maintain investment and contracting prohibitions.

Major brokerage firms are reluctant to resume conducting South Africa–related business because major U.S. cities and state governments—and big public employee pension funds—have instituted anti-apartheid policies that prohibit business with South Africa. If U.S. brokerage firms violate these policies, they run the risk of losing out on lucrative bond underwriting and other business. Oregon was the first state to reverse its ban against state pension funds investing in South Africa. According to the IRRC, in addition to state and local governments, over 200 institutional investors restrict or prohibit investing in companies operating in South Africa. According to a *Wall Street Journal* article, "far from inspiring a shift on South Africa, President Bush's decision to lift sanctions has engendered derision and scorn from some advocates of ethical investing."[56]

The clear response from the responsible investment community has been that there will be no change on South Africa investment restrictions until and unless there is majority rule. In July 1991 the Calvert Social Investment Fund reaffirmed its advisory council's statement, saying, "We will change the Fund's 'no buy' position only when representative black leadership such as the ANC call for lifting of sanctions, or the United Nations General Assembly supports a normalization of relations."[57]

The Social Investment Forum

In 1981 the Social Investment Forum (SIF) was informally organized, but it didn't incorporate until 1985 as a national association, now having a membership of over 1,000 financial professionals and research and community organizations. The first president was Joan Bavaria, president of Franklin Research and Development Corporation, a Boston-based responsible investment management company. The board of directors included Joan Shapiro of South Shore Bank in Chicago, Alice Tepper-Marlin, founder of the New York–based Council on Economic Priorities, Stuart Baldwin, Jon Blum, Chuck Matthei, George Pillsbury, and Tamsin Taylor.

The Social Investment Forum's fundamental purpose is to support and encourage the growth of socially responsible investing through the following objectives:

1. To promote the idea and use of financially sound investments consistent with a commitment to peace, a healthy environment, social justice, and other social concerns of the investor
2. To provide useful membership benefits to an expanding constituency of all interested parties who will be encouraged to actively participate in the SIF's governance and operation
3. To encourage and expect high ethical standards of professional conduct as outlined by the SIF Statement of Principles, to which all members subscribe
4. To provide a forum for the discussion of the social impact of investments and to sponsor a continuing dialogue on the development of innovative and responsible approaches to societal economic issues

The forum was the first organization that surveyed the extent of assets professionally managed utilizing some form of social or nontraditional investment criteria in addition to traditional financial criteria. In April 1985 the forum released the "Social Balance Sheet," identifying $40 billion managed as "socially invested." The amount invested in 1991 totaled $625 billion (see Figure 1.1).

The Minneapolis-based forum meets quarterly at different locations throughout the United States. John Schultz, the forum's president, believes that the forum unites all responsible investors under one roof.

> The overwhelming umbrella is the concept of "good." No correct-thinking person or human being approves of apartheid; consequently we all oppose investments in companies in South Africa. No one wants to de-

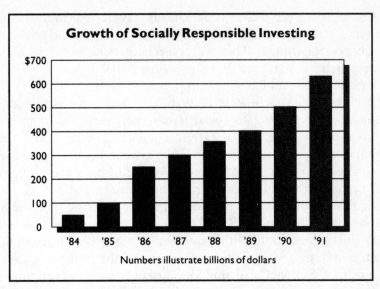

Figure 1.1   *(Source:* Social Investment Forum.)

stroy the environment, so nobody—regardless of race, creed, and color—wants environmental degradation. No one likes war. We're all for peace and social justice. These are all good and general terms. That is what unites the disparity between the groups. It's a question of prioritization. Many people are concerned about animal rights, women's issues, labor, and the environment. Different interest groups and individuals set preferential social criteria; their special interest appears at the top of the list with everything else underneath it. Then when you get down to the bottom, you have the generalized categories of peace and social justice. It's a question of priorities, but the thing that knits the whole group together is a commonality of interests and the Social Investment Forum.

The Council of Institutional Investors

In 1985 another investor-oriented group was launched: the Council of Institutional Investors. The Council was created in response to controversial corporate takeover activity and the California state retirement systems' increasing shareholder activism. Twenty private and public pension funds were the first members, but the Council was dominated by California and the personality of the late California State Treasurer Jesse Unruh. The Council now has 65 private and public pension fund members and two associate members.

Unruh was the former Speaker of the State Assembly and an unsuccessful gubernatorial candidate against Ronald Reagan. In 1975, when

Jerry Brown was elected Governor, Unruh was elected California State Treasurer. By the early 1980s he recognized the economic power held by large pension funds. This was especially evident when it came to issues such as leveraged buyouts, "greenmail," hostile corporate takeovers, mergers, and acquisitions.

Unruh had seen California Governor Jerry Brown embrace pension fund power relating to social issues, but Jesse was more interested in using his leverage to extract corporate, bank, and financial community campaign contributions and muscle his way into corporate boardrooms through the Council. As California's State Treasurer, Unruh had earlier used his considerable influence to convince the legislature to change the law and put both the State Treasurer and the State Controller (then his buddy Ken Corey) on the state's pension board. In 1986 Unruh teamed up with Governor Deukmejian's pension board appointees and, on a seven to six vote, removed the pension board's executive officer, Sid McCausland. McCausland, with the six employee representatives, had fought Governor Deukmejian's plan to divert state pension reserve funds back into the state's general fund as a budget-balancing measure. Ironically, McCausland earlier had also been instrumental in supporting my efforts to have the pension funds adopt a more activist role on shareholder issues. After McCausland's termination, Unruh was in a position of undisputed political leadership, which led to his dominance in the early years of the Council. At one time, Unruh and the Council were so feared that Ken Miller, head of Merrill Lynch's merger and acquisition group, told *BusinessWeek,* "If the institutions start speaking with one voice they could become a financial OPEC."[59]

California Pension Power

The California public employee retirement funds contribute about 16 percent of the budget of the Council and have considerable economic clout. According to *Pensions & Investments,* the two California funds have combined assets of over $113 billion and are the second and seventh largest pension funds in the country (see Table 1.1).

California pension funds and the Council have had a great deal of influence on corporate management; for instance, they convinced Exxon to agree to add an environmentalist to its board of directors, Texaco to appoint a Council member to its board, and General Motors to amend its bylaws and require that a majority of its board comprise independent directors. CALPERS, under the leadership of chief execu-

Table 1.1 Top 200 Pension Funds

	Dollars (in millions)
1. TIAA–CREF	83,100
2. California Public Employees	54,000
3. New York State & Local	43,737
4. New York City	40,763
5. AT&T	38,876
6. General Motors	36,300
7. California State Teachers	30,140
8. General Electric	27,108
9. New York State Teachers	26,689
10. New Jersey	26,609
11. IBM	25,000
12. Texas Teachers	23,734
13. Ford Motor	20,800
14. Ohio Public Employees	20,595
15. Florida State Board	19,268
16. Wisconsin State Baord	18,482
17. Ohio State Teachers	18,200
18. Du Pont	17,728
19. North Carolina Retirement	17,289
20. State of Michigan	17,268

Source: *Pensions and Investments*, "Top 200 Pension Funds/ Sponsors," January 21, 1991.

tive Dale Hanson, has also obtained bylaw changes or other assurances on various issues it had requested from ITT Corporation, W.R. Grace & Company, Armstrong World Industries, Sears, and Boise Cascade Corporation. CALPERS and many institutional pension funds that are members of the Council teamed up with the United Shareholders Association, an activist nonprofit shareholder organization, to win many concessions from corporate management in 1991. Lockheed Corporation, for example, agreed to put to a shareholder vote its golden parachutes—lucrative benefit packages given to managers if a takeover occurs; Santa Fe Pacific Corporation repealed its "poison pill" defense; and Colgate-Palmolive adopted confidential voting for shareholders. CALPERS also voted against the management of ITT because, according to Hanson, "the huge amount of compensation that ITT's board has awarded its [chief executive]...despite what we consider to be quite mediocre performance, compelled us to express our displeasure in some tangible way."[59]

CALPERS shareholder activism, which has become quite institutionalized over the past 10 years, led California Governor Pete Wilson to attempt a reorganization and fund raid of the retirement system in the 1991 fight with the legislature over a state budget. The Republican governor, like his predecessor, Republican George Deukmejian, sought to balance the budget using CALPERS funds.

Wilson's proposal was to replace the thirteen-member board with a nine-member board—five named by the governor. Six of the members who are elected by state employees and retirees would have been dropped, as would seats held by the state's elected treasurer and controller (both Democrats) who normally side with the beneficiary representatives. Although Wilson failed to take over the CALPERS board, he was able to divert $2 billion from CALPERS to reduce the state budget deficit. Many shareholder activists identified the Business Roundtable as the force behind Wilson's efforts.[60]

In August 1991 CALPERS reported on its proxy voting for the year. Wilson's attack on CALPERS has ready resulted in CALPERS' retreating on corporate shareholder issues in the 1992 shareholder season. It released its new voting guidelines on several "social/political" issues that will be on future shareholders' agendas. In a major step backwards, CALPERS has decided to take the following actions:

1. Vote against shareholder proposals asking for a report on the Valdez Principles
2. Abstain on shareholder proposals asking for signing of the Valdez Principles
3. Vote against Israel boycott resolutions
4. Vote against a report on the equal employment and environmental effects of U.S. companies' Maquiladora operations
5. Vote against shareholder proposals asking for a report on companies' role in poor and minority communities
6. Vote against all tobacco-related shareholder proposals, except the proposal that establishes minimum labeling and marketing standards for tobacco sales in Third World countries[61]

Dale Hansen indicated that CALPERS would also attempt to negotiate with corporate management rather than introduce shareholder resolutions in the future. Hansen admitted, however, "I have some trustees on our board who are not particularly happy with this approach; they would much rather we do the resolutions."[62]

Growth in Socially Conscious Investing

The tremendous growth in assets of funds managed utilizing social criteria was caused primarily by the civil war in South Africa and the popularity of the divestment campaign. Almost every state legislature, university, and local government across the country was being asked to take some form of action, from simply adopting a resolution expressing opposition to apartheid in South Africa, to halting business with companies operating in South Africa or divesting stocks, bonds, or short-term securities from companies identified with South Africa. According to the Social Investment Forum, the majority of the $40 billion in socially screened investment assets in 1985 was due to South Africa–related investment restrictions. The same is true in 1991, as the figure of socially screened assets exceeds $625 billion, mainly representing large institutional investors that have divested from companies in South Africa.

In 1989 the nation's largest pension fund, which now manages over $83.1 billion for college employees, announced that it was offering its 1.2 million participants a new social investment option. TIAA-CREF introduced a stock and bond fund that avoids securities of companies in South Africa, nuclear power companies, and some companies in Northern Ireland that have not signed the MacBride Principles. It also excludes companies with significant business stemming from weapons manufacturing, alcoholic beverages, or tobacco.[63] As of December 31, 1991, the fund has grown to over $166 million.

In 1982 Wayne Silby and John Guffey created the Washington, D.C.-based Calvert Social Investment Funds, first launching a socially responsible money market fund and later a managed growth fund, a bond fund, an equity fund, and two Calvert Ariel funds. Working Assets Money Fund was opened in San Francisco in September 1983 by eight individuals (including myself), which has strong and comprehensive social and economic criteria.

Since the mid-eighties other social mutual funds have been created: the Parnassus Fund, the Progressive Environmental Fund, Merrill Lynch's Eco·Logical Trust, the Global Environment Fund Limited Partnership, the Muir Trust, and the Domini Social Index Fund (See Chapter 8). Portfolio managers have increased their socially screened assets under management, and many traditional firms have increasingly expanded their client base and are managing "social" money. (See Chapter 7).

Most of these funds, however, are only screened for South African exposure and managed by very traditional and conservative portfolio management firms, banks, and insurance companies. John Schultz, president of the Social Investment Forum, is responsible for monitoring the growth of socially conscious assets: he projects an enormous rate of growth in the future.

> In this decade there will be $300 billion in growth and in the upcoming century there will be at least $2 trillion of growth left, especially when we start considering the issue of the environment.

In addition, since 1984, when Amy Domini and Peter Kinder wrote *Ethical Investing* (published in 1986), the popularity of responsible investing and its role in a contemporary economy was just being felt. Since then, another dozen books have been written on responsible investing, and numerous investment newsletters and a magazine are now published that are totally committed to serving the responsibly investing public. Several social investment research organizations have expanded or sprung up, as well as responsible portfolio management firms, financial planning companies, and a brokerage firm, Progressive Asset Management (PAM). There is even an alternative to the Chamber of Commerce: Businesses for Social Responsibility. In the remainder of this book you will learn more about socially conscious investing and the numerous investment opportunities and resources available to change the world through the responsible management of your assets.

If socially responsible investing is a movement to address the world's many social and economic justice issues, are the leaders of the movement up to the challenge? I believe they are, but first we must understand the policies and controversy inside the movement itself. Let's take a look at the debate inside responsible investing.

CHAPTER TWO

The Debate Inside
Responsible Investing

Professionals attribute the success of responsible investing to the public's increasing awareness of the power of money to influence political and economic decision making in America. Corporate contributions to American politicians are so large now that we almost have brand-name elected officials. Environmental, health, safety, land use, and other issues are resolved not necessarily by logic or by a democratic decision-making process but rather by raw economic power: money. We have the best Congress that money can buy. The Golden Rule prevails: "He who has the gold, rules."

Wielding economic and political power was certainly not the goal of early responsible investors. The avoidance of certain investments was an ethical issue. The American church, as an institution of society, found the investment of church funds in companies involved with alcohol, tobacco, gambling, or weapons morally reprehensible and inconsistent with the teachings and objectives of the church. The church was not taking action to economically or politically punish companies or to extract some economic or political concession. It simply chose not to take profit from what it viewed as morally suspect economic ventures. The church was merely avoiding what it viewed as "sin investments."

The Vietnam War galvanized the responsible investment movement by uniting political activists and church leaders in support of a new moral and economic order. By the mid-1960s American churches, like universities, had accumulated vast amounts of capital, much of which was invested in companies profiting greatly from the war. The churches, and later the universities, had to come to moral terms with the dividends they were receiving from their investments. It became impossible for the churches to preach love of humanity from the pulpit on Sunday while collecting napalm dividends on Monday.

The use of napalm on men, women, and children in Vietnam shocked the American public. When investors learned that profit-soaring Dow Chemical produced the napalm, many sold their stocks. Dow Chemical was, in Americans' minds, the paradigm of the military industrial complex, a concept first identified by President Dwight D. Eisenhower. The savage brutality of antipersonnel weapons used by U.S. military forces heightened public awareness of companies such as the Honeywell Corporation, which manufactured the weapons. Honeywell was a prime Department of Defense contractor and was making a staggering profit. Investors who were opposed to the Vietnam War began to see the linkage between their investment dollars, their dividend checks, and the senseless carnage abroad. The "idea people" of the responsible investment movement had a new audience.

Is Responsible Investing Political?

Shareholder resolutions were introduced in the early 1970s by churches and other concerned investors not to demand moral purity but to act as responsible owners. Campaign GM, the shareholder campaign to focus attention on General Motors Corporation, was specifically designed to impact corporate behavior and influence corporate decision making. Campaign GM successfully convinced management to nominate to the board of directors a person of color, the Reverend Leon Sullivan. Reverend Sullivan's nomination led to the creation of Sullivan's South African corporate code of conduct and eventually his call for total South African corporate withdrawal.

A church investment policy of corporate avoidance based upon moral grounds evolved into antiwar corporate campaigns to not only "purify" portfolios on ethical grounds but to financially punish some corporations for profiting from death and destruction. Acts of ethical avoidance turned to overt political acts designed to inflict economic and political damage. Is modern day socially responsible investing simply an apolitical ethical act to "feel good about investing," or is it by its very nature likely to have political and economic ramifications?

The best place to find answers to this question is inside the Social Investment Forum. The forum is the best representative of the professionals involved in responsible investing. Members include professionals in accounting, bookkeeping, legal services, portfolio management, brokerages, academia, research, and publishing as well as government, church, community, and foundation service. There are several local and regional responsible investment groups such as the Bay Area Socially Responsible Investment Professionals (BASRIP) in San Francisco, the Long Island Social Investment Forum in New York, and SRI Pacific Northwest in Portland, Oregon.

John Schultz, a Minneapolis financial planner, is the current president of the forum. He is a crusty, plain-spoken Midwesterner who believes responsible investing is part of a larger political movement:

> There's no question it's a political movement because it flies in the face of conventional corporate management wisdom which is the corporation's golden rule: If I have the gold, I make the rules. It's largely conventional financial education which is based on the nineteenth-century concept, currently endorsed by such people as Milton Friedman, that the primary goal of management is just to maximize stockholder wealth. Corporate management must work to maximize wealth of all the stake holders—that is, the shareholders, employees, debtors, customers, community—and expand the protection of the environment.

Peter Camejo is president and CEO of Progressive Asset Management, an Oakland-based brokerage firm specializing in socially responsible investing. He was a national political activist in the 1960s and firmly believes responsible investing is social, political and economic:

> It's a direct reflection of the changes in society—a movement of minority rights, the protection of the environment, a political movement for women's rights; all these movements interface or affect how people look at investments, and that's why there is a socially responsible investment community at all. I think that the movement is in essence a rainbow—a spectrum of different interests and issues which all come together through investing.

Wayne Silby, founder of the Calvert Group and president of the Calvert SIF Managed Growth Fund, also advocates venture fund investing having high social and economic impact. He reflects a more philosophical view of the world of responsible investing:

> We weren't trying to redefine previous generations but focus on our own. We also wanted a concept that was uplifting contrasted to one that was the "us against them" type of thing. We were trying to appeal to people with a sense of compassion about the world. Our mission, in a sense, was to show that you can stand by your values and get a competitive rate of return.

Lyndon Comstock, chairman of the board of Community Capital Bank, methodically implemented a five-year plan to open his development bank in Brooklyn, New York, in 1990. He considers himself a banker and a community activist:

> I like to think the movement is political and social. Maybe it's part of my own personal identification that at heart I always like to tell myself it's a political activist movement. I like to think I've gotten a little smarter in the years that have gone by on how we can create change within a particular time, place and cultural setting. To me the end result is how we can try to help.
>
> The most significant goal is to increase capital flow back into community development. That's the reason I got into this in the first place. By far the most interesting and exciting story that has happened within the movement is the South Shore Bank story and what impact they've had in lending to the Chicago community. Community lending is where we could really make a contribution. It's very important to have a social vision in the field of finance or investment.

Some professionals in the responsible investing field have contrary views on whether social investing is needed at all or whether it should be an avenue for political or social action. Trex Proffitt, a research analyst for social issues services at IRRC, a well-respected investment research organization based in Washington, D.C.—for over 20 years, sees it as a political exercise:

> IRRC does not see a *need* for socially responsible investing. IRRC sees socially responsible investing as a political exercise through a particular vehicle, economic investment activity. It is constrained by the limitations of that vehicle and is not one of the more effective ways of changing communities, cities, national policy, or foreign governments, and not even corporate behavior. Simple acts like voting in the next national election will probably have a far greater impact on our country's public policy goals than social investing. The actions of elected officials, such as a vote in favor of altering the tax code to favor certain goals, would cause, overnight, more corporate change in the desired area than social investing has in its entire history.
>
> While there are many pitfalls to the social investor, the biggest is that investing is simply not a medium that lends itself to determining or achieving any particular social goals. Despite what supply-side economists or some left-wing activists would say, investing one's money to make more money does not carry an easily identified positive good or bad for society.

David Schoenwald is a founder, director, and vice president of the New Alternatives Fund, an environmental stock mutual fund based in

Great Neck, New York, which opened to investors in 1982. David doesn't see the New Alternatives Fund as having any particular political or social agenda but believes responsible investing to some extent is political.

> People involved in responsible investing are liberal and would vote for liberal politicians and liberal positions. The Iraq War has created some confusion on what I believe on some of these subjects. I'm not trying to promote Democrats or liberals or any political candidates. Generally, I think alternative energy is good, napalm and fragmentation bombs should be avoided, and we should promote civil rights. J. P. Stevens used to be the terrible employer, but I don't agree with the unions on every issue. So, it's expressing a point of view. My particular perspective should not be fitted into somebody's dogma.

The majority of the founders of the forum see the responsible investment movement as an economic strategy for social and political change in America. The strategy is to attract a significant portion of investment capital, positively affecting the flow of capital to both geographic and economically deprived areas traditionally starved of capital. Much of the leadership also believes that an increasing array of investment products and services will lead investors to recognize that responsible investing can provide competitive—if not superior—financial returns, be socially progressive, and promote greater long-term economic benefits.

Is Responsible Investing Wall Street Hype?

Responsible investing professionals differ in opinion as to how to appeal to investors and attract capital. Some are attempting to attract the "hard" capital, which means attracting investors who are willing to take greater risk or less return or both for more social and economic impact. Chuck Matthei, Joan Shapiro, and Lyndon Comstock fit into this category. Chuck and his community and church loan funds are endeavoring to attract capital to be directly invested for less than market-rate return to finance low-income housing and community small business. Joan, along with South Shore Bank and other locally based financial institutions, is working to develop lending policies which will ensure that neighborhood capital is recycled to benefit and stay in the community. She has been successful in establishing development deposits at South Shore Bank to attract outside capital, primarily from more affluent investors, to target low-income needs. Lyndon Comstock also created his Community Capital Bank specifically to refocus attention and capital to meet the needs of poorer neighborhoods in New York.

Socially responsible venture funds such as Wayne Silby's Calvert Social Venture Partners are also oriented to attract capital to business ventures that by their very nature provide socially useful or beneficial products or services such as health care or foods that are natural or organically grown.

Loan funds, development banks, venture networks, such as Investors Circle, and socially responsible venture funds are investment opportunities for placing capital directly into projects. These types of investment ventures represent a small part of the responsible investing movement. The overwhelming majority of the $625 billion in professionally managed, socially screened money, however, is invested in publicly traded securities such as stocks and bonds and in mutual funds. This means that very little "social capital" is directly placed in local communities and neighborhoods. Stocks, bonds, and mutual funds are the fastest growing segment of responsible investing. Professionals involved in such securities and mutual fund business are the expanding market for Social Investment Forum membership.

While there is statistical evidence to support the positive social and economic impact of direct investing in communities and neighborhoods (microeconomic impact), there is less evidence of social and economic impact on society (macroeconomic impact) by secondary market investing. A notable exception, however, would be the significant impact of institutional and individual investors that refused to invest and divested from stocks, bonds, and other publicly traded securities in companies operating in South Africa. The divestment movement, coupled with the refusal of public agencies to contract with such companies, precipitated a major U.S. corporate exodus from South Africa, which caused major economic and political damage to the apartheid regime.

There is a quantifiable positive impact on employment when a loan fund makes a loan to a community-based nonprofit organization to rehabilitate housing for low-income residents. There is very little quantifiable evidence to show a direct positive impact when an investment is made in a mutual fund and then the mutual fund invests in a publicly traded stock. In the case of a company trading on the stock exchange, whether you invest in a company's stock directly or through your mutual fund, you will have little if any impact on the company's economic activity. The exception may be when you or your mutual fund are actively seeking new companies involved in economic expansion and job creation through regular business activity. Another exception is if a mutual fund invests in Initial Public Offerings (IPO) in which the newly invested capital goes directly into a new business enterprise.

Seeking to bridge the impact between direct and indirect investing is the Calvert Social Investment Fund, which places up to 1 percent of the fund's assets in high impact investments. Jerry Dodson has also created three additional Parnassus funds: a California tax-exempt municipal bond fund, a balanced fund, and a fixed-income fund. Up to 10 percent of the assets of the balanced fund and the fixed-income fund may be invested in community development loan funds that will provide a direct source of "hard" capital for neighborhood economic development.

To understand the effect of direct placement investing, one needs to consider the multiplier effect of one billion dollars invested in housing construction. According to multiplier studies and input-output models, for $1 billion invested, construction of private single-family housing generates 19,100 on-site, 14,600 indirect, and 103,100 induced jobs, whereas the construction of multi-unit housing generates 31,900 on-site, 13,500 indirect, and 172,300 induced jobs.[1]

Many responsible investment professionals differ on the benefit of continuing to increase the number of socially responsible mutual funds as opposed to concentrating more attention on attracting socially invested money currently invested in stocks, bonds, and mutual funds and channeling it into direct placements such as small businesses and housing. This can be accomplished by investing through development banks, loan funds, or venture funds. Naturally "indirect" investment proponents want to see increased capital attracted to responsible investing whether it is "direct" or "indirect." The claim is that additional capital strengthens the secondary market and the liquidity of such responsible investment opportunities.

The debate within the responsible investment community is also over the question of style or substance. Is it enough to "feel good about your money" being invested in stocks, bonds, or mutual funds that avoid specific corporate practices and support others? Or should a more active social, economic, and political course be taken? Should Social Investment Forum members join with activists such as Ray Rogers and engage in corporate campaigns?

At least eight large brokerage firms, including Shearson Lehman, Smith Barney, Prudential Securities, and Scudder, now offer portfolio management or research designed for social investors. Scudder publishes a newsletter entitled "The Socially Responsible Investor," and in

1985 Prudential Securities created the Social Investment Research Service (SIRS), which has developed 30 data bases utilized for screening portfolios for social investors. SIRS's reports are published in Prudential's *Strategy Weekly*. In April 1989 Shearson Lehman investment management announced a special personalized social screen for clients with assets over $100,000. Shearson screens 1600 companies for financial strength and then narrows the list to 300 companies suitable for the Socially Responsible Investment Program. This list can be narrowed again to 75, which may be suitable to meet specific social objectives. According to Shearson the most common criteria used to screen companies are:

- Involvement in South Africa
- Weapons manufacturing (defense contracting)
- Operation of nuclear power facilities
- Unsafe environmental practices or products
- Manufacturing of alcohol or tobacco products
- Operations of casinos or manufacture of gambling devices[2]

With so many traditional Wall Street firms getting in on the $625 billion action of responsible investing, many of the original founders are getting nervous about the political, social and economic commitment of these newcomers. The professionals who have been in the field of responsible investment for the past 20 years view themselves as hard-liners who stick to a fairly uniform set of social investment principles. They see the potential for a new generation of financial professionals simply ripping off the concept of responsible investment for their own personal financial gain.

Joan Shapiro of South Shore Bank in Chicago explains this concern:

> The thing that makes me most nervous is social investing as a marketing gimmick. You've heard me say it and I say it every time I speak publicly or privately. I think that "doing well by doing good" is trivialized and is a terrible danger. For years responsible investing was negative. I think the real test is not what's screened out, but what you are seeking. I think it is critical and a question we've been asking at the forum for the last five years, although I think most people paid lip service to it.
>
> Hundreds if not thousands of brokers and financial planners have now added the social investment shingle to their shops and put out their literature. On the one hand, having lots of people doing it is a very powerful marketing tool, but, on the other hand, will they really try to make a difference and move more money to the community level or simply screen investment products?

Randy Barber, author of *The North Will Rise Again* and a member of the board of advisors of both Working Assets and the Calvert Social Investment Fund, waxed philosophically:

> You have the financial scavengers or the people who basically take techniques evolved elsewhere and when it's safe to use they're going to use and market them. We can like or dislike their motives or their techniques, but the fact is it's going to happen and it will broaden the market.

Very few members of the Social Investment Forum have engaged in corporate campaigns, with the exception of those campaigns related to South African divestment. Tim Smith's Interfaith Center on Corporate Responsibility (ICCR), while very supportive of shareholder and consumer action, has a more moderate political agenda. With the exception of Ray Rogers' J. P. Stevens campaign, most activity has been rather staid. Most unions have so far refused to exercise their muscle to negotiate joint pension administration. When they have, few trusts have exerted significant pressure as shareholders or moved capital in any organized fashion based upon a national strategy. Strikes and national boycotts, without a centralized command structure, have had little impact on corporate behavior. Environmental organizations and activists have also failed to recognize the power of the corporate campaign.

Forum Principles

For years Social Investment Forum members have discussed membership criteria but have never come to a decision about who qualifies and who doesn't. The discussion centers around whether membership should be limited to investment professionals who sign a loyalty oath regarding responsible investing or if it should be open to anyone who pays dues. I've even suggested that new members be sponsored by fellow financial professionals. My intention is not to make the Social Investment Forum an exclusive club of people who stick to the party line, but rather to ensure that new members adhere to the same ethical standards and philosophical guidelines as those who founded the organization. Membership in the Forum presently requires a new member to affirm the Statement of Principles, as follows:

1. Members agree to support the work of and to disseminate information about the SIF and the work of its members.
2. Members commit to assist, either individually or with other SIF members, in improving the public's understanding of socially responsible

investing and in supporting the theory and practice of same, which includes the concepts of ethical and alternative investments.

3. Members endeavor to place the public interest and the interest of their client over their own. The responsibility of SIF members extends not only to the individual, but also to society.

4. Members strive to act with a high degree of personal integrity, maintaining honorable relationships with colleagues, clients and all those who rely on the member's professional judgement and skills.

5. Members seek continually to maintain and improve the knowledge, skills and competence relevant to their profession and to be diligent in the performance of their occupational duties.

6. Members make an affirmative commitment to apply honest, thorough and diligent methods of research and evaluation.

7. Members should obey the laws and regulations relevant to their profession and should avoid any conduct or activity that would cause unjust harm to others.

8. Members should use the fact of membership in a manner consistent with the SIF's by-laws and Statement of Principles. Membership in the SIF is not intended to endorse an individual member's or an organization's business qualifications, values or practices.

In the near future the forum will have to grapple with the regulation of the activities of professionals in the business. Today anyone can hang out a shingle and claim to be a socially responsible investment counselor. The advertising hype of modern America is the product of skilled manipulators who can take the best intended idea or product and trivialize it. I was contacted last year by a woman in Los Angeles who told me that she responded to an advertisement in the *Los Angeles Times* that listed a financial planner as "socially responsible." The woman found herself educating the so-called socially responsible financial advisor about the Pax World Fund and Calvert. The planner knew absolutely nothing about responsible investment but was clever enough to use the term as an attraction for new clients.

Joan Shapiro has given the issue a great deal of thought in her six years on the SIF Board:

I think it would be very useful for us, as a national movement, to figure out how to help people judge responsible investment practitioners. I think the SIF has got to figure out how to become a more dominant force in the field without a $500,000 marketing budget. This is now becoming an international movement, and by the year 2000 socially responsible investing in a sense will be business as usual.

Is Responsible Investing A Capitalist Contradiction?

In the early days of responsible investing, socially concerned investors simply avoided the Dow Chemical and Honeywells or decided to stay out of the stock market altogether because it was too riddled with capitalistic contradictions. Many people thought they were doing the right thing by simply putting their money in a bank savings account. They thought this was at least neutral. People continue to hold on to a naïve belief that when they give their money to a bank teller it goes into a vault where it sits drawing interest until it's withdrawn. Banks make loans, sometimes for socially and environmentally offensive endeavors.

In the late 1970s there was a large environmental organization that was found to be investing in major polluters. The organization's leadership reacted so negatively that they pulled out of stocks completely and invested all of their money in Treasury bills. Of course, that wasn't necessarily the right investment or social answer since Treasury securities support the national deficit. Many departments of the federal government, including the Department of Defense and the Department of Energy, support weapons research and nuclear power, and are responsible for hazardous waste. The CIA's $30 billion dollar budget is used to overthrow foreign governments and fund many terrorist organizations. Relatively naïve investors sometimes find that, while thinking they were investing to avoid defense, they were actually investing in money market funds or banks that lend to major weapons suppliers. There really is no neutral investment. Every time you, as an investor, try to make a profit, your capital investment makes a political statement. Buy stocks in a company that is a major polluter, and your profit comes from pollution. Invest in a clothing manufacturer that uses child labor in a foreign country, and your profit comes from exploiting children. Put your money in a bank that refuses to give loans locally to minority businesses, and your interest is earned through discrimination. Capital power molds our society. More and more Americans are learning that their invested money helps shape the kind of America we live in.

Wall Street has picked up on this trend. Many traditional brokerage firms have "socially responsible" departments or investment advisory services. In many cases "socially responsible" is simply a phrase used to attract clients. Brokers in many nationally recognized firms are allowed to manage clients' assets using some form of social criteria, mostly directed by the client. Having Wall Street committed to social responsibility is akin to having no bread lines in Russia—it may happen, but it takes time. Many of these national firms only support brokers who do responsible investing to the extent that they are big producers of commission revenue, which ensures their job security. They are not kept on because they are doing good work, but because they support the firm's bottom line. Many brokerage firms' largest underwriting clients are companies that are excluded from SRI portfolios. It may not be in the best financial interests of the brokerage firm to widely advertise SRI services.

PAM was founded in 1987 by five brokers and three financial planners who were either working on their own or for nationally recognized firms such as Merrill Lynch, PaineWebber, Dean Witter Reynolds, and Prudential Securities. The four women and four men decided to leave their firms because they realized that there was no firmwide support for responsible investing. They wanted to both own and manage their own business and expand socially responsible investing opportunities. Very few people have the fortitude or the client base that Bob Schwartz had in those early years to stay with a traditional Wall Street firm.

The only way to ensure that a broker or financial planner meets your criteria for social responsiblity is to question him or her personally and to seek a lot of references (see Chapter 7). There is no way the Social Investment Forum can ensure political correctness or require professionals to adopt a uniform definition of socially responsible investing. What the Forum can do, however, is serve as an information network for responsible investors to become more educated about responsible investing as well as informed about all of the professional services and investment opportunities that are available.

Many brokerage firms' largest underwriting clients are companies that are excluded from SRI portfolios. It may not be in the best financial interests of the brokerage firm to widely advertise SRI services.

The Road to Success

Financial professionals in the field of responsible investing who have witnessed its evolution are often frustrated that it takes so long for the investing public to accept social or ethical investing. Some, like Don Smart of Charing Associates in Madison, Wisconsin, and one of the first to study pension fund targeting, takes a long-term view:

> When the socially responsible activity began it was almost all coming from the Left. It was like anti-Vietnam War sentiment—it took awhile to catch on. The same is true of South African divestment. Once it infiltrated

the conservative community it just rocketed. Maybe socially responsible investing is similar to combating racism: it may take a generation for full acceptance.

Robert Zevin of U.S. Trust Company, Boston, believes that responsible investing should be carefully presented to investors:

> I would prefer that people were more cautious when indicating that social criteria will have no negative impact on performance. Some social criteria will have a negative impact upon performance. If we claim that any and all social criteria is moral and therefore positive relative to performance, we're just fooling ourselves. We know for a fact that in the case of South African divestment there was no substantial negative impact upon performance, but when we exclude tobacco companies such as Philip Morris there's no way we can duplicate the S&P 500 over the last 10 years.

Some in the community also caution about being overconfident and warn that all may not come up roses in the future. In the case of tobacco divestment, Tim Smith, executive director of ICCR, believes that it would be a mistake for the responsible investment community to expect immediate success on tobacco divestment campaigns:

> There's no way we are going to successfully convince the tobacco industry to pull back production and marketing of such a lethal product. We also haven't succeeded in encouraging many companies—some, but only a few—not to make nuclear weapons. We're winning in terms of public awareness, but we're not winning in terms of stopping the companies from producing such harmful products.

Responsible investing is, in some ways, creating a more ethical capitalism in the financial services industry, but it is still capitalism and one of the objectives is to turn a profit. Competition within the industry creates conflict, often leading to the lack of cooperation. Cooperation is a goal of many responsible investment advocates in order to expand the base and assets under the management of social investors.

Lyndon Comstock, chairman and founder of the Brooklyn-based Community Capital Bank, feels there is still a tendency to "protect our turf." Comstock knows the importance of cooperation. He relied heavily upon many of the institutional investors, especially the church community, that support socially responsible investing to capitalize his bank. The Ecumenical Development Cooperative Society (EDCS) was one of his investors; now he is working with Progressive Asset Management to help EDCS raise its capital for Third World economic development loan funds.

Alice Tepper Marlin, founder and executive director of CEP, also believes that social investment research organizations and mutual funds need to share data and information:

> We'd all work together better if we shared information. The Social Investment Forum is wonderful in facilitating sharing. But, for example, IRRC has a major environmental project and CEP has a major environmental project and we can't seem to share information on it. The different funds all have social information which is regarded as proprietary with few willing to share it. Somehow there needs to be a better community of interest.

Historically the social investment community has been fragmented. Some of this comes from geography—several small or struggling firms on the opposite ends of the country finding it difficult or nearly impossible to communicate. Some of the division comes from personalities, people unwilling or not used to sharing ideas or business.

The Social Investment Forum, which was formally launched in 1985 to facilitate networking and sharing of socially responsible investment information, initially received limited support and participation by such pioneers in the movement as Pax World Fund and Dreyfus Third Century Fund. Both of these funds owe much of their growth to the work of the founders of SIF and South African divestment activity, yet these mutual funds were late in jumping on the anti-apartheid bandwagon. Dreyfus has only one "social" fund and its social commitment, if based upon its vague social criteria, makes it suspect. Pax World is somewhat isolated in New Hampshire, and its social criteria and more conservative management limited its leadership when dealing with a South African divestment movement that was seen by many as politically radical. By the mid-eighties, divestment had become more widespread and accepted by individual and large institutional investors. Pax World and Dreyfus also received some shareholder and church pressure for a more anti-apartheid stand, especially when comprehensive U.S. sanctions legislation became a reality and the Reverend Leon Sullivan denounced his own code of conduct as unworkable.

Since its inception, Working Assets Money Fund has been the most pro-active of all the social mutual funds. In the past the research staff communicated with activists in labor, environmental, and community organizations to assist them in digging out financial information on targeted companies. Working Assets also engaged in letter-writing campaigns to corporate management both to inform management of Working Assets' position on issues as well as to assess corporate policy.

Through its management company, the Fund has also worked on national corporate campaigns coordinated by the American Committee on Africa, TransAfrica, ICCR, and the AFL-CIO.

Social investment research organizations—especially the IRRC, which was founded by progressive Ivy League educational institutions—received their initial institutional subscribers as a direct result of anti-apartheid and other social investment activity. IRRC now bends over backwards to avoid any public relationships with progressive shareholders and responsible investment activists. IRRC even goes so far as to say there is no need for socially responsible investing, even though the organization's creation stemmed from it and IRRC's financial survival depends upon it. IRRC's overwhelming financial support and subscriber base has shifted from more liberal-oriented educational organizations and foundations to conservative banks, insurance companies, and pension funds. IRRC's conservativism simply reflects its financial constituency.

Some of the competitiveness is related to egotism and "turf fights." Much of it is typical of the industry. Financial service is a very competitive field, and, like it or not, we live in a world dominated by the power of money. There is constant tension between the needs to turn a profit, share information, and work for the collective benefit of the socially responsible investment movement. It has been very difficult for many responsible investment firms to work together, jointly market, and share social data and information. On the other hand, thanks primarily to the Social Investment Forum, seminars and trade shows sponsored by the forum and its members consistently attract large audiences of investors and financial professionals and have been responsible for growth in both assets and responsible investment professionals, services, and products.

Over the last two years there has also been some change in the area of joint ventures and cooperation between different responsible investing firms. PAM, in a joint venture with the Massachusetts-based research organization of Kinder, Lyndenberg, Domini, Inc., has signed a contract to socially and environmentally screen companies for Franklin Management, Inc., the investment management subsidiary of San Mateo, California—based Franklin Resources. Franklin is managing assets for several environmental clients and has other clients that have demanded an environmental screening program. PAM also worked with AI Group in Boston to offer low-income housing tax credit programs to retail brokerage clients.

Cooperation between U.S. Trust and Calvert is evident. U.S. Trust acts as Subadvisor for the Calvert SIF. FRDC also screens the Calvert Ariel Appreciation Fund for environmental concerns as well as serving as Subadvisor for the Nader-oriented Green Environmental mutual funds being organized in Los Angeles.

As early as 1988, after PAM was created as a brokerage firm specializing in socially responsible investing, I had a vision of jointly marketing Working Assets Money Fund and PAM and eventually merging the two companies because of similar ownership, common market, similar research needs, and mutual location (the San Francisco Bay area). A merged company could serve as a larger corporate entity able to adequately raise significant capital to compete with traditional brokerage firms, mutual funds, and portfolio managers. Internal feuding at Working Assets and disagreements between Working Assets' management company, trustees, and limited partners reduced this vision to reality. In 1991 I was forced to realize that creating a larger national socially responsible financial institution would have to be postponed. Working Assets was sold to a new group of investors in November 1991.

The New York-based ICCR has had success in coordinating shareholder resolutions introduced by many in the responsible investment community. ICCR has had even greater success in working through the forum to help launch the Valdez Principles with the Council on Environmentally Responsible Economies (CERES), which was the creation of FRDC's Joan Bavaria. CERES was initially financed by members of the forum.

ICCR has also been very successful in providing a communications network among church investors, investment activists, and financial professionals. Because of Tim Smith and ICCR's leadership at the corporate shareholder level, ICCR is the first to be contacted when a group considers a corporate campaign. For example, the Business Executives for National Security (BENS), an organization based in Washington, D.C., that unveiled a code of conduct for weapons exporters, recently met with ICCR to discuss shareholder action. BENS's code calls on companies that export arms to assist in halting the spread of nuclear, biological, or chemical weapons and missiles; support the "letter and spirit of current and future laws against the proliferation of such weapons"; and refuse to knowingly export products, technologies, or services used in the "unlawful or unconscionable development of such weapons."[3]

Do We Practice What We Preach?

Profits are now being made by responsible investing institutions, from Pax World Fund to Parnassus and Working Assets. Progressive Asset Management has made a modest profit in two out of three fiscal years, while FRDC has struggled since 1987 with high overhead and internal management problems. Although Working Assets became a profitable investment for its limited partners and management company share-holders, it was consistently faced with internal personality clashes and numerous management changes. For Working Assets, the road to acceptability by investors, credibility, and financial success has been a rocky and difficult one.

The values of responsible investing and traditional capitalism often clash. Many responsible investing financial institutions and professionals have spent a great deal of time attempting to democratize the corporate decision-making process and encourage employee participation. FRDC gave all employees a share of stock, elected employees to the board of directors, and encouraged maximum participation at all corporate levels. Working Assets elected its original two employees to the board of directors and provided stock ownership; it later found out that the last thing the employees wanted was to be in the middle of board and internal management company turmoil. PAM awarded stock to all its employees and brokers; at one time a majority of its elected board consisted of brokers. PAM management found that it was difficult to run a company for the benefit of its shareholders when it conflicted with the financial interests of its brokers.

Joan Shapiro and others in the Social Investment Forum constantly warn that forum members should practice what they preach when it comes to ethical business practices, ownership opportunities for employees, advancement of women and minorities within socially responsible businesses, and participation of such on boards of directors. We must also be concerned with how we treat our employees and each other within the responsible investment community. Another question that is always being raised is who owns and controls progressive financial institutions and who will provide leadership in the future.

The leadership and social record inside responsible investing are improving, but there are still major questions. One of the largest responsible portfolio managers, U.S. Trust, is a conservative New England bank. With the exception of Robert Zevin's socially sensitive portfolio management influence within U.S. Trust, it's hard to believe the company's board of directors will provide progressive national leadership on major responsible investment issues.

The largest responsible investment mutual fund family, Calvert Group, is owned by a conservative insurance company, Acacia, based in Washington, D.C. Wayne Silby, John Guffey, and Stan Sorrell exert progressive and enlightened influence within Calvert, but ownership and control is still Acacia's.

Pax World, Global Environment, Dreyfus, PAM, New Alternatives and Parnassus are still owned by their founders. FRDC is still independent but was almost sold on two occasions—once to Sophia Collier, who then successfully purchased Working Assets. There is no union representation at any of the socially responsible investment organizations.

With the exception of Ariel's John Rogers and PAM's Peter Camejo, minorities are certainly under-represented in ownership positions in the responsible investment community. Women, however, have comprised much of the leadership of responsible investing throughout its history. Joan Bavaria, FRDC's president, was also the founding President of the forum. Joan Shapiro of South Shore Bank was the forum's second president. Alice Tepper Marlin and Margaret Carroll

Table 2.1   Board of Directors/Trustees (*Source:* Fund publications and discussion with fund staff. September 1, 1991.)

Organization	Total	Minorities	Women
US Trust Co., Boston	20	1	2
Franklin Research & Development (FRDC)	5[A]	0	2
Progressive Asset Management (PAM)	5	2	1[B]
Pax World Fund	9	2	2
Dreyfus Third Century	5	2	2[C]
Calvert SIF Funds	9	2	3
Calvert Ariel Funds	7	2	1
New Alternatives Fund	6	0	1
Muir Investment Trust	5	1	3[C]
Domini Social Index Trust	8	1	3
Parnassus Fund	3	1	1[B]
Shield Progressive Environmental Fund	5	1	0
Working Assets Money Fund	10	5	6[D]

[A] Four of the five directors are also employees.
[B] The woman is also a minority
[C] One of the women is also a minority.
[D] Two of the women are also minorities.

have been the pacesetters in the leading social investment research organizations such as the CEP and the IRRC, respectively. Amy Domini is a successful portfolio manager, a nationally recognized spokesperson for responsible investing, author of *Ethical Investing,* and head of the Domini Social Index Trust, a socially screened index mutual fund. Sophia Collier is the new 60 percent owner of Working Assets; she achieved her initial success through the creation of Soho Natural Soda.

Some of the forum's most successful brokers and financial planners are women. They have included PAM brokers Ellen Stromberg, Constance Finley, MaryAnn Simpson, Janet Ader, and operations manager and chief administrative officer Cathy Cartier. Visible and articulate Bay Area financial planners include Virginia King, Janiel Jolley, Bonnie Albion, and Kathleen Kendziorski of Seattle, Washington, and brokers such as Shelly McFarland of Dain Bosworth in Portland, Oregon. Tamsin Taylor, a nationally recognized socially responsible investment advisor, was a pioneer in writing one of the first investment targeting studies, writing institutional and social criteria, and providing leadership on many local and state government investment organizations.

Women and minorities are fairly represented on most of the boards of directors of socially responsible financial institutions, as shown in Table 2.1.

As you can see, while women are represented in socially responsible financial institutions, minorities are still under-represented. With a few exceptions, the responsible investment community also exhibits a considerable homophobic bias.

Responsible Investing is a Human Relationship

There is no universal definition of socially responsible investing. It will evolve and change with personal experiences, society, and the ability of the investment community to respond to social and political issues. There is no socially pure investment or company, just as there is no totally "politically correct" investment decision. The best we can do is make an attempt to invest using comprehensive social and financial criteria consistent with the investor's goals and objectives.

No one in American society today can escape our economic system. You have to eat; you have to clothe yourself; you have to have shelter. These essentials are all provided by a system built on investment capital. Sure, you can grow your own food, weave your own cloth, and build your own lean-to, but the pollution in the air, the contamination of the water, and the noise of an industrial society keeps you connected to the system. Purity becomes a moot point. Responsible investing seeks to exert maximum economic pressure within the system to produce the greatest benefit for all society, not just one sement of it.

Chuck Matthei, founder of the Institute for Community Economics and of the loan fund movement, once said:

> Investing is a human relationship. It's not simply a financial or mechanical or abstract transaction. In the gospel it's very clear that the purpose of investing is to help those with the greatest need.

All investment decisions will not result in helping those with the greatest need, but *some* investment decisions can. Every responsible investor is concerned about making a competitive return and at the same time improving society. Investing in moderate income housing, earning tax credits for historic rehabilitation and low income housing, and investing in small businesses in economically depressed areas of cities all stimulate a sector of the economy that is usually ignored by traditional investing. Investors may ask themselves, "Is there an inherent conflict between financial performance and doing good?" If you invest to achieve the best performance possible, does it necessarily result in harm to society, or to one segment of society? Can you improve your financial security, invest for your children's education, plan for your retirement, care for elderly relatives, and still sleep at night with a clear conscience? I plan on answering these questions in the course of this book.

From a historical perspective, we shouldn't forget that the greatest surge of responsible investing growth occurred in the decade of greed, the 1980s. The media never let us forget the deeds of Michael Milken, Carl Icahn, and Donald Trump. There are people, however, who are part of what has become known as the socially responsible investing movement. They are out to change the world, not by the power of greed, but by incorporating ethics and social responsibility into investment decision making. The next two chapters identity some of these people and tell their stories.

CHAPTER THREE

The People Who Are Changing the World

The players in the field of the American SRI movement have been at it for 25 years. They are an idealistic group of people seeking to right the many wrongs of society through economic justice. Here are profiles of some of the key shapers of the American SRI movement.

Alice Tepper Marlin
The Council on Economic Priorities (CEP)

Alice Tepper Marlin is a woman who makes a difference. She has worked for 23 years to build the most respected nonprofit social research organization in this country, the Council on Economic Priorities (CEP). Hers is a success story with heart and political conviction.

Alice attended Wellesley College, where, in her junior year, she took a sociology course and was introduced to the Moynihan Report, Daniel Patrick Moynihan's 1965 study on black family structure. She took issue with Moynihan's recommendation that the way to break the cycle of black poverty was to change the structure of the black family. Alice believed the way to break the cycle of poverty was through economic advancement, not by changing the black family structure. Her independent research not only caused her to change her major in college from art history to economics, but it also eventually changed her life.

Alice was convinced that she wanted to use her economics degree to help end poverty by financing minority business and low-income housing. She was surprised and disappointed to find that the economic development organizations she approached were not interested in her because she had no business background. With the help and advice of an uncle, she decided to get a job on Wall Street. She became a securities analyst for Burnham & Company, which later became part of Drexel Burnham Lambert.

In 1968 the "Clean Gene" McCarthy presidential campaign came along, and Alice channeled her distaste for the Vietnam War into full-time campaign activity. She left Burnham and became a "McCarthy for President" volunteer, traveling to Chicago and Boston hot on the campaign trail.

It was back to reality when McCarthy lost. Alice had used up all her savings, so she went to work as a financial/portfolio manager for Thomas O'Connell Management in Boston. One day her boss was playing golf with the administrator of a local synagogue pension fund, who mentioned that he needed someone to invest the synagogue's funds to make sure that the synagogue avoided investing in defense-oriented stocks. The boss knew he had hit a hole in one because one of his best portfolio managers was also a "peacenik"—Alice Tepper Marlin. With the help of a group of graduate students at MIT, Alice put together a "peace portfolio" that included an exclusionary screen for weapons contractors. Alice called a friend from the McCarthy campaign who worked for an advertising company. Together they developed a small advertisement for the peace portfolio. This was 1968, the height of the Vietnam War. It was so unusual for a money management firm to advertise a "peace portfolio" that other newspapers quickly picked up the story. Alice received over 600 responses to the ad.

Alice was convinced that there was a growing need for social-related investment research, not only on defense-related issues but for other areas such as the environment, civil rights, and South Africa. She tried to convince several Wall Street firms to put up the needed capital for a specialized research firm. When she was unsuccessful, she decided to start the firm herself.

Alice recruited a board of directors and staff. In November of 1969 CEP was incorporated as a nonprofit research and educational organization to provide information on corporate practices such as military contracting, minority hiring, promotion of minorities and women, environmental pollution, and investment in South Africa. Alice started CEP with a hope, a prayer, a $5,000 grant, and a $25,000 noninterest-bearing loan. The staff of 20 all worked for $50 per week, including Alice. In 1970 CEP published its first study, *Efficiency in Death* (Harper & Row), which identified 105 companies with major contracts for the manufacture of antipersonnel weapons and related weapons parts.

Alice is known as a tough and demanding boss. Some of America's best researchers have passed through CEP's doors, producing far-reaching studies on corporate behavior. Alice's days in the McCarthy campaign paid off. She knew how to run an office and shepherd a large staff on bare bones. She borrowed office space, used donated telephones, and at one time ran the office out of the National Council of Churches' office at 475 Riverside Drive (The God Box) in Manhattan. For a while CEP's offices were split between Washington, D.C., and New York. It even was donated a suite at the Mayflower Hotel for two years where researchers worked and lived. A Wall Street firm allowed CEP to use its office, telephones, and copying machines at night. The firm's staff would come in at 7:30 AM and find CEP staffers working, asleep, or both.

In those days CEP existed on budgets of less than $100,000. Today the organization's budget exceeds $1.5 million. Alice has a staff of 25, with about 30 university and college interns. However, CEP continues to struggle to raise funds because its audience is primarily the general public. CEP's income is derived from membership and subscribers, charitable contributions, and the sales of studies and reports.

For over 20 years CEP has published such studies as *Star Wars: The Economic Fallout* (Ballinger/Harper & Row), *Military Expansion, Economic Decline* (M.E. Sharpe), and, more recently, *Rating America's Corporate Conscience* (Addison-Wesley, 1987), *Shopping for a Better World* (Ballantine Books, Annually), and *The Better World Investment Guide* (Prentice Hall, 1991).

Recently CEP launched an Institutional Investor Research Service that rates companies in such areas as the environment, South Africa, women's advancement, minority advancement, nuclear power, military contracts, charitable giving, animal testing, disclosure of information, community outreach, and family benefits. CEP has also signed a contract with PAM to market CEP's corporate environmental data clearinghouse material on publicly traded corporations, which provides up-to-date, comprehensive environmental data to professional investment managers.

I met Alice and asked for CEP assistance in 1972 when I was writing my first legislative report and again in 1975 when I wrote a study entitled "California State and Local Investments: A Guide for Responsible Ownership." In 1979, when I was a special consultant to the California State and Consumer Services Agency, I worked with CEP on a study entitled "Pension Funds and Ethical Investment," which was published in 1980. This study was primarily responsible for the embarkment of California's two largest public employee retirement systems on more active course of shareholder activism, including the introduction of a resolution at Xerox Corporation in 1982 calling for corporate withdrawal from South Africa.

When Working Assets Money Fund was created in 1983 and I had the job of appointing an advisory board, Alice Tepper Marlin was one of my first choices. She continues to serve on the Working Assets advisory board and was helpful in formulating the money fund's social criteria.

I'm really glad to have had the chance to work with Alice Tepper Marlin. Over the years she has been an inspiration to me. Her work has made it possible for Americans to change the way we invest and consume. Without her invaluable research, we would still be in the Dark Ages of ethical investment. Information is power, and Alice has made it available to the American public.

Dr. Robert J. Schwartz
Dean of Responsible Investing

In the late 1960s Dr. Robert J. Schwartz was the first broker in the United States to publicly take on the investment establishment over Wall Street's support of weapons manufacturers during the Vietnam War. In 1965 Bob and his wife decided that they did not want to hold any family investments in war-oriented U.S. companies. He went on to work with Alice Tepper Marlin to manage the "peace portfolio." The number of portfolios Bob managed grew geometrically as did the increasing demand for different social screens. One of his first clients was a distinguished member of the Board of the American Friends Service Committee.

Bob holds two graduate degrees, a master's degree in economics from Columbia University and a doctorate from American University. His first job after graduate school was with the U.S. Treasury Department; he was an economist and spent two years in Puerto Rico. While there he was invited by the Puerto Rican government to become a director of a new development bank (Formento), but being young and headstrong he instead joined the Marine Corps. He was in active combat in the Pacific and was decorated. He returned to the Treasury Department post in Washington, D.C., after World War II.

Bob later became a senior officer at Amalgamated Bank of New York, a union bank owned by the Amagalmated Clothing Workers. Politically he felt comfortable at the bank, but the bank's management was conservative and didn't handle union pension accounts because of the complex legal and fiduciary requirements. He eventually moved to another bank at a higher salary. The Vietnam War broke out and Bob's life turned topsy-turvy.

Bob was so strongly against U.S. involvement in Vietnam that he organized Wall Street Executives Against the War and ran for Congress in a special primary election in New York in 1965. He was the first person in the United States to run for Congress on an antiwar platform. Naturally he was also the first ex-Marine captain to do so, which probably did not endear him to his colleagues in the banking business. He left banking and went to work for Cogen, Berlind, Weill, and Levitt, which grew by acquisitions and mergers to be Shearson Lehman Brothers. He stayed with them for more than 20 years.

Bob primarily managed union pension funds and church and individual client accounts. Many of his friends were against the Vietnam War and didn't want to invest in companies like Dow Chemical or General Electric. His antiwar, pro-civil rights, and pro-union views made him a unique portfolio manager at Shearson. In a May 1, 1979, *Wall Street Journal* article about Bob, he was described as a "maverick" after the reporter discovered a union "bug" (denoting a union print shop) on his business card. In his office at that time were personally inscribed photographs of civil rights and antiwar leaders Eleanor Roosevelt, Martin Luther King, Jr., and Dr. Benjamin Spock.

Bob commanded a great deal of respect inside Shearson even if corporate executives were not pleased about his political views. Because he went public with his political philosophy, he became a double-edged sword for Shearson. Bob brought in money for the firm even as he alienated many of Shearson's traditional corporate clients and conservative individual clients.

In 1983 he convinced Shearson/American Express to allow him to capitalize a mutual fund called the Trust for Balanced Investment. Unfortunately, management gave him less than six months to raise $75 million in commitments from institutional investors at a minimum of $100,000 per investment. To understand the difficulty of raising such an enormous amount of money in such a short period of time, we should note that Lyndon Comstock took over a year to raise $6 million in equity for his Brooklyn-based Community Capital Bank in 1990. It took the founders of Working Assets over two years of hard work and extensive advertising to raise $75 million from shareholders to invest in a safe money market fund.

Because of the controversial nature of Bob's proposed trust, Shearson was attacked in the press and elsewhere by the National Right to

Work Committee, a right-wing corporate lobbying organization. In a July 27, 1983, letter to Shearson CEO and Chairman Sanford I. Weill, a Right to Work Committee member named Reed Larson wrote that the trust "will almost certainly result in violations of the Employee Retirement Income Security Act of 1974 and other protection of employee rights."[1]

The trust received tremendous political heat because Bob had taken on several important social issues by attempting to launch such an ambitious project. His social criteria were the most comprehensive any institutional fund offered at that time. The trust was to examine corporate conduct in such areas as promoting affirmative action, employing the disabled, or establishing daycare centers. Companies that seriously violated state and federal laws governing employment relations, equal opportunity, and protection of the environment would not be purchased by the trust.

The trust singled out South Africa for investment exclusion because active support for its government was a practice inconsistent with the trust's criteria regarding human rights and equal job opportunities. The trust identified South Africa because it was the only nation whose constitution compelled racial discrimination.

By the end of the designated time period, Bob had verbal commitments from institutions for $75 million, but he only had signed documents committing $45 million. Shearson refused to open the trust. I was working with Bob then, and my own union, the Service Employees International Union (SEIU), had committed several million dollars. As Robert told me at that time:

> The top management at Shearson had difficulty approving the trust because of their relationship with corporate clients and the kind of correspondence that was rolling in. I was told about one letter which asked why such a radical man as Woodcock, who wanted to destroy all of corporate America, was being hired as chairman and CEO.

Throughout this struggle at Shearson, Bob gained new respect for his friends, both inside the company and out. Their loyalty overwhelmed him. In his semi-retirement he moved to Smith Barney and became a senior vice president. Sanford Weill, who had been the driving force in building Shearson, is now the chairman of the board of Primerica, of which Smith Barney is a wholly owned subsidiary.

I first met Bob Schwartz at a conference in New York in 1980 when I was chair of the California governor's public investment task force. We were both speaking to a group of local and state elected officials on

South African divestment issues. Bob was impressive in his three-piece suit, standing tall and distinguished with his grey goatee and professorial manner. It was clearly evident that he was a frequent lecturer on economics and finance. He always held his audience spellbound. Bob Schwartz was the unchallenged leader on the lecture circuit in the 1970s and 1980s, when the issue of U.S. corporate investments in South Africa began to make the headlines in local newspapers across the country.

During the 1980s Bob and I would bump into one another on the lecture circuit, speaking out against South Africa while advising institutional investors on divestment issues. Bob worked with numerous state legislatures and local governments, providing testimony on South African investment issues. I shared a day with him in Eugene, Oregon, in December 1985 when we both testified as expert witnesses on the first court case involving a South African divestment.

Looking back over his 25 years as the dean of socially responsible investing, Bob is most proud of working with shareholders at the Blue Diamond Coal Company. He recalled receiving a telephone call from a young Kentucky economist in the early 1980s after two mine explosions had killed 26 miners. Working conditions at the Blue Diamond mines were extremely dangerous, and the company wasn't at all interested in change.

Bob and the young economist, John Gaventa, bought some Blue Diamond stock. They were joined by the Sisters of Loretto, a Catholic order of politically progressive nuns. They hired a Washington attorney to work pro bono with them. With support from foundation grants and free legal help, they forced the company to file reports on operations and working conditions. Eventually Blue Diamond made a settlement of $8 million with the families of the 26 miners who had lost their lives. It was one of the first successful corporate campaigns in the history of the United States. John Gaventa was later a recipient of a John D. & Catherine T. MacArthur Foundation genius award.

In our recent telephone interview, Bob summarized his feelings about his work:

> Investment is the lifeblood of an economy, whether it is socialist or capitalist. The economy functions on the basis of investments. If anyone can have some kind of control on the investment stream, whether it's the government or private industry, you will have an effective hold on the most strategic part of the economy. It should be utilized in a constructive way.

Bob Schwartz has spent his entire career challenging the system, taking risks, and walking a professional tightrope. If there was ever a hero of the responsible investing revolution, it's Bob Schwartz.

Randy Barber
The North Will Rise Again

Randy Barber is my kind of guy. He is as big as the outdoors and obviously a cowboy from Colorado. When I first met Randy in Sacramento in 1977, he was moving at a fast clip and had a story to tell. It was a great story, too. We've been friends and colleagues ever since.

Randy Barber was born in Thermopolis, Wyoming, about 100 miles due east of Jackson Hole, Wind River, and the Big Horn Mountain range. When he was six years old, Randy and his folks moved to Pueblo, Colorado. Randy is the son of a liberal Methodist preacher and the eldest of five children. His mother was a homemaker, raised in a working-class family in Evanston, Indiana. Randy and his dad used to go together to Trinidad, Colorado. One day they stopped by the roadside to look at a stone marker. The marker was a monument to the Ludlow Massacre of April 12, 1914, when Colorado National Guard troops attacked a tent village inhabited by striking coal miners and their families. Two women and eleven children were killed. The event had never been mentioned at Randy's school. He remembers being shocked by all the deaths and even more shocked by the silence on the issue. This experience had a profound influence on the rest of Randy's life.

With his dad as a role model, Randy became involved in civil rights and economic justice issues. When Martin Luther King, Jr., was killed, Randy organized a march and demonstration at his high school. In 1968 he went to Dartmouth College and enjoyed teasing his family by saying he majored in antiwar demonstrating. It was in Hanover, New Hampshire, that Randy became interested in the labor movement. About three miles away, in Springville, Vermont, were several machine tool factories. These companies had had a number of strikes, and between classes at school Randy organized strike support committees.

After college Randy went to France for a year and a half to teach French to American students. There he became interested in responsible investing after reading about a watch factory near the Swiss border that was being occupied by workers because the owners were going to shut it down. While holding the plant, workers started "wildcat production" and even began selling the watches. The idea of people having power in the workplace was a new one to Randy. The French called it "autogestation," or self-management, and Randy read everything he could find on the subject.

Suddenly Randy thought, "What if worker pension funds were invested in ways to improve the quality of life for American workers?" He and a friend, Jeremy Rifkin, set off on a mission. First they had to find out how much money there was in American pension funds. No one seemed to know. They finally came up with a figure of $500 billion, which seemed to them like a lot of money. (Pension funds now total over $3 trillion.)

Three months or so after Randy and Jeremy began their pension investment research, Peter Drucker, the noted conservative economist, wrote *The Unseen Revolution* (Harper & Row, 1976). This book declared that pension fund socialism had come to America because private and public employees, through their retirement plans, were investing in common stock, virtually owning American industry. Drucker argued that employees already owned at least 25 percent of America's equity capital, which was more than enough for control. This infuriated Randy and Jeremy. They took off for the Virginia countryside and spent a weekend in a small cabin, outlining a book that was published as *The North Will Rise Again: Pensions, Politics and Power in the 1980s* (Beacon Press, 1978). The book was released on Labor Day 1978. They sent 10,000 free copies to every labor federation, central labor council, and activist organization around the country.

When Randy was researching his book in 1977, I was the consultant to the California State Senate Select Committee on Investment Priorities and Objectives. The special committee was chaired by State Senator John Dunlap, a Democrat from Napa, California. I had worked for John as a campaign volunteer in his first election to the California legislature in 1966 while I was still in the Air Force. He was elected by a conservative Democratic majority but was politically very liberal. He took an interest in the relationship between pension funds in California and the state's economy. I was able to publish several reports under his auspices.

When Randy and I got together in the fall of 1977, I had written legislation to overhaul the state retirement system's voting of stock proxies and had begun to review all of the investment policies of California's public retirement systems. Randy was interested in learning more about California's $60 billion in public employee pension plans. (Today the total is $113 billion.)

Randy and Jeremy's *The North Will Rise Again* broke new ground. Drucker had already revealed that some of the ownership of corporate stock was in the hands of employee retirement plans. This information was not that inspiring in and of itself, but *The North Will Rise Again* revealed that the true control of pension plans was in the hands of a very few large institutions—primarily banks, insurance companies, and conservative portfolio managers. The pension fund investments were not necessarily invested to benefit the beneficiaries; often it was just the opposite. In the northeastern United States, which was called the "rust belt" because of its declining industrial economy, pension funds were being invested predominately by eastern banks and insurance companies. These institutional portfolio managers were investing capital outside of the northeast, basically aiding the decline of the economy there and exporting capital.

This export of employee pension capital would occasionally end up overseas, often in an industry competitive with a declining industry in the United States. The perfect examples are steelworkers' pension funds being invested in the Japanese steel industry or New York City employee pension funds being invested in the southern garment industry.

Randy saw that employees owned capital indirectly through pension funds but had no control. Even when the beneficiaries of the funds actually held stock, they had little or no voting control. All the control was actually held by employers or portfolio managers who owed no allegiance to employees or retirees whose deferred wages they were managing.

Randy also discovered that pension fund investment performance was poor and funds could be invested more prudently to increase not only financial return but overall economic return. In other words, it would be better to invest in the local economy and thereby keep the capital invested to spur employment, housing, and small business instead of exporting capital and destroying not only the economic base of the state and local economies but undermining the security of the pension plan.

Randy had identified the northeast, but the same problem existed in other states, counties, and cities as well. There was no concerted, organized effort to take the blinders off portfolio managers, to make them realize that they needed to understand the interdependence between investing enormous amounts of capital and the viability of local, state, and national economies. Randy summed it up nicely in his book:

> A push for alternative pension investments will require true cooperation among vastly larger and much more representative segments of society. The simple reality is that no single interest or block alone is now strong enough to recast the economic fortunes of the region. Organized labor,

state governments, and the public will have to join together and cooperate if they are to insure their survival.[2]

Randy Barber spent from 1976 until 1982 traveling around the country, giving speeches, putting together training sessions, and teaching on pension-related issues. In those days most industrial unions had no control over their pension funds. Randy started a newsletter for the industrial union department of the AFL-CIO called "Labor & Investments," which reported on union and pension investment across the nation.

It was clear to Randy that just because a union had capital, it wouldn't necessarily have the ability to do anything with it. He began to work with industrial unions to bargain for control of pension plans. (Most private pension plans are still controlled by the employer, but if the employees are represented by a collective bargaining agent or a union, they can negotiate pension plan representation.) Randy worked with the International Association of Machinists (IAM) in 1981 when they were negotiating a contract with Eastern Airlines.

In 1990 Randy was hired by the AFL-CIO to develop labor's position on how pension funds should be invested and how pension trustees should direct money managers to vote proxies. In May 1991 the AFL-CIO executive committee adopted a very comprehensive pension investment and proxy-voting policy.[3]

Currently Randy is working in the area of corporate governance, which examines how corporations should be controlled and whether or not a corporation should be accountable only to its stockholders or also to all its stakeholders including employees, consumers, and the communities where such corporations are based.

Randy serves on the advisory boards of both Working Assets and Calvert. I recently asked him what his personal goal was and where he thought we were going as responsible investors. With no hesitation Randy answered:

> The goal is to resolve economic and power relationships, in that the capital that is drawn from communities, from specific workers, should be both controlled by them and funneled back to reinforce them. Are we trying to convince people to cleanse their investment portfolio by investing in companies that are at least marginally better than someone else's? Are we simply providing a vehicle for people to feel better about making money?
>
> I am convinced investment money must be viewed as a tool to achieve an end, being a more democratic economy with people having broader control over the dispersion of resources.

Perhaps in another twenty years we will have people demanding that their pension funds not be used to pollute the environment and degrade public health. I can imagine the giant food corporations being held accountable for the quality of their food and the car manufacturers responsible for the safety of their vehicles. The potential is enormous.

Ray Rogers
The Corporate Campaign

Ray Rogers is a tough street fighter who has many friends as well as enemies. He has successfully battled J. P. Stevens, a large southern textile company, and is currently assisting INFACT, an organization in the sixth year of a fight with General Electric. He is both loved and hated by organized labor and has been called "an outsider," "a bully," a "corporate terrorist," and a "genius." Corporate management has never cared for Ray Rogers. I have the greatest respect for Ray.

He struggled as a youngster, many times taking the side of the underdog. In the fourth grade several of his friends and he were beaten up by a school bully. Ray took up boxing and worked out with weights; about six months later he confronted the bully, who backed down this time.

Ray graduated from high school and attended the University of Massachusetts. He began in astronomy and physics and ended up with a degree in sociology. After graduation from college he spent two years as a VISTA volunteer working with the poor in the Tennessee mountains. He discovered that he learned more from people who could not read or write than he had learned in his five years of college.

Ray Rogers has always been an idealist. After VISTA he went to work in Washington, D.C., for the Appalachian Regional Commission, which was a large bureaucratic economic development organization. He was assigned to work with Appalachian youth. He was young, energetic, and still naive enough to believe the organization was going to allow him to politically organize poor people. He was fired when he wrote a 15-page booklet on the problems of hunger and malnutrition in Appalachia and mapped out an organizing strategy.

Ray then set up a nonprofit group, Human Love Action, which was created to bridge the gap between the poor, minorities, and the middle class. He also ran seminars and educational programs about community and economic organizing at West Virginia University. There he met several influential leaders of the United Mine Workers, the United Farm Workers, and the American Indian Movement.

In 1973 Ray was asked by the Clothing Workers to organize a boycott throughout Alabama of Farah Slacks Company, which was based in El Paso, Texas. After successfully beating Farah Slacks in Alabama, the Clothing Workers flew Ray to New York where he was told that Farah Slacks was immediately settling the national boycott due to his efforts in the South. This all happened in the course of six weeks. Overnight Ray Rogers was a star.

In 1976 Ray was asked by the newly merged Amalgamated Clothing and Textile Workers Union (ACTWU) to work on a national boycott against the textile giant J. P. Stevens. The company was well-known as violently anti-union at its plants in the Carolinas and Alabama. Founded in 1913, Stevens was originally a family-owned textile firm in New England but later merged with ten companies, closed down mills, and moved to the South. Stevens, along with other southern textile mills, paid workers low wages and provided extremely unsafe working conditions. Its facilities were so unsafe, according to the North Carolina Department of Labor, that one out of three workers was likely to develop a disabling respiratory disease known as brown lung from illegally high concentrations of cotton dust, and half were likely to suffer hearing losses from the illegally high noise levels in the plants.[4] Stevens also had a record of violating labor law and had been cited repeatedly by the National Labor Relations Board (NLRB) for bad faith in bargaining, illegal firing of employees, and coercing workers. The company had also been found guilty of health and safety standards and racial discrimination.[5] The movie *Norma Rae* was based upon the struggle for unionization at J. P. Stevens.

After six weeks of research on J. P. Stevens, Ray was convinced there was no way a consumer boycott would bring the company to the bargaining table. Using common sense, Ray began to dissect Stevens and analyze every political, financial, and business connection that the company had to the outside world. This included the board of directors, which interlocked with other corporate boards. In other words, the directors on the board of J. P. Stevens were also on the boards of such companies as Avon, Manufacturers Hanover Trust Company, and New York Life Insurance.

Ray also paid particular attention to institutions that had large stock holdings and made multimillion dollar loans to Stevens. The goal of the J. P. Stevens corporate campaign devised by Ray was to force institutions tied to Stevens to exert their influence on the company to bargain with ACTWU and to begin to treat their workers fairly. Ray knew that companies tied to Stevens would only do so if it was in their economic self-interest. Ray believed these institutions had to be drawn into the Stevens controversy so that their reputation, image, credibility, and economic prosperity would be seriously jeopardized. This would make them pay attention.

Through a variety of tactics Ray was able to isolate and pressure Stevens directors and forced them to resign from several corporate boards. Ray and ACTWU threatened to contest the election of directors at Metropolitan Life, one of Stevens's major lenders. This would have cost the insurance company millions of dollars and caused Richard Shinn, chairman of Metropolitan, to "do some behind-the-scenes maneuvering shortly before the final settlement between Stevens and the union."[6]

Ray's successful corporate campaign heralded the end of one of the nation's longest and bitterest labor struggles (17 years). More importantly, it catapulted the corporate campaign to front stage as a new strategy that labor, church, environmental, and other community-based organizations could use to exert influence on powerful corporations beyond individual shareholder resolutions, boycotts, and strikes. The strategy involved many tactics and included shareholders, consumers, workers, and lenders. It sounds very sophisticated, but in many ways the strategy simply relied on good common sense.

A. H. Raskin, a columnist writing for the *New York Times* in October 1980, analyzed the ACTWU victory and heralded Ray Rogers's creative use of a corporate strategy. He wrote, "Pressure on the giant banks and insurance companies and other Wall Street pillars was aimed at isolating Stevens from the financial community, and helped generate a momentum toward settlement that could not be achieved through the 1976–80 worldwide boycott of Stevens products or through more conventional uses of muscle such as strikes and mass picketing."[7]

In 1981 Ray left ACTWU and founded Corporate Campaign, Inc., in New York City. He and his staff provide organizing, research, communications, and strategic planning services. Since the victory over J. P. Stevens, Corporate Campaign, Inc., has worked with many groups, including meat packers at Hormel, farm workers at Campbell, flight attendants at American Airlines, and paper workers at International Paper.

Ray has been and will continue to be controversial. He developed a unique and proven strategy that can be utilized not only by labor but also by other social and environmental organizations that seek to change unjust conditions or protect the environment. Ray is a man who is not afraid to rock the boat.

In the fall of 1991 I asked Ray if he had changed his mind about the power and use of capital. He said

The overriding issue which should be raised to the highest levels of public and political debate, but never is, is who controls the flow of the huge concentration of money and for what ends. How we approach this issue will determine whether or not we improve the quality of life for living things, or whether we face social and economic chaos and possibly nuclear holocaust.

Tim Smith
The Churches

In 1992 the Interfaith Center on Corporate Responsibility (ICCR) filed and co-filed 228 shareholder resolutions with 154 companies. When people hear about ICCR they automatically think of Tim Smith. For over 20 years Tim has committed his life to corporate democracy, to shareholder activism, and to social justice.

Tim Smith was born in Winnipeg, Canada, in 1943. As a youngster he thought of becoming a minister; his passion for social justice did not emerge until he attended college. He was elected to student council and was involved in issues such as student fees and debating economic issues such as sanctions against South Africa.

After college, in the summer of 1966, Tim traveled to Kenya as part of a program called Operation Crossroads. When he left Kenya he entered Union Theological Seminary in New York where he met his wife, Ellen. They were married in 1971 and now have a 14-year-old son, Matthew. Ellen is in charge of the women's division of the social concerns unit of the United Methodist Church and has been quite controversial by taking progressive stands on many social issues. Tim found his fieldwork at Union—a public campaign to challenge banks to stop lending to South Africa—relevant to his African experience. He graduated from Union with a masters of divinity in 1971.

A great deal of his time at Union was spent researching U.S. corporate and economic ties to South Africa. He traveled to South Africa in 1968 and again in 1970. It was in 1970 that Tim and a couple of his colleagues, Tami Hilton and Reed Kramer, interviewed corporate leadership of some 25 to 30 companies operating in South Africa. The candid interviews of American corporate management became the basis for Tim's thesis at Union. The thesis was published by the Council for Christian Social Action, United Church of Christ, in 1971 and entitled "The American Corporation in South Africa: An Analysis." It was also one of the first documents I came across when I wrote my 1972 South African report for the California legislature. Tim's interview with the managing director of Ford Motor Company is worth recalling because it exemplifies American corporate attitudes toward South Africa at that time. When Tim asked the managing director if he had contact with nonwhites in South Africa, the director replied, "I didn't mix with them in the States; I don't mix with them here, and if I went back to the States I wouldn't mix with them there either."[8]

Because of that study and his ongoing leadership and advocacy for economic sanctions and corporate withdrawal, Tim was unable to return to South Africa until recently. The government prohibited Tim and many others, including me, from legally entering South Africa. That changed in 1990, when uncontrollable domestic political and economic conditions and the effects of the divestment, bank campaign, and economic sanctions forced the new leader in South Africa to finally make concessions to the international community.

In 1970 Tim went to the General Motors stockholders' meeting and watched Campaign GM unfold in Detroit. He recommended to the churches that they begin to work together, as responsible and active institutional shareholders, on South African divestment and many other social issues.

In the early years of shareholder activism, the church and Tim encountered hostility from corporate management. In 1971 Gulf Oil asserted that shareholders were being disloyal by raising questions about Gulf's operations in the Cabinda enclave of Angola. Tim recalled the difficulties in being dealt with only by public affairs people inside the corporate structure, but

> Now, 20 years later, we are an established part of the landscape. It's no longer a set of isolated church investors raising issues. It's numerous mainstream institutional investors, investing over 600 billion dollars. This is a major change. Now we talk to the line manager and the people that can make decisions about the issue rather than solely public affairs or corporate secretaries.
>
> Corporations have also changed in the way they run their meetings and conduct their business because of ICCR. We've also learned over the years how to run a sophisticated corporate responsibility program like this more effectively so that we can dialogue with corporations to advance our goals or move into a high visibility corporate campaign.

I met Tim, along with Milton Moskowitz (then a syndicated columnist and author of *The 100 Companies to Work for in America*), in April 1974 in San Francisco. Tim and I were attending the Standard Oil of California (Chevron) annual shareholders' meeting; we were both speaking at the meeting in favor of a resolution on South Africa. As we were walking down Market Street on the way to the meeting, I stopped to buy a newspaper. The headline read "Army Coup in Portugal—A Pledge of Democracy." We immediately launched into an energetic discussion about the repercussions the coup would have in southern Africa. Tim was certainly correct when he said the coup would quickly lead to the independence of the Portuguese colonies. Portuguese Guinea-Bissau gained independence on September 10, 1974, Mozambique on June 25, 1975, and Angola on November 11, 1975. Rhodesia became the independent country of Zimbabwe on April 18, 1980, and Southwest Africa became independent Namibia on March 21, 1990.

When Tim Smith and ICCR first began introducing shareholder resolutions, corporate democracy was but a idealistic dream. There were a few "corporate gadflies" like John Gilbert and Lewis Gilbert, who made speeches to shareholders on cumulative voting or asked management to change the time or place of an annual meeting. Economic and social justice issues were ignored.

The ICCR changed all of that. They have been responsible for introducing hundreds, if not thousands, of shareholder resolutions and engaging management in dialogue on issues ranging from South Africa and Chile to the environment. Tim and his ICCR staff and committee have worked with others in drafting resolutions and providing untold hours of testimony at state and local government legislative hearings on numerous social and economic issues. The Interfaith Center on Corporate Responsibility also works with churches to increase capital directed to community-based economic development projects. The center coordinates its shareholder resolutions and social justice activities with other church and nonchurch organizations, often supporting specific corporate campaigns.

About a third of the resolutions submitted by ICCR are withdrawn following negotiation with corporate management. The average supporting vote for ICCR's resolutions continues to increase. The number of resolutions receiving more than the 3 percent needed for resubmission in 1991 was 95.5 percent, or 191 out of 200 resolutions brought to a vote. In 1973 only 17.5 percent of those resolutions brought to a vote received the necessary percentage to allow the filers to bring them back the next year.[9]

Tim recently survived a bout with cancer. He never slowed up. He is an eternal optimist. During the illness, he worked regularly; he would go to the hospital on Friday afternoon for treatment and would be back at work on Monday morning. He is a man with a mission. He is currently chair of the Calvert Social Fund Advisory Board, a member of the board of advisors of Working Assets, and a member of the board of directors of the Domini Social Index Trust.

Tim recently talked at length with me about responsible investing:

First we have to ensure that our ethics and our investment practices are consistent so that our social convictions fertilize our investment practices. A second goal is to hold corporations accountable for the decisions they make that impact society and try to change corporate behavior. That's what we're about—not just about raising issues, but trying to change corporate behavior. In doing this—from the church's perspective, anyway—we're working in partnership with our churches in the Phillippines or Chile or South Africa. You'll also hear some church representatives talk about trying to be in "solidarity with the poorest of the poor." This is a theme you will hear from the churches that you wouldn't hear from other socially concerned investors.

This is a major political and social movement we're in. It's dealing with economic power centers. It's an economic justice movement, but it's also a movement that is dealing with the integrity of investors. Investors are doing this for our own integrity as well as trying to impact the companies. It's definitely a social movement that has moved into the mainstream.

Robert Brooke Zevin
U.S. Trust Company, Boston

Robert Brooke Zevin was born in Cleveland, Ohio, in 1936. His parents were very progressive politically, and much of his love for social justice and economic democracy originated in his childhood. Robert grew up as a political activist; at a young age he was involved in the civil rights and antiwar movements.

Robert attended Antioch College and graduated with a B.A. in mathematics. He later earned an M.S. in mathematics and statistics at Ohio State University. In 1962 he received an M.S. in economics at Harvard University. He taught and conducted research at Simmons, Harvard, Berkeley, and Columbia. In 1967 he drafted an antiwar document entitled "A Call to Resist Illegitimate Authority" and helped found Resist and the U.S. Servicemen's Fund, two leading antiwar organizations. He also registered as an investment advisor that year and began to manage portfolios of like-minded social investors.

Teaching, lecturing, and managing money carried Robert through the early 1970s. By 1972 he was not only meeting his clients' social criteria but was actually outperforming market indexes. Serving as a responsible portfolio manager was the perfect combination of his interest in social activism and his skills as an economist.

In 1975 Robert teamed up with the U.S. Trust Company in Boston, which had been purchased by an investment group that was interested in expanding into financial services. He took his responsible investment clients to U.S. Trust and essentially began to build a new asset management department. Assets under management increased from $50 million to over $2 billion, of which about one-half is socially screened. The department also hired Steve Moody, formerly of the CEP and Larry Litvak of Community Economics, Inc., in Oakland, California.

Robert Zevin has never lost sight of his commitment to progressive social change. He was director and treasurer of the Massachusetts Community Center and director of both the Haymarket Foundation and the Child Care Resource Center in Cambridge. One of his greatest achievements, however, was the founding of AI Group (originally Affirmative Investments, Inc.) in 1983. AI is an investment banking firm that specializes in the financing of affordable housing.

Initially, AI Group raised capital to finance small, innovative businesses. Now the organization works primarily with not-for-profit developers who are committed to building and managing quality affordable housing. AI's projects include newly constructed or rehabilitated housing developments for single-parent families, elderly, disabled, or others with special needs.

In 1988 AI worked with Oakland-based PAM to syndicate low-income housing tax credit programs such as the Peter Claver Community in San Francisco, a single room residence for homeless people with AIDS, and Visalia Garden Villas, a newly constructed 60 unit housing development for low-income independent senior citizens in California's Central Valley. I worked with Barbara Cleary, AI's executive director, in late 1986; we were successful in financing the Oaks Hotel, a seven-story low-income residential hotel located in the City Center Redevelopment Project Area in Oakland, California.

According to David Ennis, a vice-president of AI, the organization is continuing to expand its work with nonprofit housing developers, conducting tax credit seminars, structuring low-income housing programs, and assisting developers in obtaining adequate financing for low-income housing projects.

Another one of Robert's success stories is the Calvert Social Investment Fund, a Washington-based mutual fund that screens companies using comprehensive social criteria. The prime mover behind the Social Investment Fund is Wayne Silby; Robert's U.S. Trust Company serves as Subadvisor to the fund and manages the assets.

Robert and I crossed paths several times when we testified before legislative committees or study commissions on responsible investing or on the issue of South African divestment.

I have worked with University of California student and faculty groups for over 20 years, especially during the 1980s when South Africa was at the top of everyone's agenda. During the debates at the UC Board of Regents, numerous investment professionals were asked to testify to educate the UC investment staff on the effects of divesting UC's stock portfolio of companies operating in South Africa. Regent Stanly Sheinbaum asked Robert to come to California in 1986 and refute the claims of the UC Treasurer and UC's investment consultant, Wilshire Associates of Los Angeles, regarding the costs of divestment.

Prior to his testimony before the regents, Robert reviewed a study by Wilshire Associates that opposed divestment. Staying up day and night the whole weekend, Robert wrote a 12-page analysis on the impact of divesting that contradicted the Wilshire study. His analysis and testimony before the board not only successfully refuted the findings of the Wilshire study but also convinced the company's president, Dennis Tito, who announced in front of the UC Regents that he agreed with everything Robert had said.

On July 16, 1986, California Governor George Deukmejian called for no new UC investments in companies operating in South Africa and a phased divestment of all South African-invested companies. Later in the week, and after intense personal lobbying by the governor, the UC Regents voted to divest.

Robert Zevin firmly believes that responsible investing is first a political movement, second a social movement, and third an economic movement:

> This is my personal history. That's the chronological order and also still the order of relative importance. I think a lot of the more recent and younger entrants don't think in political terms. They see it more as a social movement—in the sense of a social change movement because they belong to the generation that doesn't even vote. I think everybody has wanted to see it—and some people have professed to see it—as an economic movement. The reality so far is that we're using economic language and economic instruments and economic pressure to achieve social goals. We are not truly and fundamentally changing economic structures.

Joan Shapiro
South Shore Bank

Joan Shapiro disputes, disrupts, questions, and challenges friends and foes alike. She is the South Shore Bank's most successful and articulate spokesperson. Joan has helped define neighborhood banking and has linked it to the national SRI movement. In so doing she has also redefined responsible investing to emphasize its community roots.

Joan Shapiro was born in 1942 and grew up in Hyde Park on the south side of Chicago. Joan attended Cornell University and majored in literature. She was Phi Beta Kappa in her third year and was selected as one of an 18-person theatrical troupe to tour South America as part of a U.S. State Department program of international exchange.

Joan's nine weeks in Central and South America in 1963 had an enormous impact on her. She experienced the neighborhoods of Rio de Janeiro and the poverty of Haiti. The early 1960s were tumultuous years in Latin America, the beginning of many challenges to entrenched dictatorships and right-wing governments. She experienced bombings in some cities she toured and a blackout on stage—a far cry from middle-class Chicago. It made an indelible impression on Joan's life.

Joan and her husband spent several years in Europe and abroad, returning to Chicago in late 1973. Six months after she gave birth to her first child in 1975, Joan found a job at Shorebank Corporation. In 1973, Ron Grzywinski and three colleagues had formed Shorebank, a for-profit neighborhood development corporation and holding company for South Shore Bank. By the end of 1977, after working with Grzywinski in the holding company, Joan moved to the bank, where she worked as a development loan officer. In 1982 she took over management of development deposits and has served as a senior vice president since 1988.

In early 1983 Don Falvey and Joan Bavaria, the founders of FRDC, a responsible investment management company, called together Joan Shapiro and a dozen others in order to launch a national social investment organization. At that time there were a handful of responsible investment mutual funds and portfolio managers but no national organization to address national and international social investment issues.

Joan Shapiro has been a vital link in connecting locally based economic development organizations with a responsible investment community largely made up of mutual funds, financial planners, researchers, academics, and portfolio managers. South Shore Bank has successfully shown that a bank can be profitable and have a positive social impact on the struggling communities it targets.

Shorebank Corporation not only operates a full-service commercial community bank but also manages a real estate development company for the benefit of low- and moderate-income residents, an SBA-licensed Minority Enterprise Small Business Investment Corporation that finances small businesses, a nonprofit social and economic development organization, a for-profit subsidiary that develops rental and co-operative housing for low-income residents, and a consulting firm that provides technical assistance on real estate and development banking.

Shorebank has established itself as a leader in community banking since 1973 by combining a unique strategy of capitalizing and managing several nonbank subsidiaries, expanding traditional commercial banking services, importing social capital, and dramatically increasing the financing of affordable housing in several neighborhoods in Chicago. Shorebank is continually expanding its lending to finance the purchase and rehabilitation of moderate-income rental housing and small businesses in minority neighborhoods.

Joan was the first to ensure that any national organization addressing social investment issues would be tied to community-based financial institutions and community development investing. In 1985 the Social Investment Forum (SIF) was incorporated; Joan Shapiro was its second president, serving a two-year term between 1987 and 1989.

Joan believes that for responsible investing to succeed it must be proactive and demonstrate direct, measurable impact. In her opening address to the forum's 1987 SRI Expo at the New York University Graduate School of Business, Joan drew the distinction between the then-predominant negative screening and the practical but seldom-used positive allocation of capital.

Responsible investing, Joan believes, must address community needs, ensuring that neighborhoods and other areas ignored by the conventional marketplace have access to capital:

> How do you generate real economic well-being that is a permanent fixture—not a government plan—but self-sustaining entrepreneurship? The majority of new business in this country is still generated by the small business or neighborhood environment. If we could get to the point where anyone who calls himself a social investor routinely and by definition retains between 5–10 percent of his portfolio in community-based ventures, we could begin calling it a success.

Within the Social Investment Forum, Joan is allied with Chuck Matthei, the founder of the Institute for Community Economics (based in Springfield, Massachusetts) and champion of community-based loan funds. Joan and Chuck stress that investment professionals need to educate clients about the opportunities to invest in neighborhood development organizations and enterprises that directly affect local communities. They feel that the focus of responsible investing has been on mutual and pension fund investing. As such, it is necessarily limited to stocks and bonds that are publicly traded and have little bearing on providing access to capital and credit for the majority of struggling urban communities and small businesses.

Chicago's South Shore and Brooklyn's Community Capital Bank, social venture funds, and numerous community-based loan funds around the country are examples of financial institutions that strengthen and protect community capitalism. Joan says that, unlike managing a portfolio of stocks and bonds, a portfolio manager or individual investor can't pull up a screen on the computer and make a decision to buy a loan fund, venture fund, stock, or CD in a neighborhood bank.

> Community-based investments are not all alike. There is a great deal of difference between a bank and credit union and between those and a venture capital company. The real question is how you approach this fruit salad and choose a community-based investment that allows you, the investor, to have the economic and social impact you want. . . . You can't buy a mutual fund for a client that happens to have a Student Loan Marketing Association bond in it and tell the client she's helping students get an education. . . . If you really want to help students or education you find a loan fund or a bank that focuses on adult or low-income education. You have to be honest with yourself and not give it lip service. At times a client may have to take more risk to have a greater social impact, at others, there is comparable return and no risk whatsoever. Remember, there's enormous risk in the stock market, while losses to date with loan funds and development banks have been negligible.
>
> Responsible investing isn't just one thing. It's a spectrum of investment opportunities that all have different economic and social impacts with varying degrees of risk and reward. You can invest in Working Assets Money Fund for little or no risk, and you can invest a portion of your assets in a loan fund with somewhat higher risk but much more direct impact. You don't have to do one or the other. An investor can do as much as she wants. What's important is that anyone calling herself a social investor must commit to building a balanced portfolio—one with conventional and community-based investments—if she truly wants to ensure social as well as financial return. We've just got to make sure that people know they have choices and opportunities to change this world we live in.

Other individuals have also had a tremendous impact on the world by the way they invest, participate in the community, and donate to progressive social action foundations. You've heard from some of the leaders in the responsible investment community. In the next chapter you will learn about people who have overcome the guilt of inheriting and have used their money to benefit society.

CHAPTER FOUR

Creating Wealth
Without Feeling Guilty

Anonymity is important for many with inherited wealth. Some individuals, such as Tracy Gary and Paul DuPont Haible, have gone public, while others prefer to remain out of the limelight. For this reason, the names of all of the other people you are about to read about have been changed. This shouldn't, however, detract from their stories and certainly doesn't change the impact they've had through their activities as investors and donors.

Jane Bonner

In the fall of 1990 in the Southwest, I was introduced to Jane Bonner, who is a strong environmentalist and peace activist and an heir to a family fortune that came from a well-known person in the financial community. She had inherited over a million dollars in the mid-1980s, much of it in appreciated stocks in the family company. Jane was a busy single parent of two wonderful daughters. As a committed social activist, she edited a local environmental newsletter.

Jane turned her portfolio over to a local broker and told him that she did not want to invest in nuclear-powered utilities, weapons, or defense contractors. The broker was well-known locally for investing in "out of favor" companies and making a lot of money for his clients.

Jane talked to me about her social commitment and how she felt it was aligned with her portfolio objectives. She did express concern, however, that the portfolio was not producing enough income for her to support her family. She asked me to take a look at her brokerage statements.

Jane opened six monthly brokerage statements, and we found that

- She was overspending; her portfolio income met about 50% of her spending needs.
- She was holding junk bonds, or corporate bonds with very low quality and high risk.
- The portfolio had a high percentage of risky or bankrupt savings and loan stocks.
- Several of the companies she held in the portfolio were defense contractors.
- Several of the companies in her portfolio were nuclear utilities.

The portfolio met neither her financial nor her social goals. It was a disaster. Jane seldom looked at her brokerage statements. When I asked her why she didn't pay more attention to her portfolio, which was worth well over a million dollars, she answered with one word: guilt.

Jane felt so much guilt after her father died and she inherited a portion of the estate, she simply didn't want to have anything to do with the money and didn't care where it was invested. She told me she had always thought something was wrong with her portfolio, and I had confirmed her worst fears.

In a study entitled *Coping With Inherited Wealth,* John Levy, a therapist in Marin County, California, as well as an inheritor, said that one of the most common prices that many pay for inheriting wealth is guilt. "Inheritors find it hard to accept unmerited good fortune and may not be able to find ways to prove themselves worthy of it. They are often afflicted by feelings of separation or alienation."[1] John's specialty is working with families going through emotional trauma and discord over issues of money and inheriting.

Thankfully, Jane did not stay down long. As both a dedicated environmentalist and peace activist, she soon learned that her inheritance could be used not just to provide income to her family but invested in such a way as to actually support her political commitments. Jane quickly took charge and found dozens of stocks and tax-free and taxable bonds that financially supported recycling, sustainable agriculture, alternative energy, education, and mass transit.

Not only did she restructure the portfolio to reduce risk and produce more income but she also set up a charitable trust so she could donate appreciated stocks to the trust to reduce her tax liability. She was the sole trustee of the trust and as such made tax-deductible donations to support her concerns for the environment and peace. Her wealth was now working for her by

- Producing income to meet her cost of living
- Providing growth to increase portfolio value
- Promoting the growth of environmental investing
- Reducing tax liability *and* promoting environmental and peace action through social action charitable contributions

Jane is not the only wealthy social activist in America. Many inheritors are active in a variety of social, political, and economic justice issues. They use their wealth to invest for social change as well as donate their time and money to social action nonprofit organizations.

Tracy Gary

Tracy Gary invests and donates her wealth to have a positive impact upon American society and specifically to promote women and girls' organizations throughout the country. Her leadership in national progressive philanthropy for women is unchallenged. I met her over 12 years ago at a San Francisco investment seminar. She is a terrific role model. Tracy has put her political beliefs into action.

Tracy was born in New York into an upper-class family 40 years ago. Her father was an attorney and her mother was interested in financial matters. Her mother remarried when Tracy was 4 years old, and she lived with her stepfather and her mother until she was 18. Both her mother and her stepfather were inheritors, their money coming from Pillsbury and GTE, respectively.

Tracy's memories include houses in New York, South Hampton, Long Island, Florida, Minnesota, Wisconsin, and Paris. Her mother and stepfather were very involved in philanthropic and social activities including the American Cancer Society, the Boys' Club, the Kentucky Derby, and the Flamingo Ball. Her mother came from a family of three sisters and a brother and grew up feeling that boys were valued more highly than girls. Ironically, this created a bond between Tracy's mother and her younger brother. Tracy felt her mother seemed to value that relationship more than the mother/daughter relationship. Tracy feels this experience catalyzed her own belief that women and girls needed special philanthropic considerations.

When Tracy was 14, she was told she would inherit over a million dollars and would never have to work again. However, she was also told that it was important in her teenage years to gain the experience of work, earning money, and contributing to the community. In one of her summer jobs she had a multicultural experience with Native Americans in a camp setting. It was there she learned she was a white person of privilege and that there were people of color who would never have the same financial resources she possessed.

While Tracy worked in summer camps or in the library, her older brother spent his summers working on Wall Street and in the family business. When she and her brother would have their annual meeting with their trust officer and she would ask questions, the trust officer would give the answers to her brother. It was clear that Tracy was being prepared to volunteer for social services while her brother was being trained for business and finance.

Tracy's social consciousness was raised when she began to understand class, racial, and economic distinctions between her family and the people who took care of them and their many properties. As a child she asked her nanny how much she made each month and then compared it to how much her stepfather made. Even at that young age, Tracy was shocked at the disparity. After she completed her boarding school education in the 1960s, Tracy went to Sarah Lawrence College.

Located in Bronxville, New York, Sarah Lawrence is a small school of about 800 that has a good reputation in art and literature and is well-known for its progressive politics. It was there that Tracy started learning about the black power and antiwar movements.

Tracy loved her years at Sarah Lawrence. She studied mythology under the famous Joseph Campbell. When she turned 21, she received her inheritance and found out it was in stocks of the very companies that were being protested against at Sarah Lawrence for defense contracts and weapons production. Tracy was appalled and the shock propelled her into action. She divested her stock portfolio of weapons manufacturers. In 1973 she moved to San Francisco and immediately started investing her assets in loans for small community businesses.

Her cousin, George Pillsbury, looked her up while on a trip to the Bay Area. George told Tracy about the Vanguard Foundation, a progressive, social-action organization that was located in San Francisco. Based on her conversations with George and meetings with Vanguard, Tracy decided to give away a million dollars and did so between 1975 and 1985. She also sat on the boards of about 22 nonprofit organizations, including KQED, a publicly supported television and radio station in San Francisco. She educated herself in budgeting, fund raising, and administration. In short, Tracy became an expert in philanthropy.

Tracy helped organize and raise funds for the first battered women's shelter in San Francisco. She also mortgaged her home, for which she had paid cash, to help pay the down payment for the Women's Building in San Francisco. The Women's Building now houses the Women's Foundation, which Tracy helped found.

One of Tracy's many achievements is the Managing Inherited Wealth (MIW) program. Since 1983 MIW has provided support to women with wealth. MIW's purpose is:

1. To provide ongoing emotional, technical, and social support to women who have inherited wealth
2. To empower women to take control of their finances
3. To provide individualized assistance through groups and services available to members
4. To encourage women to share their abilities and knowledge with other women and girls
5. To bring together women of diverse backgrounds, interests, and styles to work together within a feminist context
6. To promote social activism, philanthropy, and socially responsible investing with sensitivity to the diversity within the group[2]

Tracy's personal investments are in a variety of small businesses, media projects, and socially responsible films. She also works with women to encourage socially responsible investing.

Tracy is currently attempting to raise $100 million as an endowment for women and girls' nonprofit organizations across the United States. I have no doubt she will be successful.

Tracy's memories of how she was introduced to money go back to when she was about six years of age. Her mother gave her her first quarter and said to her, "You know, there are lots of choices for this quarter. You can spend it all, you can save it, you can give some of it away, you can invest it, or you can lend it to a friend." At different times in her life, Tracy has made all of those choices. She understands the power of money. She has used money to empower herself as well as others. She turned her feelings of guilt about inheriting into positive social and economic action.

Jon Ingles

Jon was born in Los Angeles in 1954. His father was a film producer and writer. His mother is an artist. Jon's parents divorced when he was about 10 years old. He and his mother moved to Santa Barbara after his mother remarried. His stepfather is a well-known politician who has served on numerous government boards and commissions.

Jon was popular in school and an accomplished athlete, but he became increasingly bored and unhappy as a student. When he was 16 he dropped out of school and went to live on a kibbutz in Israel. He stayed in Israel for most of the next three years.

When Jon returned to the United States he pursued something he had loved since his early teens—singing and songwriting. He took singing, guitar, and piano classes. He attended Santa Monica Community College for a while but then decided to transfer to a college in Olympia, Washington. He later left Washington, traveled, and ended up in New York in 1978.

Jon inherited $500,000 when he was 18. He never really had a conversation about money that he can remember. His stepfather had broached the subject once and, as Jon said,

> It just sort of blew me away. I'd been getting allowances since I was a kid of about five dollars a week or something like that. I think someone said, like, "hey, in a few more years you're going to get a half million bucks," and my head started spinning. I think my stepfather asked "Do you want to talk about it?", but I think I just wandered off. On a practical level I just couldn't conceive having that sum of money around for me, totally at my disposal.

Jon remembers that in his late teens or early twenties he

> Went to one of these trust departments downtown and sat around one of those big tables with guys in suits and my father and I were trying to tell them I wanted to get out of the stock market at that point. The reaction was real cold.

Jon will inherit more money in a few years when the remainder of his trust funds are turned over to him. He's married now and lives in New York. He is a writer and has recently finished college with a major in journalism. He believes money is,

> Like a wild card—like a wild horse. You've got to tame it somehow because it will dominate your life. If you're living off inherited wealth there's absolutely no way it's not going to dominate your life. It doesn't matter how smart you are. It doesn't matter how hard you work on understanding yourself and other people and the world. It's a double-edged sword. It's really a mixed blessing. Only people who don't have it think if they had money all their problems would be solved. But that's not the way it is at all. It didn't have an impact on me at first. It wasn't until I came back to the States in my late teens that I really felt at a loss in my life—a way I felt until I was thirty. I've come to terms with some things both inside myself and about my place in the world. I sort of realize I have a niche. I'm not sure exactly what it is yet, but having the money really stands in the way of that because it gives you no motivation to go out and do anything.

Jon has overcome the trap of becoming part of the idle rich. He's finished college and is pursuing writing as a career. His inheritance has allowed him to be a creative person without having to struggle financially. It has also allowed him to give money to political causes, candidates, and organizations that he believes will help better the world. He is now investing with strong social criteria that he and his wife developed. He is realistic about how much he can do, but he is working with a broker, an investment advisor, and his trustees in order to have a positive social and economic impact through his inherited wealth.

Christina and Charlotte Burke

Christina and Charlotte are sisters who were born into a large, politically active family. They have seven other brothers and sisters. Both Christina and Charlotte were born in a large midwestern city and later moved to a Middle Atlantic state.

The family lived in what was called "the white part of town." The children attended both private and public schools. The sisters vividly recall that their parents were politically involved in civil rights and antiwar protests. Their church was integrated, and the priest was a prominent writer and activist.

Growing up in the sixties exposed both sisters to civil rights protests and racial riots. Christina remembers the time federal troops occupied part of the city in which they lived. The sisters recall seeing troops and tanks in the streets and burned-out store fronts. They would sit on their roof and see smoke from fires raging in other parts of the city.

Although the sisters went to an integrated and socially progressive church, both had few black friends. Christina remembers first recognizing that there were people of color around her as garbage collectors and maids. She had one African-American friend who was the grandson of the family's maid; as childhood friends they would ride their bikes in the neighborhood and play together. On one such outing, when they went to a playground together, Christina recalls one little girl saying to her that she shouldn't bring her dirty friends to the playground. When her black friend would see her playing with another boy, he would say, "Oh, you like him better than me because he's white." These incidents had greatly raised Christina's social consciousness. She learned to detest racism.

Charlotte graduated in 1980 and went to an Ivy League school where she graduated in 1985 with a B.A. in music. She then moved to a large city in the east where she presently lives and works as an actress, occasionally traveling to Los Angeles for parts in films.

After graduating Christina traveled across the United States and throughout South America. She decided to attend the University of California and graduated with a degree in women's studies.

> I started as an environmental studies major because I was looking for an interdisciplinary approach to education. The problem was that, at that time, the environmental movement—which was a big part of the inspiration of having an environmental studies department—was not at all cognizant of issues of social justice. They were talking about national parks, the ozone layer, and whales but not enough about people. Women's studies felt more comfortable to me in that it was trying to address sexism in academia and was very cognizant of the issues of injustice, including racism.

Both sisters did not talk about money growing up, even though they knew they were different from other people since they went to private school and really didn't have to worry about money in college. Charlotte inherited her money when she was eighteen. She recalled her childhood:

> Growing up I knew my family had money. It's kind of weird because I think I realized we had money in grade school when it became integrated and I started having some black friends. The deal with my parents was that we lived under our means a bit. We had a nice living room, and the rest of the house was a free-for-all. There was this knowledge that the wealth came from my grandfather—when we went to his house it was very wealthy. My father was kind of the black sheep of the family because he bought an old station wagon instead of a Mercedes. We lived in a big house in a nice neighborhood that I took for granted as a child, but when I'd go to Grammy's house it was very fancy. We'd even have high tea. Both my father and mother grew up wealthy.

When Charlotte inherited she went to the bank with her stepmother to meet with a banker; she remembers signing stacks of papers. She had no idea of what she was doing. She told me she didn't have any training about money and had to work through some resentment about it.

Christina had a similar experience when inheriting. She wasn't trained to handle her inheritance. When she met with representatives of the bank where her trust was custodied,

> they were completely unhelpful. They talked in lingo that I didn't understand, and they weren't able to translate it into a language laypeople could understand. They assumed that because I was inheriting and came

from a wealthy family I knew what they were talking about. It was very intimidating.

Christina, who is more politically active than her sister, told me

I did my best to totally deny that I was a different person than most people. I hid it. The money was a big secret. I was embarrassed and ashamed and even more so because I felt that politically it was an awful thing to have so much money.

Charlotte learned from her sister of a progressive foundation on the East Coast. She attended donor meetings and potluck social events. Since then she has donated cash and appreciated stocks that in turn supported numerous social action and community-based nonprofit organizations on the East Coast. It is important to her that the funds are used locally. Through the foundation she has met other people who have inherited large sums of money and want to put it to work on progressive social causes. Communicating with others in a similar situation put her more at ease in dealing with money and recognizing that it could be invested to benefit society.

Christina's career has turned to social action philanthropy. She is now a staff member with a progressive foundation and works with other people of inherited wealth. She links them to community-based organizations that are involved in social action and community economic development.

Responsible investing was a natural extension of these women's charitable giving, but more importantly it gave them a feeling of hope that their money could be invested to provide a positive social impact. It also gave them another level of comfort and allowed them not to be embarrassed by their investments, which at one time were made by a conservative East Coast banking firm. Both feel socially responsible investing is consistent with their belief that money is an important agent of social change. Christina, however, adamantly believes that *people* are the most important agents of social change. The sisters believe it is their role—their duty—to invest and donate their inheritance in a responsible manner. Charlotte sums it up nicely:

I think, as my great-grandfather passed his money to my grandfather and my grandfather passed it on to my father, it is my responsibility now to use my inheritance actively to make the world a better place to live. I can best accomplish this through philanthropy *and* investing responsibly.

Charlotte makes no bones about the fact that she believes her inheritance will be invested much differently than her grandfathers' and

great-grandfathers' money was invested. She feels that it may ameliorate damage caused by the traditional approach to investing, which
created some of our social problems in the first place.

Rebecca Cox

Rebecca, a client of mine, recalls that when she was 21 she had worked
and saved for several years to take a trip to Europe. Upon returning she was greeted by a letter from her dad informing her that she
was inheriting over a million dollars in securities from her grandfather's trust and would later receive another million dollars in securities when she turned 35. This all came as quite a shock. No
one had ever counseled her about money or the inheritance. She
was feeling good about the fact that she had a job and had saved
enough money to take a vacation to Europe. Now an awesome responsibility was being literally dropped on her. It changed her life;
for many years, instead of Rebecca ruling the money, it ruled her.
Since most of us dream of having a large sum of money dropped
in our laps, it is difficult to imagine money causing problems. But
it can.

Rebecca had a sense of self-worth and was proud of herself for
making money and saving for a much-needed vacation. With the sudden arrival of a million dollars, she now felt that her inheritance had
changed her identity. She was now responsible for not only her life but
for the conservatorship of a portfolio of stocks.

Rebecca grew up in Ohio and has two brothers. Her father was
the mayor of a small suburban community and a corporate attorney.
Her mother worked as a volunteer for the Red Cross. Both parents
inherited, but the bulk of the estate was passed down from Rebecca's
grandfather to her father, who was an only child.

Rebecca received an allowance while growing up but was never
trained to manage money. She was not made aware of her future inheritance or the extent of her grandfather's and father's fortune. Her
family were not conspicuous consumers, and Rebecca's lifestyle since
her inheritance has been very frugal.

Rebecca lived at home until she was 15 and was then sent to boarding school. After graduation she attended a university in California and
later moved to Berkeley. She bought a house there and spent the seventies and most of the eighties teaching at an alternative high school.
She became politicized by the Vietnam War and the social unrest it
caused on the nearby UC campus.

When I met Rebecca she was in the process of selling her house and planning to move to New Mexico because of allergies. She moved to the New Mexico countryside and continues to reside there today. She is an exceptional carpenter and has a modest property where she lives with her partner and two horses.

Rebecca had learned about responsible investing and my work through a friend. She was especially eager to learn more about directly investing her assets in positive investment opportunities. After we reviewed several programs, she invested in a historical building in Berkeley and received rehabilitation tax credits for it. Later the partnership sold the building to a bed-and-breakfast facility for a sizeable profit. Even after she moved to New Mexico, she retained her interest in the Bay Area. We later worked with a Berkeley realtor who organized a real estate partnership to purchase a building for women therapists. Rebecca participated in this venture, and the building has since been refinanced.

Rebecca's responsible investment activity didn't end there. She also invested in a large low-income residential hotel in northern California. This investment provides her with substantial tax benefits. These tax benefits are used to offset her large capital gains from stock sales. With Rebecca's initial inheritance and subsequent trust inheritances, she received a sizable block of one stock having an extremely low-cost basis. As I've sold stock over the years to diversify and increase her portfolio income, the tax advantage of the Oaks Hotel has offset capital gains from stock sales.

Rebecca's investment portfolio is managed consistent with her social values. She has utilized her assets to directly invest in real estate to rehabilitate a historic building, provide offices for women therapists, and build affordable housing for low-income Oakland residents. She has been able to restructure her portfolio to increase tax-free income and diversify the portfolio. Portfolio income has increased, overall risk and tax liability have been reduced, and Rebecca is investing in a manner consistent with her ethical and social values.

Mary Bennett

Mary was raised in upstate New York. When she was a child, she recognized that she was different from her peers because her house was much bigger. At one time her brothers even wrote about it as a mansion. She was embarrassed about the size of her house but only later found out that her brothers and sisters were even more embarrassed than she was.

Mary never had a nanny, but there was always someone around to cook and clean her house. She never remembers seeing her mother cook, clean, or do laundry. While she was in public grammar school, her friends made comments about her family's wealth that made her feel "extremely uncomfortable." They had domestic helpers who were black, but Mary was never allowed to call them servants. She wondered where their children were. One domestic worker had six children, but she never talked about them. Mary wondered who took care of the children when the worker was at her house.

No one talked about money at home. When Mary was 21, her father sat her down and explained that she would receive trust money over several years ("trickle trusts"). In other words, she would receive part of her inheritance when she was 21, 25, 30, 35, and 40 years old. There wasn't enough to live on initially, but it supplemented her other income. Mary's parents were always concerned that she not be spoiled and that she work for a living. Her father, a corporate attorney, made a point of instilling the work ethic in all of the children.

After attending Smith College, she became even more involved in civil rights. She recalls that during the civil rights struggle she was asked by many black community organizers to fight for them on the "white side of the street, not the black side." She became convinced that it was appropriate to work for social change within her own family.

Mary began to conduct research on the companies in which her family owned stock: using research from public interest groups, she attempted to change the corporation's stand on a number of social, economic, and environmental issues. Unlike many inheritors, Mary believes that those who inherit should go back and organize within their own family to influence the corporation from which the majority of their wealth is derived.

> If they've inherited their money, it's come from somewhere. Most people are removed from their family wealth source by the second or third generation and actually try to distance themselves because of wealth guilt. It's important for them to go back and reconnect with the family to provide urgently needed perspectives and information. Years ago I felt totally ineffective, but today the head of the corporation is a woman who is very progressive, there are more younger people on the board, and everyone is interested in the environment. It took many years longer than I thought it would, but I'm delighted with the changes that have been made.

Not only has Mary had some influence within her family, but she has also made a career of socially responsible investing. She is an investment advisor and wrote one of the first responsible investment studies recommending targeted investing to create jobs and promote economic development. She also drafted responsible investment criteria for an employee pension fund and has served on several local government and state commissions responsible for recommending the implementation of South African divestment laws and reinvestment strategies. Mary manages her own inheritance using social and economic criteria. Something that was once her avocation has become her vocation. She not only manages her own inheritance but serves as a socially responsible investment advisor and a leader in the field.

Paul DuPont Haible

Paul DuPont Haible went public about his social activism and his famous middle name years ago. Paul and others such as George Pillsbury not only donate to progressive social action organizations but publicize their gifts and urge other inheritors to do the same.

Paul worked as a staff member and eventually became development director of the Vanguard Public Foundation, a San Francisco–based progressive social action foundation. In this capacity he helped launch inherited wealth seminars on responsible investing, tax, estate, and financial planning for progressive donors of Vanguard. He maintains his affiliation with Vanguard and is a member of the New York–based Funding Exchange.

When he first inherited he strongly believed he should give away all of his money, and he came very close to doing so. He discovered, however, that through investing he could retain some of the principal of his original inheritance and earn competitive returns, thus providing a constant stream of income and capital appreciation to donate additional funds to progressive social causes.

For years Paul has seen socially responsible investing as part of an overall economic, social, and political strategy:

> You've got to make your inheritance and your earned and investment income work for you. It's part of a multifaceted approach to social change. In my case, I've been able to work, invest, and donate to further social justice issues. I'm very lucky. Investing in low-income housing, community businesses, loan funds and, where appropriate, Native American communities is a way to direct more dollars for positive social purposes. We can't depend upon government to solve our problems. We have to take charge ourselves and use all of our available resources. I use "we" as not only people with money but individuals working with other people who don't have money to achieve major social and economic goals.

Instruments of Social Change

Philanthropic organizations have become instruments of social change, but not without the help of thousands of donors. Donors' social, economic, and political impact have been geometrically increased by their ability to supplement their gifting with responsible investing and tax planning. They have helped define responsible investing and have turned it into a comprehensive economic strategy to address serious social and economic justice issues that cannot or will not be addressed solely by government agencies.

Many social action philanthropic organizations help bridge the gap between wealthy, middle-class, and poorer communities. Most of these nonprofit organizations are community-based, although some are national foundations that have socially progressive economic agendas.

The Funding Exchange

The most politically visible of all the social action philanthropic organizations is the Funding Exchange (FEX). It was established in New York in 1979 as a national membership organization of locally based community foundations. The community funds of FEX are committed to funding grassroots organizations that address critical issues in their geographical region. The exchange receives contributions from a broad spectrum of donors and gives community activists a primary role in grant-making decisions. It is also creating a $15 million endowment whose income will be used to subsidize small, progressive community funds that are FEX members.

Until last year FEX was run by June Makela. She recently stepped down to pursue other career opportunities as well as to take care of a newborn. Her successor as executive director is Cecilia Rodriquez, who successfully ran La Mujer Obrera in El Paso, Texas, an association of garment-making women fighting for better working conditions. Cecilia is the first Hispanic to run a national foundation in the United States.

The Funding Exchange has donated over $45 million to grassroots organizations through the national network of funds to finance such projects as:

- Battered women's shelters
- Organizing for the clean-up of toxic waste
- Organizations working for racial justice
- International human rights projects
- Labor activists fighting for workplace democracy

- Gay and lesbian rights organizations
- Media projects that educate and increase awareness on social justice issues

The Funding Exchange was established chiefly by people like Jane Bonner and Paul Haible and other progressive inheritors from wealthy corporate families with familiar names such as DuPont, Pillsbury, Rockefeller, and Sears.

Member organizations of FEX include:

- Appalachian Community Fund, Knoxville, TN
- Bread and Roses Community Fund, Philadelphia, PA
- Chinook Fund, Denver, CO
- Crossroads Fund, Chicago, IL
- Fund for Southern Communities, Atlanta, GA
- Haymarket People's Fund, Boston, MA
- Headwaters Fund, Minneapolis, MN
- Liberty Hill Foundation, Los Angeles, CA
- Live Oak Fund, Austin, TX
- McKenzie River Gathering Foundation, Eugene, OR
- North Star Fund, New York, NY
- People's Fund of Hawaii, Honolulu, HI
- People's Resource of Southwest Ohio, Cincinnati, OH
- Vanguard Public Foundation, San Francisco, CA
- Wisconsin Community Fund, Madison, WI

Many of FEX's community foundations also provide socially responsible investing seminars. They educate their donors regarding investment opportunities in companies that meet social as well as financial criteria.

The Women's Foundation

There are over 70 women's foundations in the United States that have given $20 million to women and girls' nonprofit groups. One such foundation, the Women's Foundation in San Francisco, has established special programs such as MIW, which is now under a separate nonprofit organization called Resourceful Women. Resourceful Women also houses three other programs for women with wealth: Via Leadership Training Institute, the Women Donors' Network, and Managing Earned Wealth. Tracy Gary is the director of Resourceful Women, and Kit Durgin is the executive director of the Women's Foundation.

The Funding Exchange, the Vanguard Public Foundation, and the Women's Foundation all publish directories of financial professionals for their members. The most recently published is the "Bay Area Financial Professionals Referral Directory 91–92," published by the Women's Foundation. It provides information on financial consultants, financial planners, insurance salespeople, investment advisors, organizational and philanthropic consultants, lawyers, realtors, stockbrokers, and tax advisors.

The Global Fund for Women

Philanthropic support for women and girls is now global. The Global Fund for Women, incorporated in California in 1987, has supported over 115 women's groups around the world, with a total investment of over $450,000.

The fund's program continues to focus on women's rights. It has supported numerous women's organizations, especially in the Third World.

Threshold Foundation

Threshold is a community of 300 individuals who pool their resources to support social justice, peace, environmental health, and human development. The San Francisco–based foundation provides a strong community spirit and purpose to its members. The vision of the foundation is artfully reflected in the words of its president, Roger Milliken, Jr.:

> A core problem we face at the end of the twentieth century is unbridled individualism. With the ongoing collapse of communist societies, pundits here and abroad are trumpeting the victory of free enterprise democracy. Yet all around us we sense the onrushing disaster caused by undisciplined self-entitlement, be it the destruction of the rain forest or other life-giving natural systems, the fear-driven aggression of hate groups and repressive governments or even our own nation's exploding budget deficits.
>
> When a seeker goes on a vision quest, she drops the bonds of ego and opens herself to the unseen wisdom that is always available to a sincere and open heart. Opening herself to the earth, to her ancestors and to those yet unborn, she receives intimations of her true place in the universe and how best to apply her talents and position to serve the earth and her people. It's this kind of linking the self to something larger that's solely needed in our world today.
>
> In our Threshold community, we support our individual progress along chosen paths and explore how we might grow in service to life. We recognize that separation—of matter from spirit, of masculine from feminine,

of humans from nature, of rich from poor, of individuals from the whole, of black from white, yellow from red—is at the root of the suffering in our world. While we support with our funding those who tend to the symptoms of our divided world, the quintessential Threshold project is one which works to heal the underlying separation.[3]

Threshold has supported nonprofit organizations such as the Public Media Center, the Global Fund for Women, the New El Salvador Today, the New Israel Fund, the National Gay and Lesbian Task Force, the San Francisco Zen Center, Defenders of Wildlife, Friends of the Earth, the Seventh Generation Fund, the East Harlem Block Nursery/Youth Action Project, and the Institute for Southern Studies.[4]

PART II

Responsible Investing for the Future

CHAPTER FIVE

Setting Social Goals

Almost 20 years ago I gave a talk on South Africa at Sacramento State University to a group of graduate students. I was preceded by television personality Captain Carrot, who told students, "You are what you eat." Well, I believe you are what you invest. Just as food nourishes our bodies, investment capital nourishes the economy and society.

Responsible investing has changed from a reactive force that screened out unethical or socially harmful investments to a proactive force for social, economic, and political change. Responsible investing now incorporates positive (inclusionary) criteria with the negative (exclusionary). Positive social and economic change is an integral part of responsible investing.

The Moral Minimum

In *The Ethical Investor*, Simon, Powers, and Gunnemann describe corporate ownership responsibility as applying the principal of "negative injunction" or "moral minimum" to a social injury concept.[1]

Briefly, there is a distinction between injunctions against (halting) activities that injure others and duties or moral commitments that require affirmative pursuit of some sort of social good. In other words, if the owner of a corporation is made aware that his or her firm is injuring others or in some way injuring the environment, there are few reasons why the individual or institution should be excused from taking corrective action.

Simon, Powers, and Gunnemann identified churches and colleges as institutional investors, but this issue is also relevant for individuals and other institutions such as pension funds. For a variety of reasons, investors may find themselves at moral odds with their portfolio. Investors often find that they own shares in companies that act against their personal economic, social, or political interests. According to

Simon, Powers, and Gunnemann, from an ethical standpoint, the investors are required to act. If they do not act, that in itself is an act. A sin of omission becomes a sin of commission.

A shareholder moral minimum criterion is simply a form of self-regulation required to avoid corporate social injury. The duty of a shareholder is to recognize the cost of a social or environmental injury to both the company and society, evaluate its short- and long-term effects, and take appropriate action. This action could take the form of a letter directed to the company's management or a shareholder resolution if the shareholder is not satisfied with management's response.

In May of 1990 I wrote a letter to Procter & Gamble's chairman of the board, Edwin Artzt, requesting the company to reply to the issue of a nationwide boycott of their products because of animal testing and the company's connection to El Salvadorian death squads. Unfortunately, Procter & Gamble never responded to my letter and, like many companies, will again be faced with responding to shareholders and resolutions at the annual meetings. On May 16, 1991, James Gamble and 19 U.S. religious institutions filed a shareholder resolution asking the company to investigate and disclose its ties to El Salvadorian coffee growers (Procter & Gamble is the largest U.S. purchaser of Salvadorian coffee).[2]

What if an investor doesn't own stock or have rights as a legal owner of a corporation but holds a bond or corporate commercial paper? Does the investor in the company's debt have a moral minimum? Does the company have a debt to society? These questions were thoroughly discussed when we formed Working Assets in 1983. Working Assets was organized on the basis that debt holders (in this case, corporate commercial paper holders) do have a moral minimum.

Money market mutual funds cannot invest in stocks but must invest in debt securities that have maturities of one year or less. Although Working Assets can't vote stock, it does communicate with corporate management and chooses to purchase or not purchase a company's short-term securities. For example, in 1984 Working Assets informed Ranier Bancorp that the money fund would not purchase debt obligations from the bank because Ranier had participated in the Private Export Fund Corporation (PEFCO), which financed trade-related loans to South Africa.

Setting social investment criteria is easy for many people. Two clients of mine, Matthew and Liz, are in their 30s and live in New York. Our first meeting to talk about investments was in Greenwich

Village in 1990. I soon learned that they were very well-read and articulate about the social issues they cared about. They indicated the areas in which they did not want to invest: nuclear power, weapons, environmental polluters, companies operating in South Africa, and companies in Northern Ireland that had not signed the MacBride Principles.[3]

This was all stated loudly and clearly before I could even hand them my questionnaire on social criteria. They were two steps ahead of me. We had a lively discussion about exclusionary criteria.

Take a pencil and fill out this questionnaire.

Social Investment Questionnaire
Exclusionary Criteria

"Negative"

Rate from 1 to 10
(1 is the highest priority)

Companies in South Africa   _____

Companies in Northern Ireland that have not signed the   _____
MacBride Principles

Companies that violate regulations of the Environmental Protec- _____
tion Agency (EPA)

Companies that are involved in gambling   _____

Companies that produce hazardous waste   _____

Major defense contractors   _____

Companies that discriminate on the basis of race, sex, ethnic ori- _____
gin, or sexual preference

Companies that produce tobacco   _____

Companies that violate regulations of the Equal Employment   _____
Opportunity Commission (EEOC)

Weapons manufacturers   _____

Companies that violate regulations of the Occupational Safety   _____
and Health Administration (OSHA)

Companies that produce alcohol   _____

Companies that violate regulations of the National Labor Rela- _____
tions Board (NLRB)

Nuclear power producers   _____

Companies that sell infant formula to the Third World   _____

Companies that hire union-busting consultants and/or appear on   _____
the national AFL-CIO "do not patronize" list

Companies that test on animals   _____

Companies that produce livestock through factory farming   _____
and/or companies that purchase such livestock

Companies that manufacture products containing CFCs   _____

Companies that manufacture war toys   _____

Inclusionary Criteria

"Positive"

Rate from 1 to 10
(1 is the highest priority)

Companies with a record of community charitable giving and   _____
financial institutions with excellent community reinvestment
records

Companies that support environmental organizations   _____

Companies with women and/or minorities on the board of direc-   _____
tors

Companies with a history of social disclosure   _____

Companies with affirmative action hiring and retention policies   _____

Companies committed to source reduction of solid waste and/or   _____
waste management

Companies with a commitment to a clean environment (Valdez   _____
Principles)

Companies covered by collective bargaining agreements   _____

Companies with policies supporting single parents, child care,   _____
and women in the workplace

Companies whose advertising policies support a positive image   _____
of women and minorities

Companies that support a woman's freedom of choice through   _____
charitable contributions to organizations such as Planned Parent-
hood

Companies committed to alternative sources of energy   _____

Companies producing quality goods and services   _____

Companies committed to employee benefits and workplace   _____
democracy

Defense contractors committed to peacetime conversion   _____

Companies committed to sustainable agriculture   _____

Companies committed to alternatives to animal testing   _____

If there are any other concerns that you have, feel free to add them.

_____

_____

_____

Portfolio management questionnaires help the investor to focus on important social concerns and set priorities. Surveying helps managers get to know individual clients better. Surveys help managers keep on track by allowing them to identify trends or changes in the attitudes and social goals of their clientele. Managers should survey clients often.

Social Injury

In developing social criteria, I've always been partial to *The Ethical Investor's* definition of "social injury" as "the injurious impact which the activities of a company are found to have on consumers, employees, or other persons, particularly including activities which violate or frustrate the enforcement of rules of domestic or international law intended to protect individuals against deprivation of health, safety or basic freedoms."[4] When I wrote the first South African divestiture legislation for the Black Caucus in Sacramento in 1973, I needed an overall legislative definition for social injury. This definition is the one I chose to use. In 1979, Tamsin Taylor, a registered investment advisor, consultant, and the chair of Berkeley's Citizens Committee on Responsible Investments, worked with the Associated Students of the University of California Pension Fund to design socially responsible investment criteria. In a memo dated 3/5/79, Taylor defined "socially injurious operations" as operations that:

a. Deprive or contribute to the deprivation of health, safety, adequate sustenance, basic human rights (including the right to bargain collectively), or fundamental freedoms, including the right to be free from discrimination based on race, sex, sexual preference, age, disability, religious or political beliefs, of any human people.

b. Develop, manufacture, or sell weaponry.
c. Seriously degrade or cause irreversible, irrecoverable, or irreparable harm to the natural environment.
d. Seriously endanger the continued existence of any living species.

U.S. Trust Company, Boston, was eventually retained to manage the Associated Students' portfolio and still manages it using strong and comprehensive social criteria.

Developing your social criteria and evaluating social goals can be time-consuming but very worthwhile. The process is no less important than developing your financial goals and objectives. Making money is great, but making it with a clear conscience is even better. Putting your money where your mouth is moves you into the world of positive social change.

Setting social goals and priorities is highly individual for each investor. Criteria for investing should focus on your relationship to your work, your family, the environment, and your social and political philosophy. Very few investors will come up with the same list of social goals and priorities.

We leave our workplace and tell ourselves that we won't bring our job home with us. People in business leave church on Sunday and convince themselves that religion, spirituality, and ethics have no place in the free enterprise system. We believe in a clean environment for our children but don't recycle paper, plastic, and other products. Becoming a successful adult means putting your beliefs into practice so that you always feel comfortable with what you are doing. Socially conscious investors want a successful bottom line, but they also want to feel comfortable about the way in which they obtain their profits.

Investing is as important as developing a tax strategy consistent with our social and political philosophy, our consumption of goods and services, individual social action, and philanthropy. All these ingredients make up who we are and what we will contribute to society. *We are what we invest.*

Working Assets Money Fund's latest survey of its over 20,000 shareholders nationwide revealed that they invest consistent with their ethical values. The survey found that 85 percent belonged to cause-related groups, 82 percent recycled household wastes, and 77 percent donated to charities. Working Assets' social criteria certainly reflects the social goals of its shareholders.

American society, in addition to emphasizing separateness, often attempts to rationalize actions that dehumanize. Investing in and of itself has become dehumanizing and is often marketed that way to investors. It is sanitized. It is professional. We don't really have to worry about where our money is invested or what our money is invested in as long as we believe it is safe and maximizes return.

Such an investment philosophy may have a lot to do with our being comfortable while someone takes care of us. It is easy to believe in presidents, generals, doctors, lawyers, priests, and other experts who have all the answers. Money management is left to Wall Street. One of the hottest trends is indexing stock to the Standard and Poors 500 Stock Index. This means that the index manager weights a stock portfolio to mimic the total S & P 500. As they say in the business, it is a "no-brainer." This is especially true if no social criteria exists.

The fact is that money is power. Money and power can be manipulated and abused, resulting in harm to society. When investment decisions are made about money, there are social ramifications. Your decision to invest in weapons production means that capital is available for weapons to be manufactured, distributed, and sold. There will be less capital available for other investment activities. There is a relationship among dollars invested in a weapons system, our overall economy, and the national conscience. Weapons are for destruction. Is that what we want?

Social Criteria

Portfolio managers may also implement social criteria or objectives that they follow for portfolio selection or screening. For example, I use social and economic inclusionary and exclusionary criteria simply as a guide for my clients. Such criteria are easily supplemented by more stringent and/or specific criteria articulated by individual clients. The criterion I use is as follows:

> It is the intention of the Advisor to invest in securities that create jobs and develop the world economy rather than investing in firms that promote rearrangement of business enterprises through mergers and acquisitions. The Advisor attempts to seek out investments that finance housing, small business, alternative energy and in companies that contribute to the quality of human and animal life and the environment through the goods and services they produce. The Advisor will also attempt to invest in companies that promote economic advancement of women and ethnic minorities, bargain fairly with their employees and in firms that are

creative and generous in their charitable contributions and have policies that promote the welfare of their employees. The Advisor shall also attempt to invest in companies that have a positive impact upon society through the quality or safety of their products.

On the other hand, the Advisor will not knowingly invest in securities of firms that manufacture tobacco; that pollute the environment; manufacture or distribute weapons as a principal business activity or that are listed in the U.S. Department of Defense 100 Prime Defense Contractors or who generate nuclear power. The Advisor will not knowingly invest in the securities of firms that consistently violate regulations of the Environmental Protection Agency (EPA), the National Labor Relations Board (NLRB) or the Equal Employment Opportunity Commission (EEOC). The Advisor will not invest in securities of firms that appear on the National AFL-CIO "Do Not Patronize" list or that have a record, according to the National AFL-CIO, of hiring "union busting" consultants. The Advisor will not knowingly invest in corporations that have a presence in, or in any way support, the white minority government of the Republic of South Africa.

Ratings and Company Profiles

Some responsible investment advisory newsletters use a rating system for corporations they review. Franklin's *Insight,* a monthly investment advisory newsletter, rates companies by social categories on a 1 to 5 scale (1 is the top ranking while 5 is the lowest ranking). *Insight* provides an overall social rating as well as a rating for individual social categories. *Insight* ratings are listed as follows:

1 = Company is an exemplary leader in this area and has shown exceptional initiative.
2 = Company has shown strong commitment in this area.
3 = Company has an average record without major controversies, or has a mixed or conflicting record.
4 = Company has a below average record. Company has occasionally been involved in substantial controversies.
5 = Company has a poor record, characterized by many major problems in this area.

Insight gives an overall rating of 2 to Stride Rite, a leading footwear manufacturer. The social assessment ratings by category are outlined in the Equity Brief:[5]

South Africa   2
Environment   3

Citizenship   1
Energy   2
Product   2
Insight's Ranking 2

Clean Yield, an investment advisory newsletter, on the other hand, does not rank companies but profiles them in monthly reports and presents a model portfolio (see Table 5.1).

Social Goals Change

The social goals of investors evolve and change. Events and social conditions change, too. Just like the economy and markets, society does not remain static. The moral minimum of today becomes the moral maximum of tomorrow. With over $625 billion in assets now professionally managed using some form of social criteria, issues such as the environment, corporate governance, executive compensation, and family issues are already replacing South African divestment as the critical matters of the day. Don't be hesitant to amplify your criteria and develop new criteria.

I was very impressed when one of my clients in Pennsylvania, a college professor, provided me with very strong investment criteria involving suburban sprawl and growth guidelines. He was particularly concerned that I not invest in municipal bonds that promoted growth, such as sewer and redevelopment bonds. Another client has severe allergies caused by an environmental disease. She requires me to exclude chemical companies and companies producing or selling "junk" foods.

Social Criteria Are Not Black and White

Whether you do the investing yourself or through a manager, it is important to delineate as clearly as possible your criteria and social goals. Don't just say, "I want to invest in clean companies." There are no clean or pure companies. Wellman is a great plastic recycling company, but it has no women or minorities on the board of directors and makes very small charitable donations ($3/10$ of 1 percent of pre-tax income). Wellman also emits chemical wastes from its plants.

Wellman advances recycling. Companies such as Gannett promote women in the work place. Setting particular goals allows you or a portfolio manager the flexibility to evaluate a company or group of companies (industry sector) by using a more specific social, economic, or environmental criterion.

Table 5.1 Model Portfolio 5/1/91

Stock	MKT	Symbol	Recm. Date	Cost Price	Current Price	Chng.	Yield	P/E	Technical Support	Advice
Betz Labs	O	BETZ	02/28/90	29⅛	54½	87.1%	2.0%	25	46	Hold
Durr-Fillauer	O	DUFM	04/27/88	9⅞	31¾	221.4%	0.8%	23	27	Hold
Equitable Resource	N	EQT	11/30/88	33⅝	37¾	12.3%	3.8%	13	35	Buy Under 40
Gundle Environ.	A	GUN	01/02/90	14⅛	18⅜	30.1%	0.0%	30	12	Hold
Handleman	N	HDL	06/01/88	12⅝	13¼	4.9%	3.0%	18	8	Buy Under 14
Harleysville Group	O	HGIC	10/26/88	15½	30½	96.8%	2.1%	9	22	Hold
Hechinger	O	HECHA	03/27/91	8⅝	10⅝	23.8%	1.5%	16	8	Buy Under 9
Luby's Cafeterias	N	LUB	03/28/90	16½	19½	18.2%	2.4%	14	15	Buy Under 19
Nature's Sunshine	O	NATR	01/02/91	7½	13¾	83.3%	1.8%	19	11	Hold
People's Energy	N	PGL	09/26/90	23	23⅞	3.8%	7.2%	12	19	Buy Under 24
Toys R Us	N	TOY	01/31/90	24½	29⅜	19.9%	0.0%	26	22	Hold

Cash: 26.7% (in SRI money market with 5.8% yield)
Equity position: 73.3%
Performance since 3/85 *(equity dividens included, beginning 1/90)*: = +300.5% (S&P 500 = +113.7%)

Prices as of 5/1/91
Rating Changes: Nature's Sunshine
Erratum: Last month's CY Performance should have read 276.4%, not 249.5%.
Clean Yield is a copyright and trademark protected publication.

Defense Contractors

Negative criteria are thought of as somewhat more objective than positive criteria because they exclude specific investment opportunities. Although this seems simple and straightforward, it is often not the case. Companies that appear on the U.S. Department of Defense's list of the 500 largest defense contractors can easily be excluded from your portfolio. But what about a company that is on the list but sells toilet paper, clothes, and other consumer products to military facilities across the globe? Should this company be divested from a responsible investor's portfolio? What about a news-gathering organization (such as the Washington Post) that has a reporter in South Africa? Should the Washington Post be screened out for this reason?

Gray areas of social criteria—just like gray areas involving financial criteria—require subjective decision making. Most socially oriented investors screen out a weapons manufacturer but would not remove a consumer products company that was a Department of Defense contractor from their portfolio. Similarly, most responsible portfolio managers would retain the Washington Post in their portfolio since access to relatively unbiased news from South Africa is important. In addition, the African National Congress (ANC), a leading anti-apartheid organization in South Africa, has expressed the view that U.S. investors should not boycott objective news sources from within the country.

Research and most analytical resources, including available databases, only screen out objectionable corporate activities at the first level or tier. For example, you may be able to identity all weapons contractors (first tier), but what about a company that manufacturers a part of a weapons system such as a bolt (second tier) and sells it to the defense contractor as well as to other businesses? Many of these second or third tier companies cannot be identified. Even if they were identified in a database, updating the information would be an endless task.

Portfolio managers do not have access to sophisticated data that would enable them to screen second and third tier companies. It is important, however, to ensure access to information on the first tier or end manufacturer, such as IBM or McDonnell Douglas.

South Africa

For years South African divestment was a rallying cry for many investors who wished to meet a social as well as a financial goal. Many investors simply did not want to include in their portfolios companies that operated in South Africa. For some people the overriding reason was an ethical aversion to investing in any company that benefited from the apartheid system. Other investors wanted to economically penalize U.S. companies in South Africa by having them pay a higher price for being there. Many people encouraged U.S. companies to disengage or leave South Africa, advance enlightened workplace and employee policies while remaining in South Africa (Sullivan Principles)[6], and/or encourage U.S. corporate subsidiaries to lobby the South African government to change its apartheid structure.

Let's clarify the South African exclusionary criteria. There are companies not physically located in South Africa that still benefit from apartheid, fuel the apartheid government with tax dollars, and provide strategic services to government agencies in South Africa. IBM is the perfect example. Although IBM does not have a physical plant or facility or ownership (equity) in South Africa, it does maintain business relationships through a trust that markets and sells IBM products, and services and maintains computer systems. Should IBM be in a responsible investment portfolio or not? For instance, California can still buy IBM under its divestment law because the state retirement system determined that certain companies with indirect economic relationship were not covered under the divestment law. Almost all other responsible investment managers and mutual funds, however, screen out IBM.

IRRC in Washington, D.C., is a nonprofit research organization that keeps updated documentation on foreign and domestic firms operating in South Africa. This information is supplied to subscribers, many of whom are large institutional investors, including pension funds, corporations, insurance companies, mutual funds, banks, universities, colleges, and churches. The information is concise, timely, and comprehensive. The American Committee on Africa (ACOA), the United Nations in New York, and the Africa Resource Center in Oakland also keep extensive documentation on transnational corporate activity in South Africa. It is for the investor, the portfolio manager, the broker, or the financial planner to determine how comprehensive the exclusion of U.S. corporate subsidiaries operating in South Africa will be.

South African exclusionary criteria has evolved over the last 20 years. People have changed their minds about the efficacy of the Sullivan Principles. When my colleagues and I drafted the criteria for Working Assets, Jerry Dodson (the first president of the company) and I disagreed on the South African criteria. He did not support divestment and disengagement; he shared the view of Rev. Leon Sullivan that enlightened corporate conduct would have the greatest influence on the white-minority government. I wanted a total investment ban on all companies with any economic relationship in South Africa.

We compromised. I agreed to leave in a rather wishy-washy South African exclusionary policy if Jerry would agree to ensure, in practice, that Working Assets never invested in any company with any connection to South Africa. To this day, Working Assets has implemented the most rigorous and comprehensive South African exclusionary policy of any mutual fund in the country. For example, when First Nationwide Financial was purchased by Ford Motor Company, the fund took First Nationwide off of its buy list because of Ford's involvement in South Africa.

In 1990 the Working Assets board of advisors recommended that the board change the South African prospectus language to reflect the fund's current screen, continue to support South African sanctions and divestment, and continue its efforts to confer with approved banks with outstanding loans in South Africa. The board of advisors specifically recommended changing the prospectus language to read:

> Working Assets Money Fund will not knowingly invest in corporations which do business in South Africa until that country's system of apartheid is abolished and the country has established democratic majority rule. We will not invest in companies which retain non-equity ties or own a subsidiary in South Africa.[7]

The board of advisors also suggested that the "repressive regime" portion of the criteria be removed. Since only South Africa had been identified as a "repressive regime," the advisiors recommened that the fund continually review corporate impacts on countries with significant human rights violations and establish a formal review process for adding countries to the "repressive regime" status. Due to the change of ownership and control of Working Assets, the fund has not yet made these changes.

Innovative Criteria

One of the founding trustees of Working Assets Money Fund was Jack Conway, who served as chairman of the board for five years. Jack has quite a list of accomplishments with organized labor, Common Cause, and the environmental movement. At one of the first Working Assets board meetings we were discussing expanding or amplifying our social investment criteria. We had just completed a meeting with our board of advisors, a group of experts we consult in evaluating criteria. Jack suggested that we consider investing in defense contractors who were seriously committed to converting their companies from defense to peacetime business activities. Everyone thought it was an interesting idea, but the problem was in finding a defense contractor who would fill the bill. Much to our sorrow, we never found one.

Another of Jack's ideas was to consider investing in those utilities that were phasing out nuclear power while expanding their commitment to alternative forms of energy. There were a number of utilities involved in this process. This was a great idea, but it had limited application to Working Assets since a money market fund only invests in the commercial paper of a corporation and none of our candidates issued prime corporate commercial paper. On the other hand, had the fund been able to invest in utility company stock, the dialogue between management and activist shareholders may have produced interesting and positive results.

Rewarding Positive Behavior

Positive corporate behavior should be as important to investors as negative behavior. Positive behavior needs to be rewarded by publicity, award presentations, and ultimately by investors voting their approval and commitment to such conduct with their investment and consumption dollars. For example, CEP holds an annual America's Corporate Conscience Award event. In 1991 H.B. Fuller, S.C. Johnson & Son, Inc., Stride Rite, Foldcraft, and Food 2000, Inc., were recognized for charitable contributions; Hershey Foods and Time Warner for community action; Hewitt Associates, Johnson & Johnson, and Kellogg Company for employer responsiveness; the H.J. Heinz Company, Herman Miller, The Body Shop, Aveda, Celestial Seasonings, Real Goods Trading, and Smith and Hawken for the environment; and Hallmark Cards, Marriott, Levi Strauss & Co., and Southern New England Telecommunications (SNET) for equal opportunity.[8] On Earth Day, 1990, many environmental investors gathered to present awards to corporations in the San Francisco Bay area for their service in protecting or preserving the environment.

Institutional Social Criteria

Large organizations often need a long time to hammer out social investment criteria based upon the goals of the institution. Working with organizations who want to clarify their social investment criteria is the most interesting part of my job. It is exciting to see people finally figure out how much power their investment dollar has.

Church Investors

I manage portfolios for a group of Catholic day homes. The day homes are located in the San Francisco Bay area and are managed by the Sisters of the Holy Family. They provide low-income people with affordable child care in San Francisco, Oakland, and San Jose. The sisters also operate a retirement and convalescent home for nuns in Mission San Jose.

Until 1991 the sisters were governed by a board of directors under the leadership of Sister Elaine Marie Sanchez. Sister Elaine Marie has been with the order for 31 years. Her strong sense of social justice and a belief in people came from her parents, who both were blue-collar workers and had left elementary school to work and care for their many siblings.

Sister Elaine Marie and Sister Ann Maureen Murphy, who is in charge of the Holy Family Day Home, felt strongly that they could not invest the Sisters' funds in a manner inconsistent with the social objectives of all the day homes. Sister Elaine Marie hired a consultant, PAM broker Tom Van Dyck, and after many months' work adopted social criteria in October 1988 to guide the Sisters' investments.

Social Objectives

The Day Homes recognize the influence money has on the basic structure of an economy and society. That influence can be abused, or it can be used in a way that is constructive, healthy and lucrative. Such investing requires an expanded concept of investing by the investment manager. The manager needs to understand that money put into the business enterprise is reflected not only in the stock price movement and dividends, but also in a quality of life represented by what the company produces, where those products are sold and how that company treats their employees and the environment. Companies that concern themselves with these issues tend to identify business opportunities more quickly, thereby earning better returns than those companies that ignore such issues. Therefore, it is the desire of the Day Homes that investments meeting the financial objectives stated above are also screened for various social concerns.

Funds should not be invested in a company that is involved in any of the following:

- Business activities, direct or through non-equity arrangements, in South Africa,
- Manufacturing or developing weapons systems, either nuclear or conventional,
- The production of nuclear energy,
- Discrimination based on religion, race and sex or consistent violation of Equal Employment Opportunity guidelines.

Furthermore, the funds should seek investments in corporations that:

- Treat employees fairly by providing profit-sharing, benefits and incentives, while also providing opportunities to women, minorities and others for whom equal treatment have often been denied. The important factor is fair and equal treatment of employees.
- Are sensitive to the environmental impact of their business and do not violate EPA standards, but instead work to develop new ways to improve the environmental standards of their business.

Health Care Investors

The Golden Gate Nurses is a San Francisco–based affiliate of the California Nurses Association. The organization is predominately run by women and is extremely cost effective. Members of the board of directors and union members volunteer and serve on numerous local and state advisory boards and commissions. The union is actively involved at many levels to provide quality health care to the community and lobbies both local and state governments to provide improved health care standards.

Golden Gate Nurses is run by a seasoned administrator and local political activist, Jo Anne Powell, who has been largely responsible for the organization's commitment to responsible investing. Their written criterion (1984) is very brief but to the point: "Monies will be placed in socially responsible accounts." The social criteria adopted by the Nurses' finance committee is the Harrington criteria on paper, supplemented by the overall social goals of the organization. These social goals relate to the advancement of women in the workplace, quality health care, and an adequate compensation and benefits program for all employees.

A group of medical doctors and other health care practitioners in the Southwest spent over a year developing responsible investment criteria that reflected the organization's goals and objectives. Similar to many in the health care field, this organization holds a strong bias against the consumption of tobacco. They have created an alternative for their employees' retirement program that enables the individual employee to choose socially screened investments.[9]

Socially Responsible Equity Fund

Investment objectives: This investment alternative is intended to reflect a higher level of total return over time than both the Money Market Fund and Balanced Fund. In addition, this investment alternative is intended to provide an option to participants for a "screened investment" which takes into consideration concerns regarding the environment, politically unacceptable policies, weapons of mass destruction, unfair labor practices, etc.

Specifically, this investment alternative will exclude companies that primarily are involved in any of the following activities:

1. Tobacco and related products.
2. Nuclear weapons.
3. Military (non-nuclear) weapons.
4. South Africa sales (direct or indirect).

Prohibited Transactions

Any company which by its actions or investments clearly supports or contributes to policies of discrimination of any kind, including religion, race, sex, age or nation of origin.

Any company whose reputation, focus of research or major source of income is derived from the sale of tobacco.

In addition, the Investment Alternative should emphasize and demonstrate a positive focus on companies whose philosophy and/or strategy encompasses the following responsible positions:

I. Environmental protection
   A. Engages in active participation regarding environmental issues and has developed organized corporate policy.
   B. Has a favorable record and demonstrates a pollution conscious policy.
II. Labor Practices
   A. Provides opportunities for women and minorities at all levels, including professional, upper management and Board positions.
   B. Follows an affirmative action plan.
   C. Reflects a history of smooth labor relations.
III. Corporate Citizenship
   A. Has a formal code of ethical conduct.
   B. Contributes to charity, education and other local community projects.
   C. Encourages management and employees to spend time on community and charity activities.

Individual Decision-Making

Social criteria do not have to be exotic or complicated. They can be brief and straightforward. The implementation of the criteria, however, requires time and needs special attention. Investing your money requires the same care that buying a house does. People rarely buy the first house they look at. Usually they study, compare, and educate themselves before buying. It should be the same for building a portfolio.

If you are investing a few thousand dollars, you may want to implement your social and investment criteria through a mutual fund. If, for example, you are interested in investing in environmentally screened companies and have only $2,000, you could consider the Eco·Logical Trust or the Progressive Environmental Fund. If you are investing more, you can diversify your portfolio and adopt and implement more comprehensive criteria with or without the help of a financial professional. If you are working alone, use the directory at the end of this book to pinpoint sources of social investment information. They are numerous and many research services are expanding their existing databases and adding new ones. For example, the Cambridge-based investment advisory firm of Kinder, Lydenberg and Domini recently added a new 650-company on-line service to provide investors and financial professionals with direct computer access to the social records of companies in the S&P 500 as well as those in the Domini 400 Social Index.

Social Trade-Offs

Some investors implement their social criteria with a rating system similar to that provided by *Insight*. The rating of a company is based upon various criteria. It allows an investor to weight both positive and negative criteria and come up with an overall rating. Johnson & Johnson and IBM are examples of companies where an investor might weigh the positive and the negative aspects of their social performance and then make a decision to invest or not invest.

Johnson & Johnson (JNJ) has long been recognized by responsible investors as a business committed to its employees and the community. For example, JNJ was among the first corporate signatories of 10 principles endorsing the rights of workers diagnosed with the AIDS virus. The company also provided the best adoption benefits among companies profiled by CEP. Johnson & Johnson was profiled in *The 100 Best Companies to Work for in America* (New American Library, 1985) and *Everybody's Business* (Doubleday, 1990), receiving praise for its childcare programs, sick-care services, flextime for employees, and other employee and community programs. On the other hand, JNJ is one of the top 10 South African investors, has yet to appoint a woman to one of its 14 top executive jobs, and is the fifth largest corporate user of animals in testing.

Reviewed in both *Everybody's Business* and *The Better World Investment Guide,* IBM is also known for its strong community and employee social programs, charitable contributions, and its support for disabled people, minorities, education, literacy programs, AIDS research, the arts, and hospitals. The company also funds research in alternatives to animal testing. On the other hand, IBM still maintains a strong South African presence and is a major defense contractor. Additionally, IBM is a founding member of the Coalition for Workplace Technology (since renamed the Center for Office Technology), a manufacturers' group that lobbies against legislation to protect the health of workers who use video display terminals (VDTs).[10]

I recently gave a speech in Hawaii for the People's Fund, a progressive social action public foundation that supports small-scale community projects such as alternative media, immigrant rights groups, and the Hoa Aina O Makaha Peace Center. In my talk, I used similar examples of positive and negative corporate behavior. I expressed a certain uneasiness, however, about making investment decisions based on the results of a weighted rating system. I compared it to evaluating a person in your community. Let's say this theoretical person donates to many charities, is a regular churchgoer, belongs to numerous civic organizations, and, for the most part, is a model citizen in the community. He has only one problem—he is an alcoholic, and when he drinks he physically and psychologically abuses his wife and children. Should the community ignore the problem and let him continue to abuse his family? Should his 1 rating in the community offset his 5 rating in the family?

Our theoretical citizen should be respected and admired for his service to the community, but his drinking and abusive activities should not be ignored and offset by his positive attributes. The same should apply to a corporate citizen. Abusive behavior by a corporation should not be ignored. An owner, a debt holder, or a customer is responsible for exerting pressure to correct corporate social injury. Positive corporate activity should be encouraged. Negative activity or social injury should be penalized and corrective action should be taken.

Social investment information and data are becoming abundant, accessible, and affordable. Perusal of a sampling of library sources will allow you to easily identify companies that produce nuclear power, sell tobacco products, produce alcohol, or are involved in the gambling industry. If you have trouble identifying these companies, call your broker for the information. Be sure, however, not to forget companies that operate casinos, such as Hilton Hotels and Holiday Inn. On one of my trips to southern Africa I was astounded to see that

Holiday Inn operated one of the most elaborate casinos in Swaziland. The Hard Rock Cafe, a favorite restaurant of many of my clients, is, unfortunately, getting into the gambling business now.

The Four Sins

Investing in the machines of destruction influences society; likewise, investing in alcohol, tobacco, and gambling has a great effect. If no money was invested in weapons, alcohol, tobacco, and gambling, would they exist? If less money were invested in them, would it raise the cost of capital to produce such items? Investing and consumption are two sides of the same coin. Without consumers to buy products, there is no market. Without the capital to produce the products, the products are not available to the market. If weapons manufacturers are capitalized, they need to find a market for weapons. They need to convince someone to buy and use weapons and to replace old weapons.

Obviously, the production of weapons, alcohol, tobacco, and gambling has a significant impact on our society and our economy. America is a violent society. We manufacture weapons. We buy and sell them domestically and abroad, and we use them on each other or against our "enemies." Americans abuse alcohol, resulting in the premature deaths of tens of thousands of citizens. Americans smoke tobacco; lung cancer soars—and so do deaths. We're also addicted to gambling. State lotteries are now approved and run by the government, subsidizing services and reinforcing the foolish belief that we can get something for nothing.

Church restrictions on investing in companies involved in the production of alcohol, tobacco, and gambling were the genesis of investment screening. Unfortunately, gambling seems to have become more accepted—in fact, institutionalized by law. The harmful effects of addiction to gambling and the fact that the lottery is, in essence, a regressive form of taxation don't seem to sway our political leaders from recommending it at every turn as a panacea for the government's revenue woes. The poor get poorer, but with the expectation of winning the lottery.

On the other hand, the decreased acceptance of the use of alcohol and tobacco is encouraging. Mothers Against Drunk Driving (MADD) and other citizen organizations have caused the beer, alcoholic beverage, and wine industry to use advertising that promotes the reduction of excessive consumption of alcoholic beverages and to spend millions of dollars on public education programs. The National Beer Wholesalers Association is presently lobbying Congress to promote responsible drinking. The lobbying is part of a billion-dollar counterattack by the liquor industry against a strong anti-drinking campaign by citizen groups, health advocates, and others "that threaten[s] to do to booze what others have done to cigarettes."[11]

In the past alcohol and tobacco companies have aggressively advertised in minority communities. Alcoholism has been identified as the top health problem for blacks and as a growing menace to Hispanics, according to the National Institute on Alcohol Abuse and Alcoholism. Government statistics show that incidences of tobacco-related diseases, such as cancer, heart disease, and stroke, are significantly higher among blacks than whites.

In Oakland and Alameda County, California, Supervisor Don Perata released a report recommending a ban on cigarette machines, restrictions on billboard advertising, and strict enforcement of laws governing the sale of alcohol and tobacco in minority neighborhoods. Perata's study found that 60 percent of the billboards in Oakland's minority community advertised alcohol and cigarettes, while in middle-class and upscale neighborhoods only 11 to 18 percent of the billboards advertised these products.[12]

Church shareholders have been especially active in requesting alcohol and tobacco companies to provide reports to shareholders on beer and tobacco sales and promotions to minorities and minors. In 1991 the Evangelical Lutheran Church in America (ELCA) and the City of New York introduced a resolution requiring Loews, a cigarette producer, to report on the marketing of cigarettes to minorities. The Evangelical Lutheran Church in America also introduced a resolution asking the company to cease making cigarette papers at Kimberly-Clark that received 4.6 percent of the shareholder vote. The same resolution received 7.7 percent at Eastman Kodak, which makes the material used for filters.[13]

A tobacco stock divestment campaign continues to pick up speed across the United States. While director of the California State Department of Health, Dr. Kenneth Kizer sent letters to the University of California, the University of Southern California, Stanford University, and the two large state retirement systems, strongly encouraging them to divest their tobacco stocks. According to the Boston-based Tobacco Divestment Project, City University of New York, Howard University, Johns Hopkins University, Southern Illinois University, Tufts University, and Wayne State University have all divested tobacco securities. In addition, Cambridge, Massachusetts, Pittsburgh, the Episcopal Church, the Henry K. Kaiser Family Foundation, the Memorial Sloan-Kettering Cancer Center, the New England Baptist Hospital, the New England Deaconess Hospital, the Rockerfeller Family Fund, the Robert Wood Johnson Foundation and the Thoracic Foundation have all divested.[14]

It is ironic that public and private retirement systems, foundations, and university endowments invest in tobacco stocks, leading to the deaths of their beneficiaries and donors, while at the same time they spend millions of dollars to promote anti-smoking campaigns and educate their students and the public on the health hazards of smoking. According to press reports, UC, Stanford, and the two largest California retirement systems have almost $700 million invested in tobacco stocks.[15]

It would be interesting to discover how many beneficiaries of California's retirement systems have died or sought early retirement because of lung cancer or other tobacco-related illnesses, as well as the number of donors to U.C. and Stanford's endowment funds who have died or been hospitalized. This is an issue in which health, morality, and good common sense are powerful allies. In a very emotional May 10, 1990, speech in Boston, Massachusetts, on the occasion of the launching of the Tobacco Divestment Project, Patrick Reynolds said:

> Cigarettes manufactured by only six companies will kill 400,000 Americans this year. Cigarettes manufactured by only six companies will addict over one million American youngsters this year. Cigarettes manufactured by only six companies will feed the addictions, and sap the health, of over 50 million Americans this year.
>
> Philip Morris, RJR Nabisco, American Brands, British American Tobacco, Loews, and Liggett Group—these six companies are responsible for almost one hundred times as many American deaths as the Medellín Cartel and the American Mafia *combined.* Although cocaine and heroin are universally abhorred by decent people as addictive drugs which take away the freedom as well as threatening the lives of those who use them, these six cigarette companies peddle a drug which has addicted more than a dozen times as many Americans as have heroin and cocaine combined.
>
> When my grandfather, R. J. Reynolds, introduced Camels in 1913, he didn't know that cigarettes would go on to kill tens of millions of Americans—including two of his four children. One of them was my father. My grandfather had no idea how self-deceiving, how filthy, ruthless and morally bankrupt the tobacco companies would become. In 1979 I divested the stock I inherited in R. J. Reynolds because of my strong feelings about this, and today I fight with all of my resources for a smokefree society.[16]

Nuclear Power

Many responsible investors avoid nuclear power the same way churches and other institutions avoid alcohol, tobacco, and gambling. The nuclear industry has been controversial because nuclear power is dangerous, a health hazard, and extremely expensive. Poor construction and design, cracked containment walls, and cost overruns have made nuclear utilities a risky and poor investment. Tom Van Dyck (a broker at PAM) and Ted Brown (a former Merrill Lynch broker and former head of a Bay Area responsible investment group) conducted a five-year study of nuclear and non-nuclear utility stocks. From 1981 to 1985 the total return performance (dividends plus price appreciation) for non-nuclear utility stocks was a compounded average of 22.18 percent, while nuclear utilities only returned 19.08 percent.

The future of nuclear power also looks bleak from a cost standpoint. With some 66 nuclear reactors due for permanent shutdowns by 2010, the costs of decommissioning are enormous. The California Public Utilities Commission ruled in 1987 that Pacific Gas & Electric Company (PG&E) needed to put aside $53.2 million a year to fund the dismantling of its Diablo Canyon nuclear plant and to spend $578.5 million (based on 1985 dollars) to decommission the plant.[17] PG&E spent $5.8 billion dollars to build Diablo.[18] Add to this the additional cost of nuclear waste disposal. We still haven't found an adequate answer to this problem or determined its total cost.

Shareholder Resolutions

Shareholders have also raised questions about nuclear safety, the disposal of radioactive waste, and monitoring radiation releases. In 1991 a shareholder resolution requesting a report from Florida Progress on the Crystal River plant received 10.3 percent of the shareholder vote. A shareholder resolution at Philadelphia Electric requesting the company to report on radioactive waste storage received 9.6 percent. A shareholder resolution introduced by ICCR at Union Electric on monitoring of radiation releases received 11 percent of the total vote.[19]

Animal Testing

Nonprofit organizations that serve in the public interest are also tremendous resources for investors. When you evaluate cosmetic companies relative to animal testing, it is important to contact the Humane Society. Consumers can receive a guide entitled *Humane Shoppers Guide to Household Products and Cosmetics*.[20]

There are over 1000 animal protection organizations in the United States. People for the Ethical Treatment of Animals (PETA) has been the most active organization at the shareholder level, filing eight corporate shareholder resolutions in 1988. In 1989, PETA filed a shareholder resolution with JNJ that requested complete disclosure of how many animals the company used in tests, the types of tests used, and what efforts JNJ was taking to eliminate animal use; the resolution received 6.7 percent of the total shareholder votes cast.[21] The first known animal rights resolution was filed with Iroquois Brands in 1985; more resolutions were filed with IBM and Greyhound Corporation (Dial) in 1986 and Procter & Gamble and Greyhound in 1987.[22]

In 1990 PETA filed resolutions with Bristol-Myers, Gillette, JNJ, and Schering-Plough, urging them to reduce testing on animals. At IBM and U.S. Surgical, shareholders asked for reports on the use of animal testing.[23] In 1991 PETA introduced resolutions that requested Bristol-Myers Squibb and JNJ to phase out animal testing. The resolutions received 3.1 percent of the total shareholder vote at Bristol-Meyers and 3 percent at JNJ. Shareholders asked IBM and Pepsico to report on animal testing and requested U.S. Surgical to report on the company's use of animals to demonstrate surgical staplers.[24]

In May 1990 the Working Assets board of advisors[25] met in San Francisco to review social investment criteria and make recommendations to the board of directors of the management company. The research staff was concerned that Working Assets needed to respond to a significant number of letters asking the company for an animal rights screen. Twenty-five percent of the letters came from Working Assets shareholders.

The advisors learned that Calvert Social Investment Fund routinely screens for animal rights while FRDC screens for animal rights at the request of its clients. In addition, a 1987 American Medical Association poll found that 77 percent of Americans surveyed considered animal testing in medical research unnecessary. The Working Assets Advisors recommended that:

- The Money Market Fund should develop a public position on animal rights
- The position should be secondary to existing criteria
- The Money Market Fund should incorporate animal rights criteria as positive and not define it as avoidance or a screen
- The criteria should include only animal testing relative to consumer, not medical, products.[26]

The Investor Responsibility Research Center utilizes data from the U.S. Department of Agriculture and published Heidi J. Welsh's report, "Animal Testing and Consumer Products." The Council on Economic Priorities maintains an extensive database on companies involved in animal testing and research. The council's *Shopping for a Better World* includes animal testing in its rating system, provided for consumers to evaluate socially responsible products.

Defense and Nuclear Weapons

Prime defense contractors are identified in numerous government publications. The Pax World Fund and CEP utilize extensive data and information on contractors. The Center for Economic Conversion (CEC) in Mountain View, California, maintains considerable data and is an excellent source for current defense spending and defense-to-peacetime conversion issues. A nonprofit organization founded in 1975, CEC serves as a national resource center on conversion issues. It provides educational material, speakers, organizing assistance to conversion activities, and technical assistance to workers, managers, and public officials confronted by military cutbacks. *Positive Alternatives* is CEC's excellent quarterly publication for its members.

The Investor Responsibility Research Center annually updates its list of defense contractors. Table 5.2 shows the top 10 recipients of DoD awards and the total awards by fiscal year. Table 5.3 lists U.S. publicly owned corporations that are among the 100 institutions that receive the largest dollar volume of DoD prime contract awards as

Table 5.2   Top 10 Awards Recipients (Dollar Amounts in $ millions)

Parent Company	FY90 Rank	FY90 Awards	FY89 Rank	FY89 Awards	FY88 Rank	FY88 Awards
McDonnell Douglas	1	$8211.4	1	$8617.2	1	$8002.7
General Dynamics	2	6306.1	2	6899.2	2	6522.1
General Electric	3	5589.0	3	5771.0	3	5700.6
General Motors	4	4106.6	5	3691.5	7	3550.2
Raytheon	5	4071.0	4	3760.7	5	4055.3
Lockheed	6	3552.6	6	3651.5	8	3537.7
Martin Marietta	7	3492.0	8	3336.6	6	3715.1
United Technologies	8	2855.8	7	3556.3	9	3508.1
Grumman	9	2697.0	10	2373.1	11	2847.7
Tenneco	10	2409.9	21	915.9	4	5057.9

Note: The Boeing Co. ranked 10th in fiscal 1988, 9th in fiscal 1989 and 11th in fiscal 1990.
Compiled by the Investor Responsibility Research Center from Department of Defense data.

Table 5.3 U.S. Publicly Owned Corporations (Awards in $ millions)

Parent Company	Rank	Awards	Dependance Ratio*
AT&T	23	917.1	.025
Allied-Signal	28	724.5	.058
Amerada Hess (N)	96	124.7	.018
Amoco	72	186.9	.007
Arvin Industries	93	134.2	.076
Arco Products (N)	47	390.5	.020
Black & Decker	8	165.5	.034
Boeing	11	2266.6	.082
Bolt, Beranek & Newman (N)	92	138.7	.530
CFM International Inc.+	54	318.6	***
CRS Sirrine/Metcalf & Eddy JV#(N)	84	160.3	***
CSX	63	226.8	.028
Chevron	73	186.3	.004
Chrysler	65	215.4	.007
Coastal	51	370.6	.040
Computer Sciences	53	319.0	.213
Contel.	62	229.0	.067
Control Data	64	221.3	.131
Digital Equipment	88	149.6	.011
E-Systems	41	460.1	.254
Eastman Kodak	98	120.0	.006
Eaton	77	176.1	.043
Emerson Electric	67	200.7	.027
Exxon	42	437.7	.004
FMC	30	634.0	.170
Federal Express et al. JV**(N)	60	253.5	***
Ford Motor	25	768.8	.008
GTE	17	1294.5	.070

*   Dependence is measured using a ratio of total fiscal 1990 DoD prime contract awards worth more than $25,000 to total company sales or revenues for the year. The ratio does not provide a precise measure of defense dependence, but rather gives a rough indication of the relative value of such contracts to the company.

(N) Indicates that the company is new to the top 100 in fiscal 1990. Such companies may have appeared on previous top 100 listings, but did not appear in fisical 1989. In the case of Arco Products Co., the company's awards were reported in fiscal 1989 under its parent, Atlantic Richfield, so only the name has changed since last year.

\+ CFM International is a joint venture between General Electric and Snecma of France. It manufactures military and aircraft engines. The division of awards between GE and Snecma is not available, so the defense dependence ratio for GE presented here is somewhat lower than it would otherwise be if the division of the awards between the two were known.

\# CRS Sirrine/Metcalf & Eddy JV is a joint venture between CRS Sirrine and Metcalf & Eddy, two construction firms.

** Federal Air Express et al. is a partnership between Federal Express, Northwest Airlines, Pan Am World Airways, Tower Air and United Parcel Service formed to transport troops and material to the Persian Gulf as part of Operation Desert Shield.

Table 5.3   (*Continued*)

Parent Company	Rank	Awards	Dependance Ratio*
Gencorp	21	1132.8	.630
General Dynamics	2	6306.1	.620
General Electric	3	5589.0	.096
General Motors	4	4106.6	.033
Goodyear Tire & Rubber (N)	99	119.7	.011
Grumman	9	2697.0	.667
Harris	71	188.2	.061
Harsco	75	178.0	.101
Hercules	38	491.7	.153
Hewlett Packard	89	149.0	.011
Honeywell	15	1388.1	.199
IBM	18	1285.8	.019
ITT	24	870.2	.042
Int'l Shipholding (N)	87	157.1	.480
Johnson Controls	59	253.8	.056
Kaman	70	188.2	.228
LTV	20	1182.9	.193
Litton Industries	14	1576.2	.299
Lockheed	6	3552.6	.356
Logicon	86	157.3	.609
Loral	31	618.2	.485
Martin Marietta	7	3492.0	.568
McDonnell Douglas	1	8211.4	.502
McDonnell Douglas/General Dynamics JV++	33	555.0	***
Mobil	61	237.7	.004
Morrison Knudsen	50	370.7	.224
Motorola	45	402.6	.037
Northrop	26	746.4	.136
Olin	32	575.7	.222
Oshkosh Truck	58	259.2	.572
Penn Central	49	373.3	.173
Philip Morris Cos.	90	140.9	.003
Raytheon	5	4071.0	.439
Rockwell Int'l	13	2217.3	.178
Sequa	69	190.7	.085
TRW	22	1087.3	.133
Talley Industries (N)	97	122.7	.368

++McDonnell Douglas and General Dynamics were working on the A-12, an all-weather medium-range attack aircraft. The division of awards between the two companies is not available, so the defense dependence ratios for the two companies presented here are somewhat lower than they would be otherwise if the division of awards between them were known.

##World/Rosen et al. is a joint venture involving World Airways, Rosenbalm Aviation, Key Airlines, American Airlines, Evergreen International Airlines and Emery Worldwide formed to transport troops and material to the Persian Gulf as part of Operation Desert Shield.

Table 5.3   *(Continued)*

Parent Company	Rank	Awards	Dependance Ratio*
Teledyne	35	515.3	.137
Tenneco	10	2409.9	.166
Texas Instruments	29	704.2	.107
Textron	19	1190.4	.150
Thiokol	52	358.5	.301
Unisys	16	1375.9	.136
United Technologies	8	2855.8	.131
Varian Associates (N)	78	173.3	.130
Westinghouse Elec.	12	2243.4	.174
World/Rosen et al. JV## (N)	85	160.3	***

* Dependence is measured using a ratio of total fiscal 1990 DoD prime contract awards worth more than $25,000 to total company sales or revenues for the year. The ratio does not provide a precise measure of defense dependence, but rather gives a rough indication of the relative value of such contracts to the company.

(N) Indicates that the company is new to the top 100 in fiscal 1990. In the case of Arco Products Co., the company's awards were reported in fiscal 1989 under its parent,

World/Rosen et al. is a joint venture involving World Airways, Rosenbalm Aviation, Key Airlines, American Airlines, Evergreen International Airlines and Emery Worldwide formed to transport troops and material to the Persian Gulf as part of Operation Desert Shield.

Compiled by the Investor Responsibility Research Center from information provided by the Department of Defense, Dun & Bradstreet, Standard & Poor's, *Fortune* and *Forbes*.

well as their dependence on defense contracts for the federal fiscal year ending September 30, 1990.

In addition, IRRC has published a reference guide, *Stocking the Arsenal,* that contains profiles of the leading defense contractors. The organization also produced a guide to the nation's nuclear weapons industry, *The Nuclear Weapons Industry,* that identified nuclear weapons producers and delineated the effect the industry has on communities, the economy, and the political process.

INFACT's Corporate Campaign

The nuclear weapons controversy is becoming quite pronounced. Ray Rogers, who runs Corporate Campaign, Inc., was recently hired by the Infant Formula Action Coalition (INFACT) a Boston–based activist organization that has managed a five-year boycott of General Electric (GE) products. The GE boycott focuses on GE's manufacturing of neutron triggers for weapons and GE's position as the nation's second largest producer of nuclear power. In addition, GE is responsible for 47

Superfund hazardous waste sites, is the third largest military contractor, and has been convicted of overcharging the federal government and defrauding the U.S. Department of Defense. INFACT claimed that by mid-1990 GE had lost more than $100 million in sales due to the boycott.[27]

Ray Rogers is using sophisticated financial and marketing strategies in his fight against GE, including the release of a 29-minute videotape documentary, "Deadly Deception." This video is being distributed to GE managers, institutional investors, stock analysts, and customers and has been shown on cable television in Fairfield County, Connecticut, where GE is headquartered.[28]

California's Experience

In 1971, my first job with the California legislature was as a staff assistant to the joint committee on economic conversion, which was chaired by Assemblyman John Burton. The joint committee was concerned that aerospace layoffs in southern California would damage the state's economy; it was looking for ways to assist defense contractors and local governments in becoming less dependent on defense contracts.

In 1978, when I was the consultant to the California State Senate select committee on investment priorities and objectives, Gordon Adams, an expert on economic conversion issues, was working for CEP. Our committee retained CEP to study the defense industry in California and provide expert testimony at one of our public hearings.

In 1971 and in 1978, there was little change in the attitudes of contractors, local government, or state government. In the 1990s, California's state government and many local governments are again struggling with a nationwide 25 percent reduction in defense expenditures and massive layoffs. Local and state governments compete to have contractors open factories in their communities by providing lucrative tax advantages and other incentives. Because defense companies are tied to public coffers and the taxpayers' ability to pay (or borrow), it's a boom-or-bust industry.

The Bush Administration and many large defense contractors are mobilizing to provide federal loan guarantees for defense contractors so that they can compete with foreign firms in the exportation of weapons to Third World countries. As the Persian Gulf War taught us, the Third World does not need more weapons, but rather trade and a private sector commitment to economic development.

Other Sources

For much of their defense-related information, the researchers at Working Assets utilize Nuclear Free America, a nonprofit research and social action organization based in Baltimore, Maryland. Nuclear Free America, CEP, and portfolio managers such as U.S. Trust Company, Boston, and FRDC also use sophisticated defense department data compiled by Eagle Eye, a private research company in Arlington, Virginia. Eagle Eye has computerized its database, which it obtains directly from the DoD.

Screening

Working Assets Money Fund screens out defense-oriented companies. It starts with the top 100 defense contractors and then eliminates any companies that do research or development on the Strategic Defense Initiative (SDI). Working Assets leaves the possibility of investing in companies with a minor amount of nonstrategic or nonweapons defense contracts, but in reality Working Assets screens *all* defense-oriented firms.

As a portfolio manager I've found that it is very easy to screen out defense-oriented firms and that it has no impact on performance or the overall diversification of risk within a client's portfolio. This was confirmed by a recent study by Prudential Securities' Social Investment Research Service (SIRS). The study examined the Standard & Poor's 500 Composite performance when both the top 100 prime defense contractors and the top 500 U.S. prime defense contractors were excluded from investment.[29] Both the portfolio of the S&P excluding the top 500 contractors and the portfolio of the S&P excluding the top 100 contractors outperformed the S&P 500 composite 15.7 percent and 16.2 percent to 14.5 percent, respectively.

Women and the New Family

In 1990, 86 percent of all personal wealth in the United States was controlled by women and 61 percent of all family bills were paid by women. Over 66 percent of female workers have children under 18. One out of every five working mothers is a single parent. Fifty-seven percent of women with children hold jobs. For every dollar earned by men, however, women earn approximately 63 cents. Only 2 percent of women who work make more than $50,000. In 1990 there were only three women serving as CEOs of Fortune 500 industrial and Fortune 500 service companies.

If you surveyed most philanthropic organizations, you would find that most donors and the majority of volunteers are women. Although there are about 70 women's foundations across the country, a total of less than $20 million has been donated to women and girls' nonprofit organizations.

According to Ellen Stromberg, a 10-year veteran of SRI issues and currently on maternity leave from the brokerage firm of PAM,

> Child care is probably the issue most often discussed. This is not just a women's issue. Child care is an issue for men, families, corporations, and society. Corporations need to acknowledge their employees have family lives. A number of corporations have responded to their employee needs and have provided child care services. Some companies provide on-site daycare facilities, while other companies provide referral services to help employees find adequate care for their children. These companies have created child care programs which are based on real concern for their employees and on the recognition that employees who know that their children are safe and well cared for maintain higher morale, higher productivity, and lower absenteeism.

Ellen, who has conducted numerous seminars for women on socially responsible investing, is also concerned about the glass ceiling:

> Reaching pay equity and breaking the glass ceiling are issues crucial to women and minorities in corporate America. These issues are at the core of the problems that women and minorities face in their corporate work-lives. Pay equity means equal pay for work of equal value. Adopting pay equity is a course of action that eliminates gender and race discrimination in the wage-setting system. The glass ceiling refers to an invisible barrier, usually from mid-level to upper-level management, above which it seems impossible to advance. Often the excuse has been that because women and minorities are relatively new to corporate America, they are being left out of the upper echelons of management. In fact, what frequently stands in the way is a corporate culture reluctant to change and diversify in upper management.
>
> Both these issues indicate the need to eradicate the roadblocks standing in the way of women and minorities. Some companies are acknowledging the desirability oι recognizing these newer work groups. The work of transforming a company's culture can be slow, complex, and subtle. However, it is vitally important that the transformation takes place.

According to the U.S. Department of Labor's 18-month study at nine large corporations, both women and minorities are still trapped under the glass ceiling. Women account for only 6.6 percent of corporate executives and minorities 2.6 percent of executive jobs. The Department of Labor announced that it would investigate federal contractors and disqualify any companies that refused to correct discriminatory practices. Whether this investigation does occur is questionable, since the report was released at the same time President Bush announced his determination to veto any civil rights bill that would make it easier to pursue discrimination cases in court.[30]

Women are not represented on most corporate boards of directors or in the executive suites of large corporations, but the majority of small businesses are run by women. Women are poorly represented in the financial community. Very few women serve as investment advisors or brokers. Certainly more women work as financial planners, tax preparers, and accountants, but they are still a minority in these occupations.

Although no specific social investment criteria for women's issues exist, there are numerous foundations and women's organizations that are excellent sources of information on corporate policy and behavior on issues. Such organizations include the Women's Foundation in San Francisco, the National Organization for Women (NOW), and the Ms. Foundation in New York. In *Shopping for a Better World*, CEP includes women's advancement and family benefits among the categories for rating various consumer product companies. The women's advancement category measures the representation of women on the board of directors and among the company's top officers. The family benefits category rates companies in three major categories:

1. Flexibility in workplace policies: parental leave, flextime, job-sharing, and flexible benefits.
2. Child and/or dependent care assistance: reimbursement, referral, on-site or near-site day care, adoption subsidy, elder care, disabled dependent care.
3. Education and information: on-site seminars, distribution of educational materials.[31]

In addition, CEP discovered that only four large publicly traded companies have four women on their board of directors: Gannett Inc., Philip Morris, Campbell Soup, and Houghton Mifflin.[32] The Working Assets Money Fund board of trustees has six women out of a total of ten trustees, and 60 percent the company is owned by a woman. Progressive Asset Management has one woman on a five-member board of directors, and four out of eleven brokers at PAM are women. The Calvert Social Investment Fund has three women on a board of nine, while FRDC has two women on a five-member board The Muir Investment Trust has three women on a five-member board, and the Domini Social Index Trust has three women on an eight-member board (See Table 2.1 on page 60).

Additional sources of information on women's issues relative to corporations comes from magazines such as *Working Woman* and from articles written on business and social responsibility by Milton Moskowitz. Another resource is Baila Zeitz and Lorraine Dusky's 1988 book, *The Best Companies for Women*. *Ms.*, along with CEP, published "20 Corporations That Listen to Women" in their November 1987 issue. Research organizations such as Catalyst and the Conference Board, both in New York, conduct detailed studies of women in the workplace, specifically women in management. Another excellent resource is Richard Louv's book entitled *Childhood's Future* published by Houghton-Mifflin Co., Boston, 1990.

The Council on Economic Priorities has consistently maintained a database on women and family issues and has produced several excellent studies. In its November 1986 newsletter, CEP printed the article "Business Takes First Real Steps" by Steven Lyndenberg, documenting the response of business to the growing demand for child care. In its October 1987 newsletter CEP published the *Ms.* study in its entirety.

Several institutions have compiled data on feminist and family issues relative to establishing a screen for corporate behavior. The Women's Foundation is a San Francisco–based nonprofit organization that funds programs designed to improve the economic, social, cultural, and political status of women and girls. This community-based organization, founded in 1981, has worked with both Working Assets Money Fund and PAM in the San Francisco Bay area to develop comprehensive criteria on issues concerning women, girls, and family. A corporate socially responsible definition matrix was a product of that research:

Socially Responsible Definition Matrix

I. ECONOMIC STATUS OF WOMEN
   A. *Working Conditions* (Environmental and Employment Practices)
      1. Health and safety
      2. Health care benefits
      3. Child care
      4. Retirement benefits
      5. Employment training opportunities
      6. Affirmative action

      7. Workers rights
      8. Union
      9. Accessibility to moving up, in and over
     10. Pay scale/wage level
     11. Number of women in the workplace, distribution through organization

  B. *Nature of Products* (e.g., alcohol, drugs)
  C. *Marketing Practices* (e.g., internationally, national)
  D. *Use of Profits*
     Investment practices, philanthropic, reinvestment, exploitation of workers
  E. *Political Action*
     Providing political support (i.e., money, privileges, benefits) to socially sensitive issues (e.g., anti-abortion, pro-NRA, etc.)
  F. *Investment in Other Companies* that may be or not be socially responsible

II. LEADERSHIP/EMPOWERMENT
  A. *Working Conditions*
     1. Child care
     2. Training opportunities
     3. Job mobility
     4. Affirmative action
     5. Entry level opportunity
     6. Pre-employment opportunities (e.g., relationship with public sector)
  B. *Political Contributions*
  C. *External Activities* (e.g., participation in community efforts, lending employees, philanthropic activities)
  D. *Number of Women in Work Place*
     1. Number of women in organization in a decision-making capacity
     2. Distribution of women within the organization
     3. Number of women on the board of directors
  E. *Media PR Practices* (image of women)

Recently PAM conducted a feasibility study on the creation of an open-ended mutual fund addressing corporate issues that affect women and families. Harrington Investments, Inc., has incorporated an asset management firm, Hearth Capital Management, that is majority-owned by women employees. In addition, Edith Conrad, a former Merrill Lynch financial planner, has announced plans to start a mutual fund that will screen investments based on women's issues. The fund, which is slated to be out by early 1992, will be named Women$hare.[33]

Regulatory Criteria

Several responsible mutual funds and portfolio managers collect and analyze information from regulatory agencies such as EEOC, OSHA, the National Labor Relations Board (NLRB), and the EPA. State Fair Employment Practices Commissions (FEPC) are also a source of information for responsible investors.

In 1981, as a member of the Sacramento Board of Administration, Investment, and Fiscal Management (Sacramento City Employees Pension Fund), I attempted to convince the rest of the board that we should avoid investing in companies that were continually costing our beneficiaries money (as shareholders). Many companies were involved in costly litigation, defending themselves before U.S. District Courts against charges of civil rights violations and discrimination in employment. Four companies owned by Sacramento city employees had been found guilty in federal court of employment discrimination and another nine companies were defending themselves against 57 civil rights violations.[34]

In 1980, CEP published a study for the California state retirement systems showing that, between June 30, 1978, and June 30, 1979, 13 corporations held in the portfolios of the state retirement systems had been found guilty in federal court of employment discrimination. Furthermore, the study found that another 37 companies were defending themselves against civil rights violations in 206 suits.[35]

The cost of civil rights litigation falls heavily on public employees and retirement beneficiaries because they are losing money not only as shareholders but as taxpayers (since their tax dollars pay for the operations of the federal court system). Our federal dollars are also spent on the state and federal regulatory agencies that sue the companies in the first place. Usually the only monetary winners are attorneys. In addition, much of the cost of discrimination is not made public because the majority of cash settlements are out of court.

While white women are being kept out of the boardrooms, women of color are barely evident in corporate management at all. In 1988, black women made up just 2 percent of managers in companies with 100 or more employees; black men accounted for 3 percent, white women 23 percent, according to data from the EEOC. Not one black woman was named in the 1988 Black Enterprise article about the top 25 black managers in corporate America The responsible investing community is also lacking in the recruitment of minorities. (see Table 2.1).

We can no longer rely on government to support affirmative action. Responsible investors will have to look to nonprofit organizations such as CEP and mutual funds such as Calvert and Working Assets to evaluate data from regulatory agencies. This raw data, however, is insufficient for use as the sole basis for equal employment investment decision making. As regulatory agencies reduce standards and compliance becomes more questionable, investors will have to place more reliance on company research and evaluation. This is unfortunate since several responsible mutual funds, including Working Assets, have trimmed their research department staff.

Equal employment research also includes a determination of whether or not a company discriminates against gay and lesbian employees or applicants. Data in this regard is elusive, and extensive literature searches are necessary. Recent information from the ICCR's Gay and Lesbian Employment Rights Project has been helpful. Employment, however, is a research area that is extremely labor intensive, requiring an objective database and the ability to compile and analyze the data efficiently and effectively.

Labor and Employment

By far the most comprehensive labor- and employment-related criteria have been developed by Working Assets Money Fund. The criteria encompass not only equal employment, but jobs, capital flight, and labor.[36]

Equal Opportunity. We seek out firms that promote the economic advancement of women and minorities. At the same time, we do not knowingly invest in companies that discriminate on the basis of race, religion, age, disability or sexual orientation, or which consistently violate regulations of the Equal Employment Opportunity Commission.

Jobs. We purchase instruments that we believe create jobs and develop the U.S. economy rather than rearrange existing assets through mergers and acquisitions. Also, to the greatest possible extent, we choose instruments of financial institutions that reinvest deposits in their local communities.

Capital Flight. We do not purchase Eurodollar instruments which drain capital from productive use in the U.S.

Labor. We seek to invest in companies that bargain fairly with their employees and have policies that promote the welfare of their workers. At the same time, we do not knowingly invest in companies that consistently violate regulations of the National Labor Relations Board, appear on the national AFL-CIO "Do Not Patronize" list or have a record, according to the AFL-CIO, of hiring "union-busting" consultants. We also avoid multinational firms that have fewer than half their employees in the United States, unless a majority of their eligible U.S. employees are represented by organized labor.

Activist Approach

On numerous occasions Working Assets has entered into dialogue with companies involved in national or regional employee job actions. For example, in 1989 Working Assets informed Embarcadero Associates that Working Assets would no longer purchase prime corporate commercial paper issued by Embarcadero Associates. Working Assets made this decision because Embarcadero Associates was an active member of the Building Owners and Managers Association, which had recently hired the well-known union-busting firm of Seyfarth, Shaw, Fairweather and Geraldson and had bargained in bad faith with Service Employees International Union Local 87.

In some cases Working Assets simply removed a company from its buy list and informed the company of the action and the reasons for the action. For example, in 1983 Working Assets removed R. H. Macy and Company for NLRB violations; in 1984 both Equitable Life Assurance and Louisiana-Pacific Corporation were removed because the companies had been placed on the national AFL-CIO "do not patronize" list.

A rather lengthy dialogue has gone on between Working Assets and Nordstrom since early 1990. Working Assets' research department discovered that Nordstrom had violated numerous NLRB regulations along with systematic violations of Washington state labor law. In addition, Working Assets had been concerned about the company's settlement of back-pay issues that affected employees in six other states, allegations of racial discrimination, AIDS discrimination issues, and whether or not Nordstrom was committed to bargaining fairly with United Food and Commercial Workers Union Locals 1001 and 34. Although Working Assets effectively removed Nordstrom from its buy list in the summer of 1990, it did not publicize the action.

Labor-Intensive Research

Research into labor and other interactive social criteria is labor intensive and can be a virtual minefield filled with subjective decision making. Working Assets has been fortunate in having researchers such as Jon Lickerman and Pamela Swan who are dedicated to the dialogue required to uncover differences among management, social activists, nonprofit organizations, and organized labor. In addition, Working

Assets has several people on the advisory board who are members of labor unions, former union officials, and labor consultants. Working Assets research department readily acknowledges that the company's two strongest research areas are South Africa and labor.

Working Assets has been very successful at forging close ties with many local unions and sharing corporate financial information. Both Working Assets and ICCR have witnessed an increase in their influence on corporate management when they were able to foster serious dialogue on an issue.

Union Criteria

When reviewing investments, researchers at Working Assets always review the labor content of specific projects that are supported by investment vehicles purchased by the fund. For example, on new construction projects, is the job 100 percent union? Additionally, the staff reviews the project's impact on the environment and what impact growth will have on the community's quality of life. This review, research, and, ultimately, an investment decision inevitably involve subjective judgment. Adequate decision making, however, requires considerable data.

The most sophisticated labor and pension fund database was developed by Mike Locker of Locker Associates in New York. He ran Corporate Data Exchange (CDE), a nonprofit organization that published *Labor Relations: A Company–Union Guide* (1982), *Pension Investments: A Social Audit* (1979), and *CDE Stock Ownership Directory: Fortune 500* (1981). The 1979 study focused on the stock investments of 142 major private and public pension plans, identifying 99 target companies that met one or more of the following social criteria:

1. Companies that are predominantly non–unionized;
2. Firms with a poor record in the field of occupational health and safety;
3. Companies that failed to meet equal employment opportunity guidelines; and
4. Major investors in or lenders to South Africa.[37]

The 1982 study described the labor–management relationship of 80 major corporations and was the most extensive study of corporate labor–management relations to date.

Mike Locker also developed a Labor Social Performance Index for FRDC in 1986. It covered a large universe of publicly traded companies and identified the percentage of U.S. employment, percentage of unionized U.S. employees, and the trend of U.S./worldwide employment. Locker also collected corporate data on work stoppages and unfair labor practices. Mike presently works with the United Steel Workers as a consultant on employee buy-outs.

Locker believes that the decade-old empirical data and information he developed to evaluate companies from an employment and union perspective was not utilized by nonprofit organizations and SRI activists because it was seen as promoting a specific interest group. Unlike the South African data, which was seen as promoting higher moral values, the promotion of labor and union representation is often not considered. Locker had an incredibly difficult time raising grant money from foundations.

Mike was also surprised that union leadership did not understand what power they could wield if they had access to pension fund information and capital. He explains:

> Randy Barber pointed out the tremendous power of union trustees if they gained control of the capital held by pension funds, how logical it would be for them to screen their funds according to the interests of their members. But I found enormous resistance and a reluctance of labor leadership to consider having access to this data on a timely basis.
>
> The basic question is that companies have gone to war against unions, and unions have to be ready to go to war against corporate management. They are not ready. They have to take them on in a very sophisticated way. There has got to be an attempt by unions to utilize information to wage a comprehensive and long-term corporate campaign. Having access to data is the key.

South Africa

There are numerous sources of information relating to identifying U.S. companies operating in South Africa. The most traditional sources include the American Committee on Africa, TransAfrica, the Africa Resource Center (Oakland), IRRC, ICCR, and CEP (see Directory). Most brokerage firms also have extensive coverage of U.S.-based corporations operating in South Africa.

The data are objective and plentiful but are constantly changing. Almost on a monthly basis, companies are making the decision to leave South Africa. On the other hand, some are evaluating the business climate in South Africa to determine whether or not they want to return. Recently Digital Equipment sent a group of senior managers to South Africa to investigate the marketplace but decided not to return. Most are taking a very cautious approach about going back, even after President Bush removed U.S. economic sanctions on July 10, 1991.

The political situation is still tense after the March 17, 1992 Referendum vote to continue the reform process. Although there has been much talk of power sharing and election reform by the leadership of the white minority government, apartheid remains firmly in place. In July 1991, ICCR sent a distinguished delegation of U.S. citizens to South Africa to assess conditions and policies affecting economic pressures for change and to determine the likelihood of democratic structural and constitutional change in the country. With the exception of South African government and white South African business representatives, the overwhelming response was that lifting sanctions was premature and that until fundamental structural change occurs economic forces in the United States should continue to avoid investing in or conducting business with South Africa.

The South African economy is still in considerable turmoil, with inflation at 15 percent. During the 1980s, South Africa experienced a per capita decline of 12.8 percent in real gross domestic product (GDP). Forty-seven percent of the population lives below the poverty line, 55 percent have no electricity, and there is 40 percent unemployment.

About 106 U.S. companies have direct investments or employees in South Africa and another 233 U.S. companies have nonequity links through contracts, licensing, distribution, franchising, trademarks, or technological agreements with companies in South Africa.[38] The following list identifies those U.S. companies who have 500 or more employees in South Africa.

Companies	Number of Employees	Companies	Number of Employees
Caltex Petroleum[1]	2,090	Dresser Industries	757
International Paper	1,797	Union Carbide	664
Johnson & Johnson	1,495	Colgate-Palmolive	631
Albany International	1,000	Strategic Minerals	
Crown Cork & Seal	979	Corp*	550
United Technologies	939	Bristol-Myers Squibb	548
Joy Technologies*	856	Arvin Industries	512
American Cyanamid	855	Harsco Inc	500
Minnesota Mining			
& Mfg	851		

* Privately held company
[1] Jointly owned by Texaco and Chevron

U.S. Companies with Largest Relative Sales

L&M Radiator★	9.0%	Colgate-Palmolive	less than 2%
Roberston-Ceco Corp	5.1	Nalco Chemical	less than 2%
Standard Commercial		Quaker Chemical	1.6
Corp	3.5	Lykes Bros. Steamship★	1.3
Donaldson & Co	2.8	American Cyanamid	1.2
Wilbur-Ellis★	2.5	Harnischfeger	1.2
Baker Hughes	1.7	Caterpillar	1.1
Dresser Industries	1.7	Ingersoll-Rand	1.0

★ Privately held company
A breakdown showing the amount of sales to South Africa is only available for 34 of the 106 companies with South African exposure. Of those 34, 15 (or 44 percent) admitted to sales in excess of 1 percent of total. Applying the same percentage to the total, we might estimate that 47 of the 106 have sales in South Africa in excess of 1 percent.[39]

The lifting of sanctions will allow new bank lending to South Africa. The U.S. banking community will probably be reluctant to make new loans since their recent track record for both domestic and foreign lending has been poor. Some banks have renewed pre-1986 Comprehensive Anti-Apartheid Act loans, including Bank of New York, Chase Manhattan, Citicorp, Continental Bank Corp, Firstar Corp, First Bank System, First City Bancorp of Texas, Manufacturers Hanover, J.P. Morgan, NCNB, and Security Pacific.[40]

Common Sense

Implementing investment social criteria may be simple common sense. For example, the treasurer of the United Methodist Church would be sensical to avoid investing in Lockheed and GE because of their DoD contracts. Sometimes, however, common sense doesn't prevail.

Don Perata, a limited partner investor in Working Assets, is a supervisor for Alameda County, California. In 1989, when he was chairman of the board of supervisors, he was involved in a campaign to ban assault weapons in the county and the state. He organized the Citizens Coalition to Ban Assault Weapons and was a vocal critic of the proliferation of weapons in the Alameda–Oakland area. On April 5, 1989, his county treasurer bought a $5 million issue of corporate commercial paper in Colt Manufacturing, a major arms manufacturer.

This is an extreme example of political insensitivity and the lack of common sense, but not an isolated case or an exception to the rule. Institutions often make investment decisions with blinders on, or perhaps with only one eye open.

It is important to remember that people, not institutions, make subjective investment decisions. Even when a fund is indexed or when portfolio managers make investment decisions using sophisticated computer programs and mathematical models, they are based on humans programming the computer. Responsible investing is not an exact science, but rather an art. It is a continuous process that challenges you to develop an ever-expanding view of the investment universe and the world.

The economic world is in a constant state of flux. Interest rates and economic policies vary. Investment goals and objectives change; likewise, social criteria for individuals and institutions evolve and change.

In the first part of this book we reviewed the history of responsible investing and learned about its major players. In this chapter we learned how to set our social goals and to survey social information. Now it's time to make an investment, find a responsible financial professional, and pick a socially responsible mutual fund.

CHAPTER SIX

Building a
Responsible Portfolio

Once you've determined your net worth, what you can invest, how much risk you want to take, and your financial and social goals, you're ready to take the next step. You need to decide whether or not you want to do it yourself, hire a financial professional, invest in a mutual fund, or a combination of all three. For the moment, let's say you've decided to go it alone. You will do your own financial and social research, trade your own securities, and build your own portfolio.

Asset Allocation

Based on your financial goals and the condition of the economy, assets can be allocated that will meet your current and future needs. Let me illustrate by providing some investment scenarios and then by defining the major asset classes.

Profile:	Myrna is a young working mother with two school-aged children, living on marginal spousal support and needing supplemental income. She is in a low tax bracket and has minimal assets to invest ($35,000). She is a renter.

Recommended Asset Allocation:	Cash	25%
	Bonds	50
	Stocks	25
	Real Estate	0

Discussion:	Myrna is in a tough position. She will need much of her savings to supplement her work income and to have enough liquidity in case of an emergency. Because she is young she can use 25 percent of her portfolio to invest in a stock mutual fund to provide her with capital appreciation. In the future, she can use the growth portion of her portfolio for a down payment on a home.

Profile:	Ken and Polly, both professors, earn a comfortable income but have put almost all of their money into home improvements. They have no children, are in their 40s, and have $65,000 to invest.

Recommended Asset Allocation:

Cash	10%
Bonds	15
Stocks	75
Real Estate	0

Discussion:	Ken and Polly need some tax-free liquidity and no taxable income. They can therefore utilize most of their assets for capital appreciation. They will get the desired appreciation out of their stock portfolio and their house.

Profile:	Evelyn just retired on a pension and has inherited her husband's estate. She has two grown daughters and one new granddaughter. Her house

	is paid for, and she has $380,000 to invest.	
Recommended Asset Allocation:	Cash	10%
	Bonds	70
	Stocks	20
	Real Estate	0

Discussion:

Evelyn has an adequate degree of security through the ownership of her home but wishes to supplement her modest pension income. She is also risk-averse and wants to pass on her estate to her children and grand-daughter. The stocks or stock mutual funds she buys should be conservative and produce some income.

Investing covers more than just the stock market. As a responsible investor you can invest in cash or cash equivalents, bonds, stock, real estate, collectibles, low-income housing partnerships, loan funds, social venture funds, community banks, and in Third World economic development.

Cash

Cash is defined as money in the bank and money invested in money market mutual funds. If you don't want to pay taxes, you can deposit money in tax-exempt money market funds that produce dividends exempt not only from federal taxation but also from state taxation. For example, if you are a New York resident, you can deposit your cash in a New York tax-free money market fund, and you won't have to pay either federal or state taxes on the income.

Cash is also money invested in cash equivalents such as CDs, treasury notes, bankers acceptances, repurchase agreements, and corporate commercial paper. Generally, cash equivalents are defined as liquid short-term debt securities of less than one year in maturity. The asset class of cash may include a variety of the above-mentioned investment instruments. Most individuals, however, usually think of cash as either the green stuff in their pockets or the checkbook in their purses.

Bonds

Bonds are fixed-income debt securities that can have different maturities, ratings, and yields. Depending on your tax bracket, this asset class can include corporate, federal agency, treasury, mortgage-backed bonds, or municipal bonds.

If tax-exempt income is needed, both asset classes of cash and bonds can be tax-exempt. Numerous federal tax-exempt money market funds and intermediate or long-term municipal bond mutual funds are federally tax-exempt as well as state tax-exempt.

Tax-exempt bonds can have maturities as short as two or three days (tax anticipation notes) or as long as 30 years. Usually a bond portfolio holds bonds with maturities of 3 to 20 years. Similarly, taxable bond portfolios have bonds of varying maturities. It's interesting to note that both tax-exempt and taxable bond portfolios include zero coupon bonds. These are bonds that pay no coupon interest. They are purchased at a discount (less than par value) and mature at $1000 per bond on a specific maturity date.

Zero coupon municipal bonds are ideal for planning a portfolio for college education. These bonds can mature in different years, thereby allowing you to know exactly how much money you will have available for your child's education the year he or she starts college. By the same token, zero coupon corporate or federal agency bonds are perfect for retirement accounts since you'll know exactly how much money you'll have in bond maturities the year you retire.

It should be noted that when you buy bonds, it is wise to purchase at least 20 to 30 bonds. The fewer bonds you hold, the more difficult they may be to sell because they are thinly traded. You also run the risk of having a broker mark up, or charge you more in commissions, if you have to sell before the bonds mature.

Stocks

The *Wall Street Journal* can provide you with an incredible amount of information. It covers markets, stocks, bonds, real estate, commodities, company earnings, performance, tax and monetary information, special reports, news on pension funds, labor, government, and issues of general public interest. *The Wall Street Journal Guide to Understanding Money and Markets,* a small and colorful book, is a helpful guide to reading and understanding the *Journal.*[1]

For stock, option, and convertible bond evaluation and recommendations, *Value Line's* presentation and statistical reviews of data are straightforward and comprehendible. When my clients want to

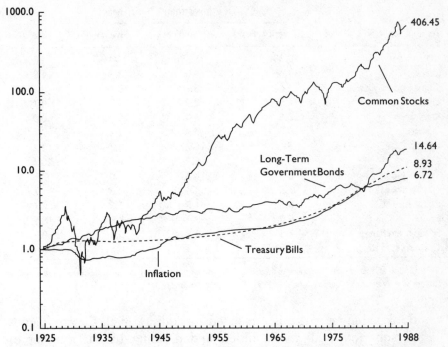

**WEALTH INDEXES OF INVESTMENTS IN
THE U.S. CAPITAL MARKETS, 1926–1988**
(assumed initial investment of $1.00 at year-end 1925,
includes reinvestment income)

Figure 6.1   Source: Stock, Bonds, Bills, and Inflation 1989 Yearbook™ Ibbotson Associates, Chicago (annually updates work by Roger D. Ibbotson and Rex A. Singuefield).

quickly review the financial statements of a company in their portfolio, I send them the *Value Line* page and *Insight's* Equity Brief covering that company. Mainstream financial information always needs to be supplemented with social information; *Insight's* Equity Brief provides both. A company's financial viability is dependent upon a society requiring a product or service from that company. Economic, social, and—many times—political factors will greatly affect a company's performance and longevity in the marketplace. It's not possible to separate the financial from the social.

Historically stocks have outperformed all other asset categories (see Figure 6.1). Occasionally there may be a period of time where stocks underperform other asset classes, but this occurrence is rare (see Table 6.1). Stocks are often selected using a variety of criteria, including book value and price/earnings ratio.

Table 6.1   The Asset Derby

Old-master paintings were the best performing investment asset over the past 20 years, a tally by Salomon Bros. shows. But stocks were best for the past 10 years, and oil was tops in 1990.

Asset Category	Investment Performance[1]			
	Twenty Years	Ten Years	Five Years	One Year
Old master paintings	12.3%	15.8%	23.4%	6.5%
Stocks	11.6	16.0	13.3	11.8
Chinese ceramics	11.6	8.1	15.1	3.6
Gold	11.5	−2.9	1.0	−0.7
Diamonds	10.5	6.4	10.2	0.0
Stamps	10.0	−0.7	−2.4	−7.7
Bonds	9.4	15.2	9.7	13.2
Oil	8.9	−5.9	8.5	20.7
Treasury bills (3-month)	8.6	8.8	7.0	7.1
House prices	7.3	4.4	4.6	4.7
Farmland (U.S.)	6.3	−1.8	1.3	2.1
Silver	5.0	−9.3	−4.8	−18.9
Foreign exchange	4.5	3.8	5.4	0.2
Consumer Price Index	6.3%	4.3%	4.5%	5.0%

[1] Compound annual return (including dividend or interest income, if any) for periods ended June 1, 1991.
Source: The Wall Street Journal, June 11, 1991. Data from Salomon Bros.

Book value per share is calculated by adding up all the company's assets, subtracting all its liabilities, and dividing by the number of common shares outstanding. The resulting number is the theoretical measure of what one share of the company's stock is worth. You can find this figure in *Value Line, Insight's* Equity Brief, or Clean Yield's newsletters. If the price of a stock is far below its book value per share, the stock may be considered undervalued.

The price/earnings ratio (P/E) is calculated by dividing the current price of a stock by the latest 12 months' earnings per share. During severe economic contractions, P/Es become distorted. Under normal conditions, however, a persistent decline in price relative to earnings results in a lower P/E. A low P/E, in turn, would be bullish (a signal to buy). A high P/E is a reflection of projected future earnings strength. These ratios are available in the same publications mentioned previously as well as from the *Wall Street Journal* and numerous other publications.

Stocks are also selected according to financial strength (ratings) and volatility. In a declining economy a company with an A+ rating (such as General Mills) would be preferable to a company with a C+ rating in the same industry sector (such as Stoneridge Resources). Similarly, in a volatile market, you may wish to purchase stocks with relatively low volatility, or beta.[2] It would be better to purchase a stock with a beta of 1.0, such as Sara Lee, than a stock with a beta of 1.3, such as Rymer Foods, whose stock is 30 percent more volatile than Sara Lee's or the market (as represented by the S&P 500 when compared to the market).

Stock diversification is often dependent upon the size of the portfolio. In a large portfolio as many as 30 stocks may be purchased. Balanced portfolios containing both stocks and bonds may have as few as 15 stocks. Market capitalization of the companies may also be important in determining the exact diversification mix.

Market capitalization is the total market value of a company's stock. It is an investment criterion that investors often use as an indication of how they value a company's future prospects. Many institutional investors, for liquidity purposes, require a company to have a market capitalization of $100 million or more to qualify as an investment. Prior to 1986, California public employee pension funds were managed with this constitutional restriction. Some managers will hold as many large capitalized companies as small capitalized firms. On the other hand, a more aggressive manager may hold all small capitalized companies. Large capitalized firms would include companies such as Archer Daniels Midland, with over $7 billion in capital, and Woolworth with almost $4 billion. Smaller capitalized companies would include Imco Recycling with $47 million, Lifeline Systems with $26 million, and Ben & Jerry's with $42 million.

The dollar size of an initial investment and the proportional representation of a stock in a portfolio may also be important. When managing larger accounts, I usually don't want to have one stock position represent more than 5 percent of the total holdings. Naturally, that protects the downside of the portfolio's performance and ensures that one stock's fall will not have an undue effect on the entire portfolio. Of course, that's why portfolio diversification is so important to a manager or for an individual managing his or her own portfolio.

Stocks require the most comprehensive industry sector diversification. Professional portfolio managers weight or apportion stocks according to a determination of how each industry sector will perform based upon a prediction of the economy, interest rates, and stock market trends.

For example, the following table shows the weighting by industry sector of the Standard & Poor's 500 Stock Index and the December 1991 sector weightings of Harrington Investments, Inc.

	Recommendation Relative to S&P	S&P Weighting
Consumer staples	U	15
Health	=	11
Consumer cyclicals	O	12
Finance	=	9
Utilities	U	13
Energy	U	13
Basic industry	=	7
Technology	O	11
Capital goods	O	7
Transportation	=	2
		100%

U—Underweight
O—Overweight
= —Equal Weighting

Industry sectors are identified by Standard & Poor, *Value Line,* and other indexes or services. To help clarify, I've identified industry sectors and listed some example stocks for each.

Basic Industry

Betz Labs (BETZ)
Wellman (WLM)

Capital Goods

Goulds Pumps (GULD)
Zurn (ZRN)
Imco Recycling (IMRI)
Thermo Electron (TMO)

Consumer Cyclical

Ben & Jerry's (BJICA)
Stride Rite (SRR)
WalMart (WMT)
Liz Claiborne (LIZ)

Consumer Staples

General Mills (GIS)
Quaker Oats (OAT)

Energy

Northwest Natural Gas (NWNG)
California Energy (CE)

Financial Services

First Hawaiian (FHWN)
Deluxe Corporation (DLX)
Wells Fargo (WFC)
FNMA (FNM)

Health Care

Amgen, Inc. (AMGN)
Merck (MRK)
Syntex (SYN)

Technology

Apple Computer (AAPL)
Reuters (RTRSY)

Transportation

Mesa Airlines (MESA)
Norfolk Southern (NSC)
Carolina Freight (CAO)

Utilities

Potomac Power (POM)
Sierra Pacific Power (SRP)

Miscellaneous/Environmental

Calgon Carbon (CCC)
Safety Kleen (SK)
Thermo Instrument (THI)
Groundwater Technology (GWTI)

Depending on your investment goals and the outlook for the economy, different industry sectors should be weighted differently. If you are a cautious investor, you would probably *underweight* (not put so much money in) technologies and consumer cyclicals and *overweight* (put more money in) consumer staples and utilities. Why? Technology stocks are usually volatile. Consumer cyclical and technology stocks don't do well when people are not spending money and the economy is contracting. In addition, in a bad economy, both consumer staples (food and basic supplies) and utilities perform well compared to other sectors. Who can be without food and utilities?

Fundamental vs. Technical

Eyes roll or glaze over when I describe myself as a "top-down, bottom-up, fundamental analyst." By this I mean that when I review and evaluate stocks I first and foremost look at the overall direction of the economy. Then I evaluate each industry sector. This is the "top-down" portion of the equation. After the sector evaluation is concluded, I evaluate each company in the industry sector from the bottom up, utilizing specific financial and social criteria.

With asset allocation, each economic sector should receive a proportional allocation based on how that sector will perform in a specific economic situation. For example, if the economy is healthy and growing, consumer demand will increase. Housing starts will increase. I'd be foolish not to increase my holdings of stocks able to take advantage of such consumer growth, such as consumer cyclical stocks (automotive, retail and appliances).

Once I've made the decision to invest more heavily in one sector, I need to identify companies that meet my financial and social criteria in that industry sector. On the financial side, this means utilizing standard due diligence to ascertain the viability of the company's management in meeting stated goals, reviewing financial documents, cash flow, balance sheets, and the like.

Using a more fundamental approach to investing does not mean turning a blind eye to technical analysis. Technical analysts study stock market data to identify patterns of stock price movements and predict future movements. Sometimes there are no explanations for certain price movements, but they may recur consistently. After all, we know the effects of electricity and current flow and what we can do with the power, but we really don't know what electricity is.

Technical analysts have been measuring and predicting stock market price changes since the late 1800s. Gurus such as Charles Dow (Dow Theory) and Garfield Drew (Odd-lot Trading) were popular in their day. In the 1990s we have Robert Prechter (Elliott Wave Theory) and Marty Zweig. Generally, a technician's popularity waxes and wanes with his or her theory's success in the real market.

Wall Street Slang

It is often said that "pigs turn into hogs and hogs get slaughtered." Essentially this phrase means once you've invested in a security (usually a stock) and it has substantially increased in value, don't be afraid to sell and take your capital gain and profit out of the market. Many investors and even some pros know when to buy but seldom know when to sell. You'll never be able to determine the bottom or the top of a stock's value. Most portfolio managers establish a level at which a stock will be sold. For example, if you buy a stock and it increases in value by 25 percent, think about selling it. By the same token, if a stock exceeds a set percentage on the downside, sell it. Many people get married to a stock: They love the stock in good times and bad. No matter how badly the stock performs, they never seem to forget the good times. Sell the stock! It may be that the downside of the stock has already exceeded the initial upside and you're down overall in the stock.

I knew a stockbroker who loved Bank of New England stock and speculated by buying more of the stock even when it was revealed that the bank was in serious financial trouble. (If you loved the stock at $10 a share, you'll really love it at $3 a share!) He has enough of the stock to paper his entire living room, and that's about all it is good for now.

For responsible investors, the ability to look objectively at owning a stock is doubly important. It may be a stock that is exemplary from a social standpoint but simply doesn't hold up when you evaluate the fundamentals and past performance. Herman Miller is a perfect example of a company that is terrific from a social standpoint but since 1985 has been a poor stock pick. There are plenty of good solid responsible companies that have good balance sheets, earnings, P/Es, and so on, and also have a strong positive social and economic impact, such as Stride Rite. Don't get married to a stock, and don't be afraid to take a gain when a stock has met or exceeded your expectations.

You often hear the phrase "don't fight the tape." This phrase is similar in meaning to the 1970s saying, "go with the flow." Essentially it means that you generally don't want to buck the market trend if there is a consistent direction to the market or to a specific stock. You don't want to sell in a weak or declining market unless you think your stock won't come back on a market rebound. You also have to be careful not to buy a stock that is falling off a ledge. You may want to find a support level to which the stock has dropped and see if the market will support the stock at a certain price. It's also important to find a resistance level, which is the price the stock hits before it gets resistance (the selling begins). When the stock hits or is near the resistance level, this is an indication that the stock probably should be sold. If a stock "breaks out" and crashes through the old resistance level, it may find a higher resistance level and you may need to re-evaluate your trading strategy.

"Buy on bad news, sell on good news." There is some truth to this saying. Many stocks are oversold because of an overreaction to a bad earnings report or because of the fact that the company's earnings didn't match or exceed the earnings forecasted by a brokerage firm's analyst. Often the stock price will pop right back up within days or weeks of such a sell-off. On the other hand, when a company has projected stronger sales or an analyst has predicted an upturn for the company's earnings, the stock may experience a sudden and dramatic spurt in price.

Initial Public Offerings

Most stock pickers know to beware of Initial Public Offerings (IPOs) of stock. Often a brokerage firm will hype and initially inflate the price of an IPO. The stock may fall in price soon after it hits the market; not until several months later will it find its true value in the market.

In a study published in the March 1991 issue of the *Journal of Finance,* three-year returns on IPOs averaged 34.5 percent, compared with returns averaging 62 percent for stocks of similar size and industry. "I always tell investors you ought to be out in less than three months because they underperform," says Robert Natale, a new-issue analyst with Standard and Poor's Corp.[3] You also need to be careful about IPOs because in many cases the stock being offered to the public is owned by selling stockholders, not the company itself.[4]

Other common mistakes many investors make are to buy last year's hot stock, put together a stock portfolio without any idea of investment objectives, buy too many mutual funds, or think that they can perfectly time the market, usually with one hot stock. In 1991 most of the increase in the stock market occurred in just a few days. No one can perfectly time the market.

Another major mistake of novices in the stock market is to feel invincible—that you never make a mistake. You buy three stocks and they immediately increase in value 20 percent. You then make three additional investments in the stock market and they increase in value 15 percent. Don't get uppity or overconfident. Stockbrokers are often guilty of overconfidence and make the mistake of trading in their own account. The longer you invest, the more bruised you become, but hopefully you'll also grow in experience and maturity. Remember, today's heros may be tomorrow's fools, and vice versa.

Real Estate

Real estate, for most Americans, represents the majority of their net worth. Home ownership is an important part of your portfolio but not one usually considered in asset allocation decisions. A home is not liquid: you need a place to live and can't sell your house at the drop of a hat. It is, however, an asset that can be borrowed against. A home is currently the major source of tax deduction for most Americans: The interest paid on a mortgage is fully tax-deductible from ordinary income.

The asset of a home is especially important when you consider the ability to borrow against the home to put children through school, finance a second home purchase, or consolidate debt. The only other assets that can be borrowed against are certain brokerage securities, such as stocks and bonds in a margin account. The interest paid on the margin account is only deductible against investment portfolio income and is not deductible against ordinary income as is mortgage interest.

Friends of mine recently decided to buy a second home at Lake Tahoe using cash from a second loan on their home in Napa as the down payment (equity) for the Tahoe house.[5] It makes a great deal of sense: They can spend their vacations, holidays, and long weekends there, and over the years the house will appreciate in value. When their children are of college age, they can sell the house and use the equity they've built up in the house to pay for higher education costs. It's one of the few investments where you can receive both present and future benefits.

Many people also invest in real estate securities such as second deeds of trust or directly in first mortgages used for rental properties. The advantages of direct real estate investing are much more limited now than they were prior to the enactment of the Tax Reform Act of 1986. No longer can you deduct real estate depreciation and maintenance costs from ordinary or investment income. The investor, however, can receive tax deductions from rental real estate expenses that can be written off against rental real estate income, but not wages, salaries, or money market income.

Several of my clients have invested a large portion of their assets in residential real estate. They are able to deduct mortgage interest on the loan they take out to buy the rental real estate. They are also able to write off depreciation of the buildings, as well as maintenance and expenses, against the rental income they receive from tenants. The other return they receive as investors is a capital gain once the real estate is sold (if the property has appreciated).

Collectibles

In viewing the whole array of assets, you should not forget such items as gold, silver, art, and other collectibles. While there may be liquidity problems, such assets play an important, though usually minor, role in a portfolio's asset allocation. Most financial planners recommend that 1 to 2 percent of a portfolio be invested in precious metals, commodities, or art.

Tax Credits

Have you ever said: "If the priorities were changed in Washington and if the tax structure were more equitable, I wouldn't mind paying taxes." Or have you said: "If only I could direct my tax dollars to my own set of human priorities." If you feel you're paying too much in taxes and/or would like to redirect your tax dollars to a priority of your own selection and not that of Congress and the President, then low-income housing tax credits are for you.

According to a new Census Bureau study, 57 percent of all U.S. families and other households are unable to buy the median-priced home in the region where they live. In the West 63 percent of all households couldn't afford the median-priced home, 59 percent in the Northeast, 56 percent in the South, and 51 percent in the Midwest. Ninety-four percent of households headed by people under 25 years of age are unable to afford a median-priced home.[6]

Millions of Americans are being priced out of moderate- and low-income housing. Without direct public taxpayer subsidies or indirect federal and state tax credits, low-income housing couldn't exist in this country. Local and state governments have been marginally successful in raising capital through the issuance of municipal bonds for moderate-income housing. But what about low-income housing now that the direct federal subsidies of the 1960s and 1970s are ending?

Low-Income Housing

Although the 1986 Tax Reform Act reduced tax-advantaged investments, there are still exciting opportunities for the responsible investor in the low-income housing and historic rehabilitation tax-credit programs provided through limited partnerships. Such limited partnerships are higher risk and illiquid but provide substantial federal tax credits to individual and corporate investors. Some California low-income housing investment opportunities have provided California state residents with state tax credits as well.

Federal and state tax credits are literally subtracted from the taxes you owe on a dollar-for-dollar basis. If you owe $5,000 in federal taxes and have a $2,000 federal tax credit, you will have a $3,000 tax liability. Tax deductions, on the other hand, reduce your taxable income, which may reduce your taxes but not on a dollar-for-dollar basis. Credits are bottom-line tax reducers and can also be carried forward to the next year if you can't use them all in one year.

In 1989, PAM teamed up with Boston-based AI Group, Inc., to raise almost $1.5 million for the construction of a 60-unit low-income senior facility in Visalia, located just south of Fresno, California. The investment provided an estimated $83,000 in state and federal tax credits for a six-year installment investment of $50,310. The same year both firms teamed up again to raise about a million dollars from individual investors to rehab a two-story, 34-unit, single-room residence, primarily for homeless people with AIDS in San Francisco. The Visalia facility is managed by the Tulare County Housing Authority, and the San Francisco facility (the Peter Claver Community) is managed by Catholic Charities.

Other low-income housing tax credit programs to rehab historic buildings and to house senior citizens are sold by traditional brokerage firms to individual and corporate investors. Some are sold as private placements and finance only one project. Others are public offerings and finance numerous projects around the country. Public offerings may only require one initial investment that provides the investor with 10 years of federal tax credits, some minimal cash return, and a capital gain at the end of the investment when the property is sold. The property, however, must be held to provide low-income housing for at least 15 years.

Programs that are syndicated by private general partners will normally expire in 15 years, and the housing will revert to market rentals. For the socially responsible investor, the concern is that people may be forced to move and seek other affordable housing. Low-income housing that is managed by nonprofit organizations will be available for low-income families in perpetuity. Generally there is no additional return for investors other than significant tax credits. On the other hand, if the housing remains low-income, there is a very meaningful return for society.

There are also public offerings that allow individuals to invest and receive federal tax credits for the rehabilitation of historic facilities such as beautiful old hotels and other buildings on the National Register of Historic Places. Some tax-credit programs not only rehab historic sites but also provide low-income rental housing for seniors. How many other investments can you make that help you reduce your tax burden by rehabilitating a beautiful historic building and providing low-income senior citizens a nice place to live?

High Impact Investing

The responsible investor is able to diversify his or her portfolio by investing in loan funds, social ventures, and other private placements that maximize positive social and economic impact.

Loan Funds

Community development and low-income housing loan funds are financial intermediaries that borrow money and then lend in lower-income areas to assist community economic development. Loans support home ownership, community-based businesses, microenterprises, and nonprofit rental housing. Loan funds also provide technical assistance to ensure that the recipient has the necessary skills and resources to become and remain economically self-sufficient. In the past 32 years these loan funds have created jobs and affordable housing nationwide, as well as a sense of self-determination for the communities affected.

Loan fund financing is derived primarily from socially responsible individuals and institutional investors looking for a way to effectively generate economic self-sufficiency and transfer capital to sectors of the American economy that are most in need. Since it is very difficult for low-income people to establish credit and qualify for loans from traditional lenders, loan funds fill an important community need and provide access to capital at very low interest rates.

A loan fund receives loans from lenders with a rate of return that can range from 0 percent to a rate equivalent to money market. Depending on the loan fund the lenders may have the option of setting special conditions on their loan. They may designate their money to a specific geographic area or to a type of group or project, depending on their preference. Loans are made for periods of time ranging from a few months up to 20 years. Loans are often unsecured and, if the recipient defaults, the loan fund will use its loan loss reserve to pay back the lender if no collateral is held. Historically, the default rate for loans made by community development loan funds has been extremely low.

Most loan funds succeed financially because they operate with very low overhead, often receive nonprofit or public agency financing, and are very efficient in what they do; that is, they provide capital to areas that are capital-starved. One of the oldest funds, the Institute for Community Economics (ICE) was founded in 1967 and committed itself to the principle that local communities should have a significant role in planning their own economic development and should be primary beneficiaries of that development. The Institute focuses on the problems of people in lower-income communities, who suffer from limited access to land, housing, and, most importantly, capital.

In northern California, the loan fund is the Northern California Community Loan Fund (NCCLF). I was very honored to be on the first board of directors. According to Paul Sussman, executive director of NCCLF, the fund has raised almost $1 million and provides responsible investors with an investment vehicle that directly finances Bay Area low-income housing and community economic development. Many of my clients loan money to NCCLF, and the majority have added significantly to their original loan amounts.

There are numerous examples of successful high-impact loan fund activities. A group called Adelante, located in Berkeley, California, provides courses ranging from English literacy to computer literacy and other services. Adelante needed $20,000 to make an initial deposit on a building it was purchasing. Traditional lenders were not helpful, but the NCCLF enabled Adelante to meet its obligation to the seller of the building by making a loan to the organization. The loan was for a period of 60 days at 10 percent interest and was secured by a deed of trust on another building. The loan was repaid after the deal was closed, allowing Adelante to remodel the building and expand its services. The loan from NCCLF was a key financing commitment that helped the project get off the ground.

In Trenton, New Jersey, a low-income neighborhood was being threatened by encroaching gentrification. The revolving loan fund of ICE made a loan to a local community land trust that allowed it to move quickly and acquire its first two houses. This provided affordable homes to two families and created the economic and political climate for community control to become established and later to expand.

Social Venture Funds

If responsible investors would rather invest in equity than lend to many small businesses, they can now do so through social venture funds. Similar to traditional venture funds, social venture funds invest in the equity of small, private companies, hoping to capitalize on the company's growth. Investing in social venture funds will allow investors to participate in a portfolio of responsible small businesses that may be in the forefront of technologies or human services that have a positive social impact.

One such fund is managed by Michael Kieschnick, one of the founders of Working Assets. The Sand County Venture Fund located in Menlo Park, California, has invested in a daycare provider who cares for mildly ill children, a water-purifying company for industrial cooling towers, a sustainable agricultural company, and a small business that produces rehabilitation devices serving the quadriplegic population.

Calvert Social Venture Partners was capitalized in 1989. Wayne Silby, president of the Calvert Social Investment Fund, John Guffey, Michael Tang, and John May comprise the general partners of the fund. Calvert invests in the middle Atlantic states, primarily in high-growth companies in energy and the environment, health services, or medical products, in education, and in human services.

These venture funds are not liquid. Investors need to consider both the lack of liquidity and inherent risk in venture-oriented investments. The offering documents of such venture funds should be reviewed carefully so that you clearly understand how you can eventually exit this investment.

Community Banks

Everyone needs to have access to capital to build or rehabilitate a home, start a business, or send their children to college. Unfortunately, many people don't have access to capital. Development or community banks and other financial organizations have been capitalized by social investors in order to serve the needs of low-income urban and rural communities.

Shorebank

In 1972 Ron Grzywinski, the former president of a small bank in Lockport, Illinois, and a former fellow at the Adlai Stevenson Institute, University of Chicago, decided to run a financial institution in one of Chicago's most depressed economic areas. He and his colleagues, Mary Houghton, Milton Davis, and Jim Fletcher, were determined to structure a bank that would focus entirely on local community economic development. Shorebank was incorporated as a for-profit neighborhood development corporation. Initially the founders raised $800,000 in capital and borrowed $2.4 million from 11 corporate, foundation, church, and individual shareholders. In August of 1973 Shorebank purchased the South Shore National Bank, which had about $42 million in assets and had made only two single-family mortgage loans during the entire prior year. The U.S. Comptroller had earlier prohibited the bank from abandoning its poor and predominately black service area in the South Shore community of Chicago.

After 20 years, Shorebank has become a premier community development organization. Its model has been copied in rural Arkansas—Southern Development Bancorp incorporated in 1986 and raised $6 million in equity to boost small business, agriculture, and manufacturing in a 32-county area of southwestern Arkansas. In 1988 Southern created the Opportunity Lands Corporation, a community development company, to focus on industrial and commercial properties and residential housing for low- and moderate-income residents. Shorebank's influence has now even spread overseas to Poland, where it is opening small loan operations in eight existing Polish state banks and establishing up to three private banks to provide loans primarily to small private businesses and development projects.[7]

Joan Shapiro, senior vice-president of the South Shore Bank, the banking subsidiary of Shorebank, has been with the bank almost since inception. She is in charge of one of South Shore's most successful programs, development deposits, which exceeds $94 million (52 percent of total deposits). These development deposits have conventional yields and liquidity and can take the form of savings accounts, money market accounts, IRAs, CDs, or checking accounts. Most of the large investors are from outside South Shore's service area and are investors who demand social as well as financial returns. South Shore's development deposits are used specifically to renovate unlivable apartments, start small businesses, and help young people get an education.

Shorebank has been successful in mobilizing capital to rehabilitate neighborhoods and generate community spirit and initiative. As Ron Grzywinski said:

Deliberate, disciplined development banking in a disinvested community can revive a local economy, rekindle the imagination of its people, and restore market forces to their normal health and interdependency. . . . We should grant new privileges that bankers are seeking for themselves—mutual fund management, interstate banking, securities underwriting and more—only to those banks that demonstrate the most exemplary performance in meeting the credit needs of their community service area. Indeed, these privileges should go only to banks that actively apply their "unique combination of financial and managerial resources" to help remedy the nation's social ills.[8]

Community Capital Bank

It took Lyndon Comstock over five years to organize, register, and capitalize his Brooklyn-based Community Capital Bank and raise $6 million in equity. January 8, 1991, was proclaimed Community Capital Bank Day by Brooklyn Borough President Howard Golden when the bank celebrated its opening.

Equity capital was raised from individuals, corporations, religious organizations, community groups, and foundations in 22 states. Initial depositors included the Franciscan Sisters of the Poor, Brooklyn Ecumenical Cooperatives, the Brooklyn Law School, the School Sisters of Notre Dame, the National Federation of Community Development Credit Unions, the Common Good Loan Fund, the American Baptist Churches of Metropolitan New York, and the Cooperative Assistance Fund based in Washington, D.C. The city of New York, Seventh Generation (an environmental products company), and Calvert Social Investment Fund initially deposited funds.

Comstock, Community Capital's chair of the board, was inspired by South Shore Bank's success in community housing and development loans. Community Capital plans on lending primarily in the lower-income areas of New York City, including Manhattan, Queens, Brooklyn, and the Bronx. According to the Community Service Society of New York, there is an estimated shortage of affordable housing in New York City of approximately 230,000 units; over the next 12 years 372,000 units of housing, costing an estimated $30 billion, will be required to ease the housing shortage. The society also estimated that over 450,000 units of existing housing in New York City are in need of major repair.[9]

The bank has already made seven loans and has 15 loans pending. All the loans made have been housing and small business loans, including a loan to the New York–based Settlement Housing Fund to rehab 40 units of moderate-income housing in the Ocean Hill/Brownsville section of Brooklyn and a letter-of-credit for an AIDS hospice in the South Bronx.

Third World Investing

Ecumenical Development Cooperative Society

Responsible investors can also invest in Third World nongovernmental economic development through the Ecumenical Development Cooperative Society (EDCS). Since 1978 EDCS has approved loans, investments, and guarantees for local bank loans to over 157 enterprises in 42 countries in the range of $5,500 to $1 million. Thirty-two million dollars has been loaned or committed to projects. Another 18 projects have been approved.

In 1975 EDCS was incorporated by the World Council of Churches in the Netherlands. This international economic development organization has a capital base of over $60 million, raising most of its money in Western Europe. However, EDCS has an office and a USA representative, Elywn Ewald, in Chicago, and support associations are located in Pennsylvania and California.

The society raises investment dollars from individuals and institutions in two ways: through $250-a-share subvention certificates (ordinarily paying 2 percent annual dividend) and through a $50,000 10-year, 5 percent bond issue for accredited institutional and individual investors. Other offerings are also being planned.

Operating on less than a 3 percent administrative overhead, EDCS employs project development officers (PDOs) in every continent of the world. Cooperative business enterprises are funded and operated in a way that disperses profits among all participants. Preference is given to projects that incorporate women in all aspects of the enterprise. Projects include housing, mining, fisheries, and numerous rural agricultural and urban industrial enterprises.

What has impressed me most about EDCS is its low overhead cost and its success in some of the poorest parts of the world in lending money so that Third World cooperative business enterprises can be developed with no government assistance. Its successful business lending has led to over 6000 permanent jobs being created and has benefited over 400,000 people.

Accion International

Accion International is a nonprofit organization that was founded in 1961. It provides credit and technical assistance to microentrepreneurs or small businesses in Latin America. It is funded by private and public dollars; in the past decade it has provided over $75 million in loans and helped create nearly 100,000 permanent jobs that ultimately benefited more than 500,000 family members.

In 1984 Accion created the Bridge Fund to leverage funds in Latin America. The Bridge Fund is capitalized with loans and donations from individuals, churches, and institutions. The funds are invested in CDs at either Chemical Bank in New York or South Shore Bank in Chicago in order to collateralize letters of credit in favor of banks in Latin America so that money can then be loaned to microentrepreneurs in local currencies.

The Bridge Fund acts like a domestic loan fund in that it accepts loans of no less than $10,000 from individuals and institutions at a 0 to 5 percent interest rate paid semiannually for a minimum of 18 months' maturity. The funds borrowed from socially responsible investors is then used to collateralize letters of credit in Latin America.

The Bridge Fund maintains a loan loss reserve both in the United States and in the country where the loan originates. If a loss exceeds both of the reserves, it will be distributed evenly throughout the total loan portfolio. The Bridge Fund has not suffered a single loss since its inception in 1984.

You don't have to be wealthy to invest with a social conscience. You can work with a broker or a financial planner, or you can pick your own mutual fund to meet your financial and social goals and objectives. In the next chapters I will discuss the role of financial professionals and evaluate socially responsible mutual funds.

CHAPTER SEVEN

Selecting a Responsible Financial Professional

Most people don't want to or cannot manage their money full-time. Actually, most don't even want to do it part-time. Managing money is serious business. It's similar to politics: everybody has an opinion. Unfortunately, in our society money talks, and often politics is indirectly, if not directly, tied to money. Just as not everyone can run the country, not everyone can run money. You vote at the ballot box, and you vote with your dollars by investing or consuming, either directly or by hiring a financial professional. In this chapter we will explore the world of financial professionals and identify those that work in the responsible investment arena.

Many financial professionals and investors have their own horror stories when it comes to bad advice or unprofessional conduct. Many investors have devised unique strategies in dealing with money, while others have attempted to have the least amount of contact with Wall Street. I have a few of my own stories to tell.

The Case of the Bad Broker

One March afternoon in 1989 I received a telephone call from Nancy Feiner, a tax preparer I work with in Berkeley, California. She and I share clients, and we understand the frustration many of them go through with tax preparation, planning, setting financial goals, and dealing with investment professionals.

While preparing a tax return for one of her clients, Nancy discovered a very large end-of-the-year statement from a well-known brokerage firm. The statement chronicled all the trades in the client's account for the calendar year. There appeared to be far too many trades. Nancy suspected the broker was *churning* her client's account. In other words, in order to generate large commissions, the broker did a large amount of buying and selling of stocks. The broker and brokerage firm made considerably more money, but the client had to pay excessive brokerage fees.

The client was 68 year-old Mary Samuelson, a partially disabled, retired county worker living in San Francisco on a small pension and the income generated by her portfolio. She had inherited $250,000 from her family. Mary had continued to employ the family broker, a man whom she considered a true and trusted friend.

This trusted broker had placed Mary's money in a brokerage margin account and had managed the portfolio on a discretionary basis. He had the legal authority to buy and sell securities in the account but could not remove cash except, of course, to cover his commission. In that one year alone Mary's portfolio had generated over $100,000 in commissions for the brokerage firm. The broker probably received more than 40 percent of that total commission. Brokers receive a percentage of gross commissions, called payout. Most firms compensate by paying a larger payout to larger-producing brokers, thus giving them an incentive for more production.

The activity in Mary's account looked like churning to me. I called Alan Wilson, a colleague of mine in Los Angeles who specializes in representing brokerage customers in arbitration before the National Association of Securities Dealers (NASD) against brokerage firm management. I sent him three years of Mary's account statements. He reviewed all of the trades, dates of the trades, the stocks traded, the average time between trades, and the loss or gain associated with each trade. He told me that Mary's situation was a classic case of churning and that she had a very good case against the broker and the brokerage firm.

You can imagine Mary's shock when she was told what her broker had done. This man had managed her family's stocks for over 10 years. Mary and her family had trusted this broker.

Throughout most of the 1980s, in the boom years of the stock market, the portfolio had earned Mary a handsome return. What she didn't know was that her brokerage house was earning 10 times more each year off her portfolio than she was earning. Even though she was retired, Mary was busy during this time in her life: She spent a great deal of time with her children and grandchildren and she had also suffered some health problems. Mary rarely looked at her brokerage statements.

Margin

Let's take a look at what Mary's broker had actually done. When Mary inherited the $250,000 from her mother, her broker suggested they put the portfolio into a margin account. Thinking her family broker could do no wrong, Mary readily agreed. She had no idea what this meant to her portfolio, nor was it explained to her. A brokerage margin account is for individuals who wish to borrow money from the brokerage firm, using as collateral the value of certain securities in their portfolio, for the purpose of buying more securities. The margin loan from the brokerage firm is at an adjustable rate of interest. There are restrictions on the amount of money that can be borrowed against the value of certain marginable securities in the portfolio. Simply stated, margin accounts allow a client to speculate on the stock market by borrowing money tol buy securities.

Regulation T of the board of governors of the Federal Reserve Board establishes the initial margin requirements on transactions. A client must put up a portion of the market value of marginable securities held in the account to collateralize the margin loan.

When the stock market is rising, the client can make a great deal of money by borrowing increasing amounts of money to buy more stocks that are increasing in value. In this way, speculative investors maximize their financial leverage.

If the market moves lower, the value of the stocks used to collateralize the margin loan will decrease to the point where it won't cover the margin loan. The brokerage firm is then required to issue a margin call. The client must either add cash or securities that qualify for margin to the portfolio or sell stocks in the portfolio to raise cash.

In the crash of 1987, many people who borrowed on margin lost their entire portfolios. The value of the stocks and securities kept dropping so fast that stocks had to be sold to raise cash. As quickly as the brokerage firm liquidated stocks, the downward spiral accelerated and more selling was required until there was nothing left.

In 1988 there were hundreds of trades in Mary's account. She had received numerous margin calls from the brokerage house. Upon receiving a margin call, Mary promptly called her broker, who always told her, "Not to worry. I'll take care of it." Because Mary had allowed her broker to manage her account on a discretionary basis, he had the legal authority to buy and sell stocks and securities in the account.

Discretionary Trading

Brokers normally manage assets on a nondiscretionary basis: Before a broker can execute a trade, she or he must first contact the client and receive approval. Most brokerage firms don't want brokers to have discretionary power or limited power-of-attorney. There is an inherent conflict of interest between a broker's fiduciary obligation to the client and the fact that a broker's compensation is tied to the buying and selling of stocks, bonds, and other investments. Brokers work on commission. If brokers trade a great deal, they make more money for themselves and their brokerage firms. Often the office manager or branch manager of a brokerage firm receives an incentive bonus from the head office if overall revenues increase. On the other hand, the office manager is subject to disciplinary proceedings if churning occurs.

Arbitration

Nancy Feiner, Alan Wilson, and I convinced Mary to leave her unethical broker. Over the course of a year she talked with all of us about taking the broker before NASD, and she consulted an attorney. In March 1991 she filed for arbitration with the NASD. Alan testified as an expert witness. In 1992 Mary received a settlement from the broker-dealer of over $100,000, but she is both embarrassed and saddened that her "family friend" treated her in such a way. She never spoke to the broker about his unethical, if not illegal, activities.

Mary's broker is still working in the securities industry but has gone to another firm. It may take years to get the broker out of the brokerage business. This is not unusual. In a highly publicized case, the New York Stock Exchange took four years to discipline a Shearson broker for alleged improper sales practices and excessive trading of customer stocks.[1]

Unfortunately, Mary's story is not unique. There are unscrupulous brokers. Consumers, however, have a way to protest. Professional arbitration services are available to represent wronged investors. I recently saw this advertisement in the financial section of the *Los Angeles Times:*

> Burned by your Stockbroker? Have you lost money due to churning (excessive commissions), unsuitable recommendations, misrepresentation, unauthorized trades, limited partnership losses or junk bond losses?[2]

Caveat investor—let the investor beware. Just as consumers have learned to educate themselves when making purchases, so must investors educate themselves when seeking financial advice. Fortunately, the overwhelming majority of brokers are honest and hardworking.

Dealing with Money

When a family member dies, people need emotional support. Many times the death also opens up the quagmire of inheritance. The dollars inherited may look like numbers on a ledger sheet, but often the inheritor is filled with frustration and anxiety toward the money.

Anxiety

Several years ago, the father of a friend of mine died. My friend and her husband discovered that her father had a unique way of dealing with his savings. The father's mother (my friend's grandmother) had given her son cash for birthdays, holidays, and special occasions. In his safety deposit box, my friend found bags of old coins and hundreds of individual holiday cards, birthday cards, and notes stuffed with cash of varying denominations. She also discovered dozens of $25 savings bonds with maturities going back to the mid-1950s.

It took a long time to redeem the bonds and to have a coin dealer appraise the value of the older coins and bills. To this day, my friend refuses to deal with a small insurance policy left to her by her dad.

Many times inheritance is intertwined with loss and grief. People are unwilling to become involved with what they see as someone else's money. They feel that since they did not earn the money they somehow do not deserve it. Inheritance can be tied to feelings of guilt about not having done enough for the person who died. These emotions often lead to a feeling of paralysis—of simply not knowing what to do with the money or how to do it. It's no wonder many people simply leave their inheritance with whoever was managing it prior to the death of a loved one.

The Lively Lady from Dallas

The grandmother of a friend of mine, a colorful, lively lady who traversed the world in the 1950s as a travel writer for a Dallas paper, was greeted as if she were a multimillionaire every time she went to her Dallas bank. Her husband had done their banking at this bank until his death in 1951. The lovely woman never stopped raving about the service and kindness offered to her at the bank. When it came time for her to move into a retirement hotel, she claimed not to have enough money to pay the rent. Her family asked to see her bank statements. They were shocked and later outraged to discover the bank was paying the same low interest rate on her money that they paid her husband in 1951. Grandmother may have been treated royally, but her bank account was that of a pauper.

When you receive an inheritance, have accumulated savings, or suddenly discover that you need assistance in making investment decisions, it is best to seek a diversity of opinions. You can start with your bank, brokerage firm, or a financial planner. Ask all of them to educate you. You are, after all, a client or a potential client.

Let them tell you all they know about managing your money.

Don't be shy about taking notes. Don't plan to do business after the first meeting. Do the same thing with two or three other financial professionals. Some financial planners and investment advisors will charge you for a visit; others won't. Before you visit in person, call in advance and ask about charges for initial consultations. If they do charge, it could be the most important money you ever spent. After listening to the second or third opinion, go back to the initial advisor with additional questions. A passive attitude toward money management permeates our society. It is ironic that Americans are aggressive money makers but turn into jelly when confronted with the task of taking care of their hard-earned capital. This passivity is especially true of people who inherit money.

Many people have unique ways of dealing with money, especially when they feel they can't trust anyone. While I wouldn't advise you to seriously consider the following method, it was quite brilliant in its day.

The *Life Magazine* Story

Bob Moore, Jr., told me this story about his dad. Bob Moore, Sr., was a smalltown schoolteacher in Oregon who retired after 30 years of service to tend his dairy farm. He did not trust banks and had devised a unique scheme to stockpile his money. When he passed away, the family looked under all the mattresses, but there was no money to be found.

It wasn't until Bob's brother started paging through one of the hundreds of editions of *Life* magazine their father had saved that they discovered their father's secret. For years he had been carefully putting money between the pages of *Life* and stacking the issues in the barn. Forty years of *Life* magazine! It took the family several days to retrieve the money. There was over $5000 between those pages.

The irony of this method of saving is that, in one respect, it worked. When burglars robbed the house and barn while their father was in a nursing home, the magazines went untouched. The burglars had even blown open an antique safe that was in the barn, only to find it empty.

Asking the Right Questions

Mary Samuelson did not put her money under a mattress or between the pages of a magazine, but she might as well have. Let's look at a few other things Mary could have done to protect her money. She needed to develop financial goals and to state these goals loudly and clearly to her broker. A good broker will help a client develop these goals. Since Mary was retired and living on a fixed income, her portfolio needed to be managed conservatively to maximize income. She should not have given discretionary power to her broker, nor should she have agreed to a margin account. How could she have known all this? A visit or two with another financial professional would have helped.

No doubt, the question in your mind is, "How do you tell an honest financial advisor from a dishonest one? How do you go about finding a reputable person?" The Yellow Pages won't help much. It is really best to just ask around. Find the most affluent person you know and ask who advises him or her. To cover their bases, some people will divide their money equally between financial professionals and see who does the best.

Good brokers and investment advisors educate their clients even if their clients say they don't want to be educated. They inform clients of the potential risks as well as the rewards of particular investments. They make no inflated claims to inside information. Good brokers and financial advisors are considerate, even-minded, and well-versed on the market and the economy.

There are excellent resource guides and directories available for selecting financial professionals. The responsible investment community and progressive foundations issue annual directories and listing of investment advisors, brokers, financial planners, attorneys, estate planners, tax preparers, insurance agents, bookkeepers, and accountants. Directories are published by the Funding Exchange, Vanguard Public Foundation, Resourceful Women, the Social Investment Forum, and the Bay Area Socially Responsible Investment Professionals.

In their guides, SIF, Vanguard Public Foundation, and Resourceful Women have also outlined tips for selecting a financial professional. Resourceful Women's guide is particularly helpful in evaluating the financial professional's background:

Questions to Ask a Potential Investment Manager

Description of Firm
   Amount of money under management.
   Background of principals (experience, # of years with the firm).
   Number and types of accounts.
   Future goals for the size of the firm.

Investment Structure
   Minimum investment.
   Fees/commissions.
   Structure (i.e., partnership, fund, segregated accounts).

Philosophy and Process of Investing

What are your investment goals, objectives and philosophy?

How do you achieve the investment goals?

Do you manage both stocks and bonds?

What aspects of the economy most influence your investment decisions?

Each field requires slightly different questions, but thanks to various sources we are including a few basics:

How long have you been in the field?

How many clients do you have and what is your average account size?

What can I expect from you as an advisor?

What specific licenses or training do you have?

How do you keep informed about your field?

How have you done (i.e., annual report) and over what period of time?

What is your investment philosophy? Describe your approach to your work. Do you consider yourself to be an aggressive or conservative investor? What is your philosophy on management?

How are you compensated? How does this compare with the industry?

What are you licensed to sell? From which products do you receive commissions, if any?

Do you or does any member of your firm act as a general partner or receive compensation from the general partner or from investments which may be recommended to me?

What types of investments do you recommend?

How often will I hear from you? In what form? What do you need from me?

How do you do your research? How many people work in research at your firm?

How would most of your other clients describe you?

What distinguishes you from other advisors in your field?

Describe the support services offered by your firm.

Can you provide me with references and samples of your work?

AND THEN ASK YOURSELF:

Do I trust this person enough to have her/him represent me?

Do I like this person?

You can obtain a copy of this guide at a cost from the Womens Foundation in San Francisco, CA; see Directory.

An investor who wants to invest in enterprises that are consistent with socially responsible values can refer to the appendix of this book. I have provided a list of financial professionals, mutual funds, and other resources that are dedicated to responsible investing.

A Responsible Professional

A prudent investor uses the same criteria for selecting a socially responsible investment professional as he or she would for any investment professional. On the other hand, it is important from the very beginning that you and the financial professional are on the same wavelength. Do you both mean the same things when you use the term socially responsible? Just as many heavily polluting industries have begun to tout their products as ecologically sound, there is a trend in the financial community to claim socially responsible investing when in fact they are investing the same old way. If your broker claims to invest in a socially responsible manner, ask him or her a few questions. Ask whether he or she votes. Ask whether her or she supports school bond measures or environmental measures on the ballot. What environmental or other nonprofit organizations does the broker support or contribute to? What boards does he or she serve on?

It's always important to ask brokers, planners, or advisors where they invest. Where do they invest their IRA or retirement plans? In which particular stocks do they invest and why? What is their goal in managing funds in a socially responsible manner? How long have they been doing it? Have they written articles or published anything in the field of socially responsible investing? Do they invest corporate or personal funds in community banks, loan funds, or socially responsible mutual funds? Ask them to identify such investments.

Ask the financial professional for a copy of the quarterly or monthly statement you would receive if you were a client. Request a list of stocks or bonds the professional would purchase or a buy/sell recommended stock list. You may also want to know the specialty of the professional—if they primarily manage bonds, growth stocks, or options. Are the majority of his or her accounts balanced, growth, or income? Are the majority of accounts institutional or individual? If the advisory firm has more than one manager, how many accounts does each manager handle? How many social researchers does the firm employ?

Almost all my clients come from referrals. Personal referrals are the most important source of business for investment professionals. You should ask for the professional's client referrals, but you should seek others, too. When you ask for client referrals, also ask for the names of former clients and the reasons they left. If the professional gives money to a nonprofit organization or sits on a board, call and ask about the professional. Try and find out how the socially responsible investment professional relates to his or her colleagues in the same field. Ask the professional why he or she believes in socially responsible investing. Does the professional belong to the Social Investment Forum or a local or regional profession association?

If someone makes a claim to be managing funds utilizing social criteria, you have a right—and a duty to yourself—to determine how the professional interprets that criteria. After all, you will be turning your financial future, your retirement, and your economic power over to the professional. You are giving this person your economic proxy.

Complex issues can become reduced to buzzwords in our modern media-driven society. Investment advisors, planners, and brokers are people with their own set of goals and objectives. It is very important that you communicate with them *before* as well as after you've made the decision to empower them with your assets. It is also important that your goals and objectives become their goals and objectives and that they receive compensation based on meeting your goals. It's your money and your goals that should come first.

Stockbrokers

Stockbrokers generally work with clients who have as little as $250 for an IRA to as much as millions of dollars. Most brokers manage accounts on a nondiscretionary basis and have qualified to be brokers by passing exams administered by NASD, a professional association in charge of setting standards for brokers and broker dealers. Brokers are registered representatives of broker dealers such as Merrill Lynch, Dean Witter, Prudential Bache, PaineWebber; smaller regional firms such as PAM; or discount brokers such as Fidelity and Charles Schwab.

There are usually no educational requirements to be employed as a "registered rep," although many hold advanced degrees. The brokerage firm, as well as the individual broker, must be registered with every state where a client of theirs resides.

Stockbrokers are usually supervised by an office manager. In larger firms there are independent research, due diligence, underwriting, and merger and acquisitions (M&A) capabilities. Some brokerage firms are discount firms and only execute trades at your direction. Unlike brokers at full-service firms, discount house brokers are salaried and not compensated by commissions. The discount firm offers no research.

Brokers can also conduct their own research or employ outside resources. Normally stockbrokers work market hours and conduct much of their business on the telephone. New brokers must usually cold call in order to build a book of clients. Brokers are hired because of the quality and quantity of the clients they bring with them or if the brokerage firm believes they have potential to aggressively market themselves and establish a solid record of production.

Since brokers at full-service brokerage houses are usually compensated solely by commissions, they need to actively trade. This can be accomplished with an established group of clients or a growing group of clients. The broker is constantly under pressure to produce, as is the office manager of large brokerage firms. Contests are held and bonuses are provided for big producers. The firm's management is constantly required to be innovative in attempts to maintain or to increase production.

Full-service brokers can be highly compensated for selling private and public partnerships and other high commission ticket items. The trading of stocks and options is also encouraged because these commissions are higher than those for bond trades. How many times have you seen a brokerage firm and its research staff turn bearish on the market and actively discourage the public from buying stocks? How many brokerage firms issue sell recommendations? It could have something to do with the fact that the same firm may be underwriting that particular company or making a market in the company's stock. It's also easier for brokers to encourage clients to buy stock than to sell stock. It could be hard for a broker to explain to a client why his or her firm is asking a client to sell a stock that the brokerage firm earlier recommended the client to buy.

About a week before America West Airlines declared bankruptcy, Shearson Lehman Brothers downgraded the stock to a sell recommendation. For years Shearson had been recommending a buy and the company's clients had accumulated about 13% of America West's stock. Some insiders at Shearson said they believed the company continued to recommend the stock because so many Shearson clients had accumulated America West on Shearson's buy recommendation. Investment bankers in pursuit of underwriting and other business have been known to mention big holdings of stock in a company in which they vie for deals.[3] It's no wonder investors are so skeptical of Wall Street.

Progressive Asset Management

This was one of the reasons why several brokers, financial planners, and I decided to open PAM, a full-service brokerage firm specializing in socially responsible investments. Progressive Asset Management was organized in 1987 and opened in San Francisco about the time of the 1987 Crash. Later the firm moved to Oakland. It was the brainchild of stockbrokers working for traditional Wall Street firms, including Tom Van Dyck (Dean Witter), Peter Camejo (Prudential Securities), Eric Leenson (Merrill Lynch), and Ellen Stromberg (E.F. Hutton). The founders also included San Francisco Bay area financial planners such as Bonnie Albion, Virginia King, Duncan Meaney, and Lincoln Pain, as well as Cathy Cartier, a sales assistant with Prudential Securities.

Peter Camejo, a sixties political activist and a former Merrill Lynch and Prudential Securities broker, was the first president and CEO of the company. Camejo had unsuccessfully attempted to have both Merrill Lynch and Prudential Securities endorse his concept of using a portion of the revenue normally used to set up IRAs donated to nonprofit organizations for AIDS research. He left the traditional brokerage world to create an independently owned, broker-run firm that was committed to economic and social justice and that specialized in socially responsible investing.

Peter's first innovative product was "The IRA That Cares." For every customer that opened an IRA of at least $1000, PAM would contribute $10 to the San Francisco AIDS Foundation. The firm made a profit in the first year of business. In the first two months of operation PAM opened over 500 new accounts and averaged 10 walk-ins per day.[4]

Since 1987 PAM has grown and diversified, creating a housing subsidiary, PAM Housing, which has been responsible for over a half-dozen low-income housing construction and rehabilitation projects in California. The firm was also successful in convincing Merrill Lynch to open the Eco·Logical Trust on Earth Day 1990. Eco·Logical is the first environmentally and socially screened unit trust in the country. Progressive Asset Management screened the companies in the portfolio for Merrill Lynch and currently serves as Subadvisor to the Schield Progressive Environmental Fund, an open-ended mutual fund that also uses a comprehensive social and environmental screen (see Chapters 8 and 9).

In 1991 PAM successfully launched an innovative, $20 million bond offering to raise capital from institutional and high net-worth investors for Third World economic development. The program, sponsored by EDCS, will provide funds to loan to cooperative business ventures in countries in South America, Asia, Africa, and Latin America, as well as some projects in Eastern Europe and North America.

Until late 1991, Peter Camejo and his family owned the majority of PAM's stock, making it one of the first Hispanic brokerage firms in the country. From 1988 to 1991 PAM diversified its ownership base by distributing additional stock to employees as compensation, eventually diluting Hispanic stock ownership. The company then created a Hispanic subsidiary, PAM Latina Americana, to continue to provide services to the responsible investment community through a majority Hispanic-owned enterprise. This subsidiary has been responsible for initiating projects in Latin America, as well as co-underwriting municipal bonds to finance housing and community improvements in California's central valley.

Camejo, who is a member of the board of the Environmental Federation of America, traveled to Peru in June 1991 as part of a delegation preparing for the 1992 United Nations World Environmental Conference on Sustainable Development, which is to be hosted by Brazil. He also traveled to Australia in July 1991 to help environmentalists there set up an Environmental Federation of Australia. Progressive Asset Management's international environmental and economic development work has become an important part of the global SRI movement.

Gallegos Institutional Investors Corporation

In 1990 another socially responsible Hispanic firm was opened in San Francisco by Herman Gallegos, a former colleague of Cesar Chavez, and Norm Berryessa. Gallegos is the chairman of the board of Gallegos Institutional Investors. He also serves on the boards of directors of Pacific Telesis Group, Union Bank, and Transmetrics, Inc. He has served on the boards of the Rockefeller Foundation, the Rosenberg Foundation, KQED, and the University of San Francisco, and he was executive director of the National Council of La Raza.

Berryessa, who serves as chief executive officer of the firm, is a colleague of mine who was a co-founder of the Northern California Interfaith Committee on Corporate Responsibility (CANICCOR) and is publisher of "Global Perspective," an investment advisory newsletter. He serves on the San Francisco mayor's Office of Business and Economic Development and is Co-chair of the bishop's Task Force on Implementation of Economic Justice, Archdiocese of San Francisco.

Gallegos's brokerage firm trades through the Pershing Division of Donaldson, Lufkin, Jenrette. It chiefly serves institutional, corporate, municipal, and union pension clients. Gallegos identifies his firm as "committed to the success of the socially conscious investor." Gallegos said that his firm is selling not only stocks but social responsibility. "We believe we can help corporations achieve their financial goals and at the same time help them become more socially responsible."[5]

Financial Planners

There is no universal definition of a financial planner. About 90 percent of financial planners are compensated by commission revenue.[6] To receive a commission they must trade through a registered broker dealer. Some planners sell insurance and are therefore registered with large insurance holding companies and/or broker dealers. Many financial planners are licensed, and some are certified by professional associations after completing coursework and passing examinations. Continuing education may also be a requirement for certification.

Financial planners may be compensated by commissions or for preparing a financial plan for a client. Some are totally compensated by preparing a plan or simply charge by the hour, anywhere from $75 to $250 an hour. Remember: Follow the money. Find out first how a planner is compensated.

Financial planners can assist in helping an individual put together a total financial plan, including a personal budget, insurance, and an investment strategy; they can refer a client to an attorney to draft a personal trust agreement, will, or estate plan.

Depending on how the planner is compensated, all of their business may be hourly, commissioned, or charged by the plan. Unfortunately, some planners could be compensated in all three ways. It pays to ask the compensation question first. It also pays to determine if the planner is certified or registered as an investment advisor, how long he or she has been in business, and the number of clients he or she has. Above all, ask for several referrals.

A growing number of commission-based planners are adding fee-based services to their practices and calling themselves fee-based planners. The risk is that you could end up paying for what might essentially be a sales presentation disguised as a consultation and still pay commissions. Many fee-based planners split fees with brokers.[7]

There are many socially responsible financial planning firms in the United States; most of them are one- or two-person offices, such as John Schultz's Ethical Investing firm in Minneapolis. Two San Francisco Bay area financial planners known for their responsible investing outlook are Bonnie Albion of Berkeley, California (who is also a board member of the Social Investment Forum), and one of the founders of PAM and Janiel Jolley of San Francisco, California.

Progressive Securities

One of the most successful advocates of socially responsible investing in the Pacific Northwest is Carsten Henningsen, president and founder of Progressive Securities, a financial planning firm and investment advisor. Carsten, a member of the board of directors of the Social Investment Forum, has been particularly successful in extending his business to Eugene and Portland, Oregon, as well as setting up an office in Seattle, Washington. His Seattle office is run by Darrell Reeck, a former portfolio manager with FRDC. Progressive Securities has also joined with Pacific Northwest Trust of Portland to manage SRI-screened retirement plans.

First Affirmative Financial Network

Another socially responsible financial planning firm is Colorado Springs–based First Affirmative Financial, which opened its doors in 1981 on a fee-for-service basis. The founder, president, and chairman of First Affirmative is Ed Winslow, who is both a CPA and a certified financial planner. In 1984 Winslow also started a nonprofit, member-owned cooperative, First American Financial Cooperative.

First Affirmative trades through Walnut Street Securities, a traditional broker dealer located in St. Louis. In 1987 First Affirmative teamed up with Co-op America, a nonprofit member-owned organization based in Washington, D.C., that serves as an advocate for cooperative business enterprises. In 1989 First Affirmative and Co-op America agreed to merge; it is estimated that Co-op America will own 100 percent of First Affirmative's stock in about three years.[8] First Affirmative has approximately 50 registered representatives serving as independent contractors (financial planners) in 21 states.

Like Progressive Securities, First Affirmative is a strong advocate of socially responsible investing. Recently the firm announced that they had developed socially screened fixed annuities and term and cash life insurance programs through First Affirmative Insurance and the Miami-based American Bankers Insurance Group.[9]

Registered Investment Advisors

Registered investment advisors (RIAs) are registered with the SEC and with a state agency such as the State Department of Corporations. These advisors pay a registration fee to the regulatory agencies, and their records and premises can be inspected at any time. An extensive and regularly updated disclosure document must be provided to a potential client prior to the client signing an investment contract. Advisors can manage portfolio assets of a client on a discretionary or nondiscretionary basis, but they usually select the former, not the latter. In addition, RIAs can charge an hourly fee for their service. Ordinarily they do not receive commissions on products purchased by a client, and many states severely restrict the activities of RIAs as well as the kind of compensation they can legally receive.

Registered investment advisors manage assets as fiduciaries and require clients to sign investment advisory contracts. These contracts are legally binding and disclose the contractual relationship, its limits, and the RIAs legal responsibilities to the client.

There are no educational standards or licensing requirements for investment advisors. Many RIAs, however, do hold advanced degrees and hold various NASD licenses. All of this information is disclosed in their disclosure document or their brochure. Before you sign a contract with an advisor be sure to review and understand all of the information in the disclosure document. Don't be afraid to ask questions.

Most RIAs manage institutional and individual portfolios for a percentage of assets managed, typically ¼ of 1 percent to 3 percent. The fee usually decreases as the assets increase. It is in the interest of the RIA to increase the client's asset value, thereby increasing the RIAs overall annual compensation. Most investment advisors establish a minimum account size for portfolio management, usually $100,000 to $400,000. Many larger management firms set a higher minimum, such as $1 to $5 million, normally for institutional or high net-worth clients. Some RIAs will charge clients a fee based upon their performance.

Brokers and RIAs can assist a client in setting and meeting financial goals. They can also refer the client to competent attorneys, financial and estate planners, insurance professionals, and others in an effort to assist the client in a comprehensive and long-term financial and professional relationship.

United States Trust Company, Boston

In 1974, U.S. Trust began managing money for clients; thanks to Robert Zevin, the company started managing money for socially responsible investors in 1975. U.S. Trust is a publicly traded corporation, trading on the NASDAQ National Market System under the symbol USTB. It is a conservative bank with a 20-member board of directors, of which two board members are women and one is a minority.

The asset management division of the bank, under Dominic Colasacco, has grown from less than $50 million in funds under management in 1974 to over $2.4 billion as of December 31, 1991. The socially sensitive balanced assets of U.S. Trust total approximately $1 billion. Client funds are managed using a variety of screens based upon the demands of the client. Accounts are managed as balanced, fixed income, or equity. U.S. Trust also manages portfolios that only screen for South African investment and manages the Calvert Social Investment Fund (SIF) managed growth fund.

U.S. Trust's fees begin at 1¼ percent per annum on the first $200,000 market value and 1 percent per annum on the next $800,000 market value for investment management accounts, somewhat less for pension and profit-sharing accounts. Assets are normally custodied at U.S. Trust, and additional charges to the client may be incurred. U.S. Trust requires an additional $500 per annum for all accounts utilizing a social screen. The minimum account size is $500,000.

U.S. Trust has identified five categories of social interest:

1. Environmental impact, including pollution control, waste utilization, and nuclear power related concerns
2. International operations, especially operations in South Africa
3. Product purity, safety, and desirability, including concerns about tobacco, alcohol, and honesty towards consumers
4. Production of weapons systems, especially nuclear weapons systems
5. Employment and workplace issues, including fair labor practices, equal employment opportunity, and safety and health[10]

U.S. Trust applies its screening process first to a basic standard that all companies must meet in all five categories. Failure to meet the standard in any category would make a company ineligible (exclusionary) for investments. The second level of screening (inclusionary) is met by those companies that perform at a higher social level *and* meet U.S. Trust's financial criteria.

U.S. Trust employs three full-time social researchers and nine portfolio managers; it manages 250 individual and institutional accounts. Account managers generally have an average of 35 accounts each.

A sampling of U.S. Trust's institutional accounts includes the United Mine Workers of America 401K, the Commonwealth of Massachusetts Pension Reserves, the New York Legal Aid Society, the Sisters of Notre Dame, the American Academy of Arts and Sciences, the Manhattan Country School, the *Ms.* Foundation for Women, the Lotus Development Corporation, and Wellman, Inc.

U.S. Trust is an active shareholder, voting proxies on behalf of clients as well as sponsoring shareholder resolutions. In recent years shareholder proposals have been introduced on such issues as the Valdez Principals, South African divestment, and treatment of labor.

For the period from 1982 through December 31, 1991, the socially sensitive balanced portfolio had an average annualized return of 15.7 percent (see Table 7.1).

Table 7.1 United States Trust Company Asset Management, Balanced Accounts Performance Summary

	1981	1982	1983	1984	1985	1986
UST unscreened balanced*	8.3	24.8	19.1	10.0	27.4	19.0
UST socially sensitive balanced**	7.1	32.4	14.4	11.3	28.3	18.2
Median Balanced Fund†	3.3	25.5	15.1	9.2	24.7	15.4
S&P 500	−5.3	21.5	22.6	6.3	31.8	18.7
SL/GC bond index	7.3	31.1	8.0	15.0	21.3	15.3
90-day Treasury bills	14.7	10.7	8.6	9.6	7.5	6.0
CPI/Inflation	8.6	3.9	3.3	3.6	3.6	0.7

* Balanced accounts in these composites are managed against a 50:40:10 stocks:bonds:cash benchmark with a 20–80 percent equity allocation range.
** Composite of accounts using a comprehensive set of social screens, relating to South Africa, the environment, products (including tobacco), weapons contracting, employment practices, etc.
†Source: Wilshire Cooperative Fund—Performance Database
Returns reflect deduction of all transaction and custody costs but are calculated before management fees.

U.S. Trust has a competitive performance record and an outstanding staff of portfolio managers and social researchers. The firm is quite disciplined and professional in their approach to asset management and has a history of being quite public about their commitment to responsible investing, social change, and high-impact social investing.

Because U.S. Trust is a larger, more institutionalized portfolio manager, they have somewhat less flexibility in responding to the needs of individual clients who require brokerage firm custody or who fail to meet the minimum asset level.

Franklin Research and Development Corporation

Franklin Research and Development was created by Don Falvey and Joan Bavaria. Falvey's Franklin Management capitalized FRDC as a private, worker-owned cooperative venture. The firm started managing socially responsible client assets in 1982. FRDC is managed by a five-member board; two board members are women, but there are no minorities. Four of the board members are employees of FRDC.

Franklin Research and Development manages balanced, fixed-income, and equity accounts, tailoring the accounts to the social needs of the client. As of December 31, 1991, FRDC managed approximately $260 million in socially responsible assets for about 250 individual and institutional clients. Portfolio performance from 1982 through 1991 is shown in Table 7.2.

Table 7.1   *(Continued)*

	1987	1988	1989	1990	1991	Av. Annual 1981–1991
UST unscreened balanced	9.4	13.4	18.8	4.6	21.8	15.8
UST socially sensitive balanced	8.1	11.9	18.8	4.7	20.5	15.7
Median Balanced Fund	4.6	10.9	19.0	2.6	23.1	13.7
S&P 500	5.3	16.6	31.7	-3.1	30.5	15.3
SL/GC bond index	2.3	7.6	14.2	8.3	16.5	13.1
90-day Treasury bills	5.9	6.7	8.2	7.8	5.5	8.3
CPI/Inflation	4.5	4.4	4.7	6.1	3.6	4.3

Portfolio management fees for equity and balanced accounts are 1 percent per annum up to $1 million and ½ of 1 percent per annum for fixed-income accounts up to $5 million. The minimum fee is $4,000. Shawmut Bank of Boston is the preferred custodian for FRDC clients. The bank charges a fee of 2.7 percent on all income collected. The fee for nonprofit organizations is 2 percent. The minimum account size is $400,000.

Researchers at FRDC evaluate more than 1,800 companies in seven categories:[11]

1. Sensitivity to the environment
2. Quality and breadth of employee relations
3. Substance of citizenship in local and world communities
4. Nature of involvement in South Africa
5. Character of energy production and use
6. Participation in weapons production
7. Value and social usefulness of product/services

In addition to providing client portfolio social research, FRDC publishes *Franklin's Insight* and *Investing for a Better World,* a monthly investment advisory newsletter that provides specific company reviews, commentary, investment advice, and social commentary on responsible investing. Patrick McVeigh, FRDC vice-president, is in charge of research and is the editor of *Franklin's Insight.* Along with Jon Lickerman at Working Assets and Steve Lydenberg at KLD, Patrick is probably the top social investment researcher in the country.

Franklin Research and Development has seven portfolio managers with a maximum of 45 clients per manager; FRDC also employs six full-time social researchers. The company serves as Subadvisor

Table 7.2 Portfolio Performance Time-weighted Total Return (%) After Advisory Fees

	Institutional Accounts			Individual Accounts	
	Balanced	Equities	Fixed	Balanced	Equities
Fourth quarter, 1991	7.07	9.37	5.16	6.83	10.07
1991	25.00	39.76	16.08	25.25	43.33
1990	5.70	1.00	9.41	2.37	(1.98)
1989	19.53	30.12	12.38	18.81	30.99
1988	9.57	12.44	7.22	10.26	12.31
1987	4.96	0.67	3.23	2.97	(0.49)
1986	17.68	19.60	12.69	18.45	22.57
1985	23.41	30.65		25.08	30.81
1984	8.85	9.48		4.88	3.61
1983				17.30	25.65
1982				31.08	25.15
Comp. annual return					
8 years 1984–1991	14.09	17.06		13.15	16.60
10 years 1982–1991				15.24	18.31

Past results are not necessarily indicative of future performance. Returns reflect the reinvestment of all dividends and interest earned for balanced accounts and the reinvestment of dividends for equity accounts.

Returns represent the median unweighted return of representative accounts of the Franklin Research & Development Corporation and FRDC California Corporation. The number of accounts in each group differs over the period shown. All accounts are fully discretionary and have a minimum size of approximately $300,000. For balanced accounts, not less than 25% of each account's market value is equity securities and not less than 20% is fixed income securities. No more than 10% of the market valaue of each account is in securities that are not within the investment guidelines established by FRDC. The equity returns include the equity portion of all equity accounts and the equity portion of balanced accounts. Cash reserves are excluded from equity and fixed income returns.

The advisor's fees are described in Part II of its Form ADV. Returns do not reflect the deduction of management fees, and returns would be reduced if such fees were included. For example, if management fees were deducted from the balanced individual accounts for the annual periods from 1986 through 1990, the annual return for this period would have been 9.27%, assuming model fees equal to the highest fee charged to any account.

Source: Franklin Research & Development Corporation.

providing social screening services for Calvert Ariel Appreciation Fund and the Nader-inspired Green Earth Mutual Fund in Los Angeles.

Institutional clients of FRDC include Amnesty International, Consumers United Insurance Company, the Episcopal City Mission of Boston, the Friends Committee on National Legislation, the General Board of Pensions of the United Methodist Church, the National Cooperative Bank Development Corporation, the Pathfinder Fund, the Sisters of Mercy, and the Needmor Fund.

Over the past three years, FRDC has lost staff and has had trouble maintaining its presence in both California and Washington since key staff members in Sausalito and Seattle resigned. Internal divisions have been exacerbated by the divorce of founders Don Falvey and Joan Bavaria.

Franklin and FRDC shared space since FRDC was created in 1982, but recently Falvey's Franklin Management moved from Boston's Atlantic Avenue to Lewis Wharf while FRDC moved to another floor in the Atlantic Avenue building. The independent status of FRDC is questionable since, on two separate occasions, sales fell through at the last minute. The first potential buyer was Sophia Collier, who later purchased Working Assets Management Company.

Despite the turmoil, FRDC has been able to hang on to its client base, continue its commitment to socially responsible investing, and maintain its national presence. The president of FRDC, Joan Bavaria, has been a tireless crusader for the Valdez Principles and continues to have a high media profile that benefits the firm. In addition, FRDC benefits from excellent staff support, exceptional research, and a popular monthly newsletter.

There is no doubt that Falvey's Franklin Management, which manages over $50 million in assets, will also continue to contribute to the national SRI movement, separate from FRDC. Don Falvey, Franklin Management's president, is a seasoned portfolio manager and already has built a solid national reputation as a leader in the responsible investment movement.

Clean Yield Asset Management

The Clean Yield Group based in Portsmouth, New Hampshire, began publishing a newsletter for socially conscious investors in 1985 and created Clean Yield Asset Management in 1986. Rian Fried and P. Douglas Fleer were the founders of the newsletter. Benjamin Lovell joined Clean Yield Group in 1986 to assist in the creation of the portfolio management company. Lovell is a CPA and before joining Clean Yield was an auditor for Tyco Laboratories, Inc., and Price Waterhouse. Fleer was an independent building contractor before co-founding Clean Yield; his partner, Rian Fried, was the director of the Brockton Regional Economical Development Corporation. There is no board of directors per se since the company is owned and managed by Fried, Fleer, and Lovell.

Social research follows that of the Clean Yield newsletter and client portfolios are tailored to meet the social and investment goals of the client. Clean Yield Asset Management invests in companies that have many of the following characteristics:

- Products and/or services that offer value to society, such as water, utilities, or health care
- Enlightened management structures that allow employee input to the decision-making process and respond to the changing environments in a rapid and productive fashion
- Women in line management and director positions
- Employee benefit plans that are comprehensive
- Employee ownership plans that give the worker/owners voting rights

Clean Yield will not purchase stocks in companies that pursue the following activities:

- Weapons manufacturing
- Nuclear power generation
- Environmental pollution violations
- Labor conflicts
- Tobacco production
- Liquor production[12]

As of December 31, 1991, Clean Yield managed approximately $12.5 million in assets and charged a fee of 1 1/4 percent per annum under $500,000 and 1 percent per annum on assets between $500,000 and $1 million. The minimum account size is $150,000.

Clean Yield's Performance	
1988	12.39%
1989	16.12
1990	−6.67
1991	19.84

Although Clean Yield Asset Management is small, its assets are growing. The Clean Yield newsletter is popular and has become helpful to many socially responsible portfolio managers. Despite Clean Yield's size and geographic isolation, its commitment to responsible investing will result in continued asset growth, as well as growth in its subscriber base.

Christian Brothers Investment Services, Inc.

Many other registered investment advisors provide socially responsible portfolio management to institutional investors. One of the largest is Christian Brothers Investment Services, Inc. (CBIS), which manages over $700 million in assets of Catholic religious institutional investors. Providing financial advice and investment management services, CBIS works solely with Catholic organizations from around the country (about 800 organizations).

The firm works with ICCR and has sponsored shareholder resolutions on South Africa, Northern Ireland, and the Valdez Principles. According to CBIS's brochure "Commitment to Socially Responsible Investing," the investment firm involves itself in research and dialogue with corporate management on issues concerning affirmative action, equal employment, comparable worth, safe working conditions, support for human rights, and defense. In addition, CBIS involves itself in research and corporate dialogue on a variety of environmental issues and has a unique bioethics criterion.

Sister Carol Coston is the director of the CBIS Partners for the Common Good Loan Fund, which is a high social impact fund of over $3.5 million. The Fund invests in community loan funds and other investment vehicles that have a positive social impact. CBIS is owned and operated by the eight U.S. districts of the Christian Brothers, whose governance comes from Rome.

Advent Advisors, Inc.

Advent Advisors, based in Durham, North Carolina, is owned by former Smith Barney broker Steve Dibble, who serves as president and chief portfolio strategist. F. Farnum Brown, Jr., is vice-president and director of research.

Advent is a two-person shop that manages about $40 million, of which 70 percent is socially screened. There are 70 clients, all individual investors. The social criteria are entirely client-oriented. Accounts are primarily managed as balanced, with assets diversified and comprised of stocks, bonds, convertible securities, and cash equivalents.

The annual fee at Advent is 1 1/8 percent of assets managed under $1 million, decreasing to 7/8 of 1 percent on the next $2 million. The minimum fee for portfolio management is $2,000. In 1991 Advent's equity accounts returned an annual return of 30.7 percent, and balanced accounts increased 16.2 percent.

MPT Associates

Many traditional portfolio management firms have found it advantageous to their financial bottom line to manage socially responsible clients, especially institutional clients that demand South Africa-free portfolios (mandated by many state and local government pension plans). New York–based MPT Associates is one such investment advisor, managing three institutional accounts that require SAF portfolios.

MPT Associates manages $89.3 million in SAF accounts. Their performance has been impressive, beating the S&P 500 South African-invested portfolios since inception in 1987 (see Table 7.3).

SRI portfolio managers and other financial professionals have provided investors with competitive performance while meeting social goals. In the next chapter we will review SRI mutual funds and see how they stack up.

Table 7.3   MPT Associates South African Free Equity Investment Performance

Year		MPT Gross of Fees	S&P 500 Less South Africa	Year		MPT Gross of Fees	S&P 500 Less South Africa
1987	1	23.9%	0.6%	1990	1	−0.7%	−3.2%
	2	2.7	0.6		2	6.4	5.7
	3	7.0	0.6		3	−16.5	−14.7
	4	−23.5	0.6		4	9.5	8.8
		4.2	**2.6**			**−3.2**	**−5.0**
1988	1	9.6	5.1	1991	1	19.9	14.9
	2	5.4	6.9		2	−1.7	−0.5
	3	0.6	0.5		3	7.5	5.3
	4	1.6	2.5		4	9.9	7.9
		18.1	**15.9**			**39.2**	**30.1**
1989	1	9.3	6.7				
	2	8.0	9.3				
	3	14.7	10.3				
	4	−1.5	1.4				
		33.4	**30.7**				

Annualized Results (Ending 12-31-91)

	MPT Gross	S&P 500 Less South Africa
2 years	16.1	11.2
3 years	21.6	17.3
4 years	17.2	13.9

MPT's SAFE equity composite for 1991 and thereafter is weighted by account size to conform to performance presentation standards of the Association for Investment Management and Research. On December 31, 1991, this composite had a market value of $89.3 million. Certain portfolios within the composite have restrictions in addition to South African investments.

CHAPTER EIGHT

Responsible Mutual Funds

Mutual funds provide an investment vehicle that enables investors to take advantage of diversification and professional portfolio management. Many investors utilize mutual funds if they don't have adequate assets to hire a portfolio manager and don't want to rely solely on a broker or financial planner for day-to-day portfolio management. Many investors also find that mutual fund investing is preferable to personally selecting individual securities. They appreciate the ease and convenience of buying and selling mutual fund shares through a brokerage firm or directly with the fund over the telephone.

Mutual funds are popular with investors because they provide a way to invest a small amount of money in a large diversified and managed portfolio to meet specific portfolio objectives. Mutual funds can be invested in stocks, bonds, treasury and government agency securities, real estate, and other securities.

Mutual funds are sold or issued by prospectus and can be tailored to meet different financial and social investment objectives. The main financial objective of mutual funds is growth of capital or income through interest, dividends, or capital appreciation. Generally, mutual funds should not be considered for short-term trading since you may pay a fee or commission when you invest or redeem shares in a mutual fund. Responsible investment mutual funds meet a wide variety of traditional investment objectives and are categorized in Table 8.1.

Mutual fund sales reached $150 billion dollars in 1990. The mutual fund industry has seen assets skyrocket from $495 billion in 1985 to $1.36 trillion at the end of 1991. A mutual fund industry study conducted by Heidi Fiske Associates, a New York–based consulting firm, found that by the year 2000 mutual funds will account for 18 percent of U.S. households' discretionary financial assets, compared to 14 percent today. Their research also predicts robust mutual fund asset growth at an average rate of about 12 percent a year during the 1990s. From $1

Table 8.1   Responsible Investment Funds

Growth Fund	Parnassus Fund	Balanced Fund	Dreyfus Third Century
	Calvert Ariel		Fund[NL]
	Appreciation Fund		Calvert SIF Managed
	Calvert Ariel Growth		Growth Fund
	Fund		Pax World Fund[NL]
	Calvert Equity Fund		Parnassus Balanced
	Schield Progressive		Portfolio
	Environmental	Bond Fund	Calvert SIF Bond Fund
	New Alternatives		Parnassus Fixed Income
	Domini Social Index		Portfolio
	Fund[NL]	Municipal Bond	Muir Investment Trust
Specialized Fund	Merrill Lynch	Fund (Tax Free)	Parnassus California
	Eco·Logical Trust		Tax-Free Portfolio
	Schield Progressive	Money Market	Working Assets Money
	Environmental	Fund	Fund[NL]
	New Alternatives		Calvert SIF Money Market
Index Fund	Domini Social Index		Fund[NL]
	Fund[NL]		

Each fund may fit more than one category.
[NL] No-Load

trillion at the start of the decade, mutual fund assets could reach $3.5 trillion by the year 2000. Sixty-nine percent of mutual funds are no-load. If money market funds are excluded, 47 percent are no-load.

There are now several hundred more mutual funds than there are companies on the New York Stock Exchange. During the past five-year period, the number of mutual funds has more than doubled to 3108 funds. Less than $\frac{1}{4}$ of 1 percent of the over 1 trillion dollars in mutual fund assets is currently in socially responsible funds. As mentioned earlier, Heidi Fiske projects 12 percent mutual fund asset growth per year during the 1990s. Assuming SRI funds maintain their share of fund assets, social mutual funds will have the following asset levels:

End of Year	Assets ($billion)
1992	1.67
1993	1.86
1994	2.09
....	....
2000	4.2

Fourteen of these 3108 funds can be classified as socially responsible:

Fund Name	Objective	Assets ($mil)	Established
Calvert-Ariel Appreciation	Growth	90	1990
Calvert-Ariel Growth Fund	Growth	262	1986
Calvert SIF:			
Managed Growth	Balanced	365	1982
Bond	Income	38	1987
Equity	Growth	51	1987
Dreyfus Third Century	Growth	361	1972
New Alternatives	Growth	24	1982
Parnassus Fund	Growth	31.8	1985
Pax World Fund	Balanced	270	1971
Progressive Environmental	Growth	3.8	1990
Calvert SIF:			
Money Fund	Money Market	186.8	1982
Working Assets Money Fund	Money Market	236.8	1983
Muir Investment Trust	Income	4.3	1991
Domini Social Index Trust	Growth	3.6	1990

The Calvert Group controls 55 percent of social mutual funds assets. Fees charged by social funds and their expense ratios in percent are shown in the following table. Load is the sales charge, 12b–1 is the annual distribution fee, the management fee is the annual percentage fee charged for portfolio management, and the expense ratio is the operating expenses of the fund expressed as a percentage of average net assets.

Socially responsible mutual funds have often outperformed market indexes. See Table 8.2 for the responsible investment mutual fund performance for six years and a comparison of the funds with the S&P 500 Stock Index, the Shearson Lehman Government Corporate Bond Index, and the 90-Day Treasury Bill Index.

Fund Name	Load	12b-1	Management Fee	Expense Ratio
Calvert-Ariel				
Appreciation	4.75	0.25	0.75	1.55
Calvert-Ariel				
Growth Fund	4.50	0.25	1.00	1.56
Calvert SIF:				
Managed Growth	4.75	0.25	0.70	1.32
Bond	4.75	0	0.65	0.75
Equity	4.75	0	0.70	1.00
Dreyfus Third				
Century	0	0	0.75	1.08
New Alternatives	5.66	0	1.00	1.19
Parnassus Fund	3.50	0	1.00	1.86
Pax World Fund	0	0.25	0.58	1.10
Progressive				
Environmental	4.50	1.00	1.00	2.50
Calvert SIF:				
Money Fund	0	0	0.50	0.90
Working Assets				
Money Fund	0	0.22	0.50	1.05
Muir Investment				
Trust	4.50	0	0.74	1.00
Domini Social Index	0	0.05	0.08	0.75

Note: numbers rounded

Socially responsible mutual funds cover a variety of financial and social investment objectives. All open-ended mutual funds are owned by their shareholders, but ownership of the investment advisor is different. I'll discuss social criteria, the owners of the investment advisors, and companies presently in the funds' portfolios as well as identifying the performance and management of each fund.

Pax World Fund

Dr. Luther Tyson teamed up with Jack Corbett, a colleague on the United Methodist Church's board of church and society, to create the Pax World Fund in 1971. A Methodist woman from Ohio had written to him asking if it were possible for churches to avoid investing in war

Table 8.2 Mutual Fund Performance 1986 through 1991

Fund:	1991	1990	1989	1988	1987	1986
Calvert Ariel Growth Fund	32.72	−16.1	25.1	39.9	11.4	2.0*
Calvert Ariel Appreciation	33.16	−1.2				
Calvert Equity	21.93	−4.9	27.5	14.8	−14.1	
Calvert Managed Growth	17.79	1.8	18.7	10.7	5.0	18.1
Calvert Bond	15.75	8.3	13.6	8.0	3.8*	
Dreyfus Third Century	38.12	3.5	17.3	23.2	2.6	4.6
Parnassus Fund	51.89	−22.0	2.8	42.4	−6.8	2.5
Pax World Fund	20.8	10.5	24.9	11.5	2.6	8.5
New Alternatives	25.6	−7.6	26.0	23.9	−2.6	22.5
Progressive Environmental	−1.97	4.1				
Merrill Lynch Ecological	31.6	0.1				
Domini Social Index	37.84	1.47*				
Global Environment LP	24.17	0.17				
S&P 500	26.31	−3.1	31.7	16.6	5.3	18.7
SL/GC Bond Index	16.12	8.3	14.2	7.6	2.3	15.3
90-Day T-Bills	6.45	7.8	8.2	6.7	5.9	6.0

* Partial year
Source: Weisenberger Mutual Fund Panorama. Warren, Gorham & Lamont. New York, 1991.
Individual Mutual Fund Advisors.

weaponry. He checked around and discovered that this had become a major concern among church people. The Pax World Fund was created as an alternative to traditional funds that supported the American military industrial complex. Today Pax concentrates on supporting health care, education, pollution control, and alternative and renewable energy.

Luther Tyson was a minister in New England for eight years after graduating from Southwest Nazarene University, Boston University School of Theology, and Boston University Graduate School, where he received a doctorate in the sociology of religion and social ethics. Dr. Tyson holds a doctorate in economics; Dr. Corbett has a Ph.D. in international relations and was the founder of the National Coalition to Ban Handguns.

The Pax Fund recently celebrated its twentieth birthday, and Luther reflected on its founding:

> Jack and I developed a social criteria around the question of life-supporting goods and services. This is what we emphasized—something that supports life and detracts from military expenditures and pollution. We also wanted to support minority and women's rights. In the process we developed an extensive questionnaire which we have used to question corporate officers about policies and corporate practices.

Pax World Fund's investment advisor, Pax World Management Corporation, is still owned by the original four founders: Luther Tyson, Jack Corbett, Anthony Brown, and Paul Brown, Jr. Their social criteria causes them to avoid the 100 largest U.S. DoD contractors and other DoD contractors if 5 percent or more of their gross sales is derived from such contracts. Pax World also avoids companies involved in liquor, tobacco, and gambling. Pax World endeavors to invest in companies that have adopted and administer fair employment and pollution control policies and that invest in companies that produce life-supportive goods and services and are not to any degree engaged in manufacturing defense or weapons-related products. By the way of illustration, the fund will invest in such companies as housing, food, leisure time, education, retailing, pollution control, health care, household appliances, publishing, and building supplies, among others.

Although Pax World does not have a specific South African exclusionary policy in the prospectus, the fund has not invested in companies that operate in South Africa since 1989. I remember having several conversations with Luther Tyson in the early 1980s, trying to convince him that Pax World should totally divest from companies operating in South Africa. At that time, Luther believed that Pax World should support the Sullivan Principles, which he felt would be more effective in eliminating apartheid than total divestment and disengagement. Historically Pax World has invested only in those companies operating in South Africa that were involved in food and medicine.

Pax World Fund is a very conservative balanced stock and bond fund, investing about 37 percent of its assets in stocks and 59 percent in bonds.[1] Cash is invested in short-term government agency bonds. Most of the bonds are in government agency securities of less than 10 years in maturity. The nine-member board of directors of the Pax World Fund includes two women and two minorities.

Pax has a minimum investment of $250 and is a no-load fund. It charges a 0.56 percent management fee and a 0.23 percent 12b–1 fee. Total fees charged (as a percentage of average net assets) total 1.17 percent, making it one of the least expensive of all the responsible investment funds. As of December 31, 1991, Pax World Fund's assets were $270 million. Most of the growth at Pax occurred after 1982. The fund increased over $150 million during 1991.

Pax World Fund is one of the most consistent and competitive performers of all the social funds. For its no-load and low operating expenses, it can't be beaten for a conservative balanced social fund. In 1990 Pax World was ranked the top-rated mutual fund in the balanced fund category by Lipper Analytical Services, a national mutual fund rating service. Nelson's Directory of Investment Managers, which tracks investment managers' performance, ranked Pax World Management Corporation among the best performing balanced account managers in 1990. In the February 17, 1992, edition of *Business Week,* Pax World was listed as a "top-performer" with an average annual return of 13.8 percent for the last five years.

Pax World's Performance			
Date	**Return**	**Date**	**Return**
8/71 to 12/71	1.70%	1982	18.4
1972	.8	1983	24.2
1973	−19.9	1984	7.4
1974	−16.1	1985	25.8
1975	34.1	1986	8.5
1976	24.8	1987	2.6
1977	1.9	1988	11.5
1978	−0.04	1989	24.9
1979	19.6	1990	10.5
1980	17.4	1991	20.8
1981	1.0		

Stocks in the Pax World portfolio include Brooklyn Union Gas, Bay State Gas, H.J. Heinz Co., Hechinger, Equitable Resources, Sierra Pacific Resources, DPL, Inc., Black Hills Corp., and Advanced Logic Research. Pax World does not invest in U.S. Treasury bonds "since the money could be used for the military."[2]

Pax World created the Pax World Foundation to permit shareholders to donate some or all of their income or capital gains to support sustainable agriculture, water purification, and reforestation in the Third World as well as friendship tours to promote international understanding and reconciliation around the globe.

In the early days of socially responsible investing, Pax World was seen as a somewhat politically conservative and passive mutual fund. Pax was not active in the South African national divestment campaign. It was not one of the founders of the Social Investment Forum, nor has a representative of Pax served on the board of directors of the forum. In recent years, however, Pax has become more active in forum programs, pays a higher institutional membership fee, and includes forum material in mailings to its shareholders. Pax World Fund votes its shares by proxy at annual shareholder meetings but has never introduced a shareholder proposal.

Dreyfus Third Century Fund

The Dreyfus Third Century Fund was opened in 1972 by Howard Stein, who was a major fund raiser for Eugene McCarthy's 1968 presidential campaign. He has been chairman of the board and CEO of the fund since its inception. Third Century is the only social fund of the Dreyfus family of funds.

Third Century's social criteria are vague at best. Tim Smith, executive director of ICCR allegedly said, with tongue in cheek, that Third Century's social criteria were wide enough to drive a tank through. Third Century seeks to invest in companies that "enhance the quality of life in America," specifically evaluating a company's record in the areas of "protection and improvement of the environment and the proper use of our natural resources, occupational health and safety, consumer protection and product purity, and equal employment opportunity." In 1985 Dreyfus Third Century Fund decided to discontinue investing in companies that operate in South Africa.

Third Century's primary goal is capital growth, holding approximately 75 percent of its assets in stocks and 24 percent in cash or U.S. Treasury Bills.[3]

Stocks in the Third Century portfolio include Coca-Cola, Magma Power, FNMA, Becton Dickinson, Merck, Rubbermaid, WalMart Stores, Safety Kleen, General Motors, and Thermo-Electron. Dreyfus has adopted a more restrictive policy regarding investment in South Africa but did not exclude companies with licensing agreements.

Third Century's Performance			
Date	Return	Date	Return
1980	41.5%	1986	4.6
1981	−11.0	1987	2.6
1982	4.6	1988	23.2
1983	19.9	1989	17.3
1984	1.4	1990	3.5
1985	29.7	1991	38.12

Dreyfus will not hold stock in a company in South Africa if the company has a 10 percent or more direct interest in South Africa. Several companies in its portfolio maintain licensing or franchise agreements with other firms in South Africa. There are also companies in the portfolio that are large defense contractors.

Dreyfus Third Century's assets more than doubled in 1980 and in the first quarter of 1991 grew from $199.3 million to $280.5 million. Assets as of December 31, 1991, were $360.9 million. The minimum investment is $2500. Like Pax World, Dreyfus Third Century is a no-load fund; there is no 12 b–1 fee. The management fee is 0.75 percent and operating expenses total 1.08 percent, making it—along with Pax World—one of the most inexpensive of the social funds.

The board of directors has five members, including two women and one minority. Dreyfus votes its stock at annual shareholders meetings by proxy but has not introduced a shareholder resolution at an annual meeting.

Dreyfus is an active member of the Social Investment Forum and pays an institutional membership fee. The fund was not a founder of the forum. Dreyfus has never had a representative serving on the forum's board of directors.

Dreyfus Third Century is a safe, conservative balanced fund that is an extremely passive social investor. The fund has not taken a leadership role in the responsible investment community, probably because it is part of a larger nonsocial family of funds. The social criteria for Dreyfus Third Century are limited to broad social statements, and its South African criteria are of limited use. It is, however, an inexpensive fund in which to invest if you're willing to accept a somewhat questionable commitment to social investment criteria and change. Dreyfus Third Century received high marks for performance from *Business Week,* and the *Mutual Fund Forecaster* ranked Dreyfus Third Century a "Best Buy" in January 1992.[4]

Calvert Social Investment Funds

The first of the Calvert Social Investment Funds was launched in 1982. In 1976, however, Wayne Silby and John Guffey, both graduates of the Wharton School of Business, decided to create a guaranteed government loan market and later a variable rate fund.[5] They teamed up with Robert Zevin, who was involved with Cambridge-based ICE, and created a family of mutual funds that reflected social as well as financial values. By the early 1980s Calvert had assets of over a billion dollars. The founders decided to capitalize on their popularity and sold the Calvert Group to the Washington-based Acacia Mutual Life Insurance Company.

Although Calvert is now owned by an insurance company, Wayne and John still serve on the Social Investment Fund board and provide leadership throughout the SRI movement. Within the Calvert Group there is a sense of mission. Stan Sorrell, Calvert's president, CEO, and vice chairman, is very articulate in expressing the company's commitment to socially responsible investing:

> When Wayne talked to our management team about starting a socially responsible mutual fund, there wasn't a whole lot of support, but a year later there was a lot of excitement created by the press in terms of our asset growth. People were investing because they believed the story that no one would have to sacrifice investment performance for principles. Ten years later we have a clear track record that substantiates faith investors had in us.
>
> Today's environmental and social issues are going to be tomorrow's economic issues. They are all part of the infrastructure we live in, and here at Calvert we want to be on the leading edge of social issues and concerns of the 1990s.

Wayne Silby thinks responsible investing is here to stay:

> We've become more institutionalized. People can relate to responsible investing in a mainstream sense. I find to some extent it is more widespread and accessible. In the early years we would always run into antagonism, but now it's much more accepted.

The Calvert Social Investment Funds (SIF) include the Money Market Portfolio, the Managed Growth Portfolio, the Equity Portfolio, the Ariel Growth Fund, the Ariel Appreciation Fund, and the Bond Portfolio. With the exception of Working Assets Money Fund, Calvert's SIF implement the most comprehensive social criteria of any of the responsible investment mutual funds. The social philosophy of Calvert's SIF is to invest in companies that "enhance the human condition and the traditional American values of individual initiative, equality of opportunity and cooperative effort."[6]

The Calvert SIF prefers to invest in a company that:

1. Delivers safe products and services in ways which sustain our natural environment. For example, the Fund looks for companies that produce energy from renewable resources, or that show a sensitivity to animal rights issues while avoiding consistent polluters.
2. Is managed with participation throughout the organization in defining and achieving objectives. For example, the Fund looks for companies that offer employee stock ownership or profit-sharing plans and use quality circles or incentive production teams.
3. Negotiates fairly with its workers, provides an environment supportive of their wellness, does not discriminate on the basis of race, gender,

religion, age, disability, ethnic origin, or sexual orientation, does not consistently violate regulations of the Equal Employment Opportunity Commission, and provides opportunities for women, disadvantaged minorities, and others for whom equal opportunities have often been denied. For example, the Fund considers both unionized and non-union firms with good labor relations.

4. Fosters awareness of a commitment to human goals, such as creativity, productivity, self-respect and responsibility within the organization and the world, and continually recreates a context within which these goals can be realized. For example, the Fund looks for companies with an active commitment to community affairs and charitable giving.

The fund will not invest in an issue primarily engaged in:

1. The production of nuclear energy or the manufacture of equipment to produce nuclear energy.
2. Business activities in South Africa or other repressive regimes.
3. The manufacture of weapons systems.[7]

The Calvert SIF also does not invest in companies engaged primarily in the manufacture of alcoholic beverages or tobacco products or in the operation of gambling casinos.

The Fund believes that social and technological change will continue to transform America and the world for the balance of this century. Those enterprises which exhibit a social awareness measured in terms of the above attributes and considerations should be better prepared to meet future societal needs for goods and services. By responding to social concerns, these enterprises should maintain flexibility and further social goals. In so doing they should not only avoid the liability that may be incurred when a product or service is determined to have a negative social impact or has outlived its usefulness, but also be better positioned to develop opportunities to make a profitable contribution to society. These enterprises should be ready to respond to external demands and ensure that over the longer term they will be viable to provide a return to both investors and society as a whole.[8]

Calvert SIF Money Market Fund

The Calvert SIF Money Market Fund was the top performing money market fund in the country in 1983, according to the Donoghue Money Average. It was in the top quartile of performance in 1984 and 1985 and continues to perform at or above the Donoghue Average for all money market funds in the country today. As of December 31, 1991, assets totaled $186.8 million. Sixty-six percent of the assets were invested in corporate commercial paper, 5 percent in Repurchase Agreements, 7 percent in CDs, 8 percent in Government Agency Obligations, 11 percent in Variable Demand Notes, and 3 percent in corporate notes.[9] Securities held in the fund include Melville Corporation, U.S. West Communications, Walt Disney, Nebraska Higher Education, South Shore Bank, and Federal Home Loan Mortgage Corporation. The nine-member board of trustees for all the Calvert SIF Funds includes three women and two minorities.

The minimum investment in the Calvert SIF Money Market Fund is $1000. It is a no-load fund and has a management fee of ½ of 1 percent. Total operating expenses are 0.87 percent.[10]

Calvert SIF Managed Growth

The Managed Growth Fund is Calvert's premier fund, which has retained U.S. Trust Company to act as Subadvisor. The Managed Growth Fund is a conservative balanced fund. Forty-eight percent of the portfolio is invested in stocks, 45 percent in government agency bonds, 2 percent in corporate bonds, 1 percent in CDs, and 1 percent in direct private placements.

The minimum investment for Managed Growth is $1000. It is a low-load fund with a 4.75 percent sales charge, a 12b–1 fee of 0.25 percent, and a management fee of 0.70 percent. Total fund operating expenses are 1.32 percent. As of December 31, 1991, assets in the fund totaled $365 million. Asset growth has steadily increased, with a spurt of growth occurring from 1985 to 1986, when assets jumped $70 million at the height of the national South African divestment struggle.

Calvert SIF Managed Growth Fund Performance

Date	Return	Date	Return
1983	11.3%	1988	10.7
1984	6.8	1989	18.7
1985	26.9	1990	1.8
1986	18.1	1991	17.79
1987	5.0		

The Calvert Managed SIF Growth Fund includes companies such as Digital Equipment, Ametek, Clorox, Magma Power, Groundwater Technology, Quaker Oats, Wellman, Washington Post, Kelly Services, Humana, Oregon Steel Mills, Sigma Aldrich Corp., and Bell Atlantic.

In September 1990 Managed Growth shareholders approved a new high social impact investment program designed to invest up to 1 percent of fund assets at below-market rates where there is a probability of direct positive social impact. The fund purchased shares in the Sand County Venture Fund, a social venture fund on the West Coast, and in Accion International, a Third World fund which makes microenterprise loans to people in Central and South America. Calvert's SIF Managed Growth Fund has invested in numerous community loan funds to build and rehabilitate low-income housing, in market rate CDs in South Shore Bank, and in numerous community-based credit unions. Calvert recently invested $100,000 in 10-year, 5 percent bonds issued by EDCS, which lends funds mainly to Third World cooperative enterprises.

Calvert SIF Bond Fund

The Calvert SIF Bond Fund is designed to provide high current and conservative income to fund shareholders. About 75 percent of the Fund's assets are invested in government agency securities, 19 percent in corporate bonds, 1 percent in convertible bonds, and 1 percent in stocks (First Union Real Estate).

The minimum investment is $1000. It is a low-load fund with a 4.75 percent sales charge and a management fee of 0.65 percent. Total fund operating expenses are 0.75 percent; on December 31, 1991, assets totaled $38 million. The asset growth has been steady since the fund was opened in 1987, with growth doubling annually since 1988.

Calvert SIF Bond Fund Performance			
Date	**Return**	**Date**	**Return**
1987	0.8%★	1990	8.3
1988	8.0	1991	15.75
1989	13.6		

★Partial year

The Calvert SIF Bond Fund includes such government agency securities as FNMA, Federal Home Loan Bank, and GNMA. Corporate bonds include such companies as Deluxe Corp., Goulds Pumps, The Limited, MASCO, Maytag, Pitney Bowes, McGraw-Hill, and U.S. Wind Power.

Calvert SIF Equity Fund

The Calvert SIF Equity Fund is a growth fund for investors who are interested in capital appreciation. Ninety-one percent of the fund is invested in stocks, while 1 percent is invested in convertible bonds (Illinois Tool Works).

The minimum investment for Equity Fund is $1000. It is a low-load fund with a 4.75 percent sales charge and a 0.70 percent management fee. Total operating expense is 1.00 percent. As of December 31, 1991, assets totaled $51 million. The fund was opened in 1987 but didn't really start growing until 1989 and 1990.

Calvert SIF Equity Fund Performance

Date	Return	Date	Return
1987	−14.1%★	1990	−4.9
1988	14.8	1991	21.93
1989	27.5		

★Partial year

The Equity Fund includes such companies as Albertson's, Digital Equipment, Dun & Bradstreet, H.J. Heinz Co., Melville, Smuckers, Student Loan Marketing, and Toys'R'Us.

In discussing the future of Calvert Social Investment Funds, Stan Sorrell, president, CEO, and vice chairman of Calvert Group, said that they are opening a global equity social fund in June 1992 named the Calvert World Values Fund. The fund will be managed by Glasgow-based Murray Johnstone International Ltd. Minimum initial investment will be $2000.

Calvert Ariel Funds

In 1983 John Rogers founded the Chicago-based Ariel Capital Management as a black-owned and operated portfolio management firm. By 1990 the firm was managing $1.2 billion. Ariel is the largest minority-owned money management firm in the United States and currently the only minority firm that manages mutual funds.

Calvert began marketing Ariel Growth Fund in November of 1986. The fund was so successful that it was closed to new investors on April 30, 1990, while the Calvert Ariel Appreciation Fund was opened in January 1990. Eric McKissack is the senior vice-president, director of research, and portfolio manager for the Ariel Appreciation Fund.

John Rogers is what is known as well-connected. His family is well-known in the Chicago area. His mother is an attorney and is on the boards of directors of several corporations; his father is a judge with the Chicago Juvenile Court.[11] The facts that Rogers is well-connected and that his family owns the largest minority-owned money management firm in the country explain in part why Ariel Capital Management has experienced such explosive growth. As well, Rogers's relationship with Calvert as the distributor for Ariel explains the increasing exposure Ariel Funds have had in the recent past.

The Ariel Growth Fund manages a portion of Howard University's endowment fund and initially picked up a great deal of assets from institutions that wanted to avoid companies in South Africa, achieve superior performance, and have assets managed by a black-owned money management firm.

Although the Ariel funds do not have as comprehensive a social screen as Working Assets Money Fund and the Calvert Social Investment Funds, Ariel avoids companies operating in South Africa, companies that primarily manufacture weapons, and nuclear-powered utilities.

The Ariel Growth Fund invests 92 percent of its assets in stocks but is closed to new investors. Assets as of December 31, 1991, were $262 million. The seven-member board of trustees for both Ariel Funds includes two minorities and a woman.

Calvert Ariel Growth Fund Performance

Date	Return	Date	Return
1986	2.0%*	1989	25.1
1987	11.4	1990	−16.1
1988	39.9	1991	32.72

*Partial year

The portfolio of the Growth Fund includes American Greeting, Armor-All Products Corporation, Caesar's World, Ecolab, Handleman, Interface Floors, Omnicom Group, Sealwright, T. Rowe Price, and Western Publishing.

The Calvert Ariel Appreciation Fund is structured to provide long-term capital appreciation to shareholders by investing a majority of the fund's assets in stocks. About 87 percent of assets are invested in stocks and 13 percent in cash.

The minimum investment is $2000. It is a low-load fund with a 4.75 percent sales charge, a 0.75 percent management fee, and a 0.25 percent 12b–1 charge. Total fund operating expenses are 1.55 percent. As of December 31, 1991, assets totaled $90 million. Assets at the end of 1990 were $26.2 million.

Calvert Ariel Appreciation Fund Performance	
Date	**Return**
1990	−1.2%*
1991	33.16

*Partial year

The Ariel Appreciation Fund includes companies such as Bausch & Lomb, Bergen Brunswig, Carnival Cruise Lines, Church & Dwight, Houghton Mifflin, National Medical, Stanhome, Topps, and Walgreens. Both Ariel Growth and Appreciation Funds have been questioned by individuals in the responsible investment community about their holdings of gambling casinos such as Caesar's World and Carnival Cruise Lines. Calvert Ariel has no prohibition on gambling, tobacco, or alcohol. Ariel Appreciation has retained FRDC to provide environmental screening for the advisor. The advisor, Ariel Capital Management, is privately owned by John Rogers, Jr., and his mother, Jewel S. Lafontane.

On May 1, 1991 the Ariel board of trustees approved a resolution reorganizing the Washington Area Growth Fund into the Calvert Ariel Appreciation Fund.[12] It was approved by shareholders September 3, 1991. The Calvert Washington Area Growth Fund was a regional stock fund with limited growth potential and appeal as a specialized fund and had only $8.7 million in assets.

Calvert Group is the powerhouse family of socially responsible mutual funds. Calvert has one of the best national distribution networks. Under the leadership of Stan Sorrell, its future is indeed bright.

The New Alternatives Fund

Maurice Schoenwald and his son, David, who is now vice president and portfolio manager of the fund, opened New Alternatives to the public in 1982. Originally the fund was named the Solar Fund and was incorporated in 1978 as a limited partnership. Maurice and David started the fund in their home and taught themselves to conduct research — or due diligence — on companies involved in alternative energy, conservation, recycling, cogeneration biomass energy, hydroelectricity, natural gas, and passive and active architectural systems. David's investigative research experience as a newspaper reporter in Newark, New Jersey, helped their studies a great deal.

According to David, the founders of the New Alternatives Fund did not consider their mutual fund a social fund but one that concerned itself with solar and other alternative energies. The fund specifically excludes nuclear power "due to the potential for an accident, unresolved radioactive waste disposal problems, excessive cost and frequent community opposition to such programs."[13] The fund also excludes investments that relate to the Strategic Defense Initiative, atomic warfare, and South Africa.

New Alternatives clearly advertises itself as a social fund, and its asset growth is a reflection of the popularity of responsible investing, South Africa divestment, and environmentalism. Prior to 1985 New Alternatives had less than 1 million dollars in assets, but as of December 31, 1991, the fund had $24 million in assets.

The New Alternatives Fund is a very specialized environmental mutual fund that has an economic and social agenda: the achievement of national energy independence through investing in alternative and renewable energy.

The primary objective of New Alternatives is to invest for long-term growth. About 81 percent is invested in stocks, 16 percent in money market and treasury bills, and 3 percent in cash.

The board of directors consists of five men and one woman, with no minority members. Another woman serves as vice president and officer of the fund but is not a director.

Minimum initial investment in New Alternatives is $2650. The fund charges a 5.66 percent sales commission and a management fee of 1 percent. Total fund operating expenses are 1.19 percent. The fund's cash is invested in South Shore Bank, Vermont National Bank, and Alternatives Federal Credit Union as well as in treasuries. According to David, the fund is not concerned with disarmament issues and "not against the government having an army."

New Alternatives Fund Performance

Date	Return	Date	Return
1982	10.4%	1987	−2.6
1983	13.5	1988	23.9
1984	−0.5	1989	26.0
1985	23.3	1990	−7.6
1986	22.2	1991	25.6

Stocks in New Alternatives include Air Products, Archer Daniels Midland, Betz Labs, Burlington Resources, Corning, Energy Conversion Devices, Hawaiian Electric, Mycogen, Ogden Projects, Thermo Instrument, and Zurn Industries.

Hawaiian Electric

For several years there has been an environmental controversy regarding Hawaiian Electric's plan to eventually develop a 500-megawatt geothermal power plant in Hawaii. The project has been delayed pending the completion of an environmental impact report (EIR). The plant is opposed by native Hawaiians who believe that the volcanoes are sacred and should not be tapped for geothermal production. Another environmental and technological problem with the project relates to the construction of major underwater cables needed to transfer the power from the island of Hawaii to the population centers on Oahu.

Environmentalists and native Hawaiians have established a Pele Defense Fund. The National Resources Defense Council (NRDC) is concerned about the cultural and environmental effects of the project. The council has stated that, until a hard look has been taken at the economics of the project and a comparison has been made of other alternatives, "NRDC believes that any further exploration and development of geothermal power in the Wao Kele forest is premature."[14] The Rainforest Action Network issued a press release on August 15, 1991 entitled "A Bad Investment for the Socially Responsible," stating that "the Rainforest Action Network, together with a coalition of environmental and native Hawaiian rights groups, is urging investment funds and stockbrokers to divest from companies directly associated with geothermal energy development in Hawaii."

New Alternatives holds 23,000 shares of Hawaiian Electric. Schoenwald has indicated that he is aware of the Hawaiian geothermal controversy and continues to hold Hawaiian Electric stock. He said that the project has been delayed in order to complete another EIR but didn't hint at whether or not New Alternatives had lobbied Hawaiian Electric.

In March 1988, when I first read of the controversy, I wrote the president and CEO of Hawaiian Electric, C. Dudley Pratt, Jr., about the concerns of my clients who were holding 20,000 shares of the company's stock. I asked for Hawaiian Electric's side of the story. Five months later Mr. Pratt finally responded:

> While I respect the right of the organization which placed the advertisement in West Coast newspapers opposing the development of geothermal

energy in Hawaii, I strenuously object to the gross misstatements of fact and the sweeping assumptions contained in the advertisements.

As one whose great-grandfather arrived in Hawaii in 1832 as a missionary, I can assure you that geothermal energy will not be developed in Hawaii unless it can be done with great care and with respect for our unique environment and culture which all Hawaiians and Hawaiians-at-heart are pledged to protect. I also bring to your attention the fact that our courts recently considered the right of these people to halt geothermal development on religious and cultural grounds and specifically rejected their claim of this right.

By developing Hawaii's own natural energy resources, we seek to reduce the amount of imported fuel oil required to generate electricity in our State, and thereby to improve the quality of Hawaii's environment. I am enclosing several brochures describing our company's wind energy projects and trust these endeavors will be favorably received by your clients.

Despite Mr. Pratt's convictions that Hawaiian Electric will protect the interests of Hawaiian culture and the environment, the controversy continues. With so little factual information to substantiate the company's side of the story, I decided to sell my clients' holdings in the stock. In August 1990 Working Assets Money Fund also decided not to invest in Hawaiian Electric's corporate commercial paper.

New Alternatives Fund is closely held by the Schoenwald family and has unique social and environmental criteria. The fund is not aggressively marketed, and the Schoenwalds seem content to continue relatively passive social investment and marketing policies. The fund is somewhat removed from the mainstream and isn't helped much by its high sales load (the highest of all the social funds).

The performance of the fund has picked up over the last six or seven years and, compared to the S&P 500 Index, has performed well. Portfolio management and stock picking is not as disciplined as that at U.S. Trust or Parnassus, but David Schoenwald is proving himself a very capable manager. This is an environmental fund to watch.

Muir California Investment Trust

In June 1991 the newest of the social investment funds arrived on the scene in San Francisco. The fund's founder, Michael Kieschnick, was a co-founder of Working Assets Money Fund. Keith Goodlett, vice-president of Muir's Investor Relations, is also a former director of Working Assets Management Company and was manager of its customer service and sales.

The Muir Investment Trust is an open-ended municipal bond fund investing in investment grade California municipal bonds that provide social, environmental, and economic benefits.

Muir restricts investments in projects or programs that do not have a positive social and economic effect on California. For example, Muir will not finance the construction or the maintenance of correctional facilities, highways, parking garages, toxic waste dumps, dams or other water utilization facilities, golf courses, country clubs, power transmission, or utilities relying on nuclear power.[15]

Muir's portfolio manager and distributor is Sand County Securities, L.P., and Sand County Ventures, Inc., both of which are owned by Michael Kieschnick. Sand County has retained GMG/Seneca Capital Management as the fund's advisor. The chief investment officer and managing general partner is Gail Seneca, the former senior vice-president and chief investment officer of Wells Fargo Asset Management Division (Wells Fargo Bank). The five-member board of trustees includes three women and one minority.

Securities in the portfolio include the California Housing Finance Agency, San Francisco Bay Area Rapid Transit, Sierra California Joint Community College Certificate of Participation, Sacramento Light Rail Transit, and the California Veterans Home Revenue Bonds.

The minimum investment in Muir is $2500. It is a low-load fund with a 4.50 percent sales charge and a 0.74 percent management fee. Total operating expenses are 1 percent. As of December 31, 1991, assets in the trust totaled $4.3 million.

Muir is implementing an extensive marketing campaign in California but will be competing against several no-load state tax-exempt funds, such as Fidelity. Parnassus is also planning to offer a competing social California tax-exempt bond portfolio.

The Muir Investment Trust could have a difficult and short life if aggressive marketing in California doesn't pay off. Not only is Muir going up against several large California tax-exempt municipal bond funds, but its social market is very thin and Dodson's Parnassus California tax-exempt portfolio could cut into its market share. The Muir's market is limited to wealthy California individual investors (eliminating the institutional market), and only those whose social sophistication recognizes the difference between a regular tax-exempt California bond fund and the unique characteristics of a socially responsible fund such as Muir. With a low interest rate environment, bond funds have also lost much of their appeal.

Muir's future is also clouded by its load (which is high compared to other California municipal bond funds), its management fee, and its limited distribution. It is also not broker friendly, since it takes a portion of the commission for itself to the disadvantage of selling brokers.

Domini Social Index Trust

In February 1989 Peter Kinder, co-author with Amy Domini of *Ethical Investing* (Addison-Wesley, 1984), announced the results of a year-long study on the feasibility of indexing stocks screened for a broad range of social constraints. No company qualified for the social index if more than 4 percent of its gross sales came from weapons, alcoholic beverages, tobacco, gambling, or nuclear power, and no company with South African operations could qualify. The index included firms with positive records in the areas of the environment, manufacturing methods, employee relations and programs, and corporate citizenship.

The social index ended up with a universe of 400 stocks by taking the Standard and Poor's 500 and the next 500 largest corporations by market capitalization. The study compared the 400-stock social index to the Standard and Poor's 500 for a period of five years, ending with the fourth quarter of 1988. The social index provided an average quarterly return of 5.5 percent (market-weighted) and 4.6 percent (unweighted), compared to 4.0 percent for the Standard and Poor's 500 Index.[16]

In August 1990, armed with the Kinder study, the Domini Social Index Trust opened as a no-load, diversified, open-end investment company. This Social Index Trust is managed by State Street Bank of Boston; the fund's administrator and distributor is Signature Broker-Dealer of Boston. Kinder, Lydenberg, Domini & Company, Inc. (KLD) is the portfolio's investment advisor. The investment objective is long-term capital appreciation by investing (indexing) all of the trust's assets to duplicate the price performance of the Standard and Poor's 500 stock index through the screened Domini Social Index.

The minimum investment is $1000 and there is no sales charge. The trust charges a 0.08 percent management fee and a 0.05 percent 12 b–1 fee. The total operating expenses are 0.75 percent. The trust is managed by an eight-member board of trustees, including three women and one minority. Tim Smith, executive director of ICCR and a trustee, is also on the advisory board of both Working Assets and the Calvert Social Investment Fund. As of December 31, 1991, the trust had $3.6 million in assets.

The promotional literature is attractive and designed to appeal to the socially conscious investor. "Investing for Good" is a service mark used by the Domini Social Investment Trust. The promotional brochure for the trust reads: "Thousands of starfish had washed ashore. A little girl began throwing them in the water so they wouldn't die. 'Don't bother, Dear,' her mother said, 'it won't really make any difference.' The girl stopped for a moment and looked at the starfish in her hand. 'It will make a difference to this one.' "

Total return for the first half of 1991 was 16.73 percent.[17] Total return for 1991 was 37.84 percent.

The Domini Social Investment Trust has Amy Domini's popular name and reputation as the author of *Ethical Investing* and her very capable marketing skills. The trust also has the advantage of professional management and the research skills of Peter Kinder and Steven Lydenberg, two of the best social researchers in the business.

The Domini Trust also has a wide open market for those social investors that look on indexing as the most inexpensive way to at least match the performance of the stock market. Domini is also hoping to team up with Sophia Collier and offer the trust to Working Assets shareholders. The only problem is whether or not Kinder, Lydenberg, and Domini can convince the social investment community that its social criteria will not be sacrificed for index performance. Look for this trust to gain acceptance, respect, and credibility as social investing continues to swell in popularity.

The Parnassus Fund

In 1984, Jerome L. Dodson resigned as president and CEO of Working Assets Management Company to try his hand at contrarian portfolio management. The contrarian philosophy of picking stocks is to look for undervalued and out-of-favor companies that are fundamentally sound but whose stock is selling at a depressed price.

Dodson also looks for companies that have enlightened and progressive management. He specifically keeps his eyes open for Renaissance factors, which he defines as:

1. The quality of the company's products and services;
2. The degree to which the company is marketing-oriented and stays close to the customer;
3. The sensitivity of the company to the community where it operates;
4. The company's treatment of its employees; and
5. The company's ability to innovate and respond well to change.[18]

The Parnassus Fund excludes companies that manufacture alcohol or tobacco products or are involved with gambling. The fund also screens out weapons contractors, firms with operations in South Africa, and companies that generate electricity from nuclear power. Additional positive social factors that Parnassus considers include a company's "good environmental protection policy, an effective equal employment protection policy, an effective equal employment opportunity policy, a record of civic commitment and a history of ethical business dealings."[19]

Dodson started Parnassus on a shoestring budget, not taking a salary for several years. To cut down on expenses he even served as his own transfer agent, which is rare in the mutual fund business. He has a small staff but employs numerous university interns.

As of December 31, 1991, Parnassus had invested over 95 percent of its portfolio in stocks, with the remainder in short-term CDs and a Margaux Inc. convertible debenture. Assets as of December 31, 1991, were $31.8 million, up from $20.7 million at the end of 1990.

Parnassus Fund Performance			
Date	**Return**	**Date**	**Return**
1985	18.5%	1989	2.8
1986	2.5	1990	−22.0
1987	−6.8	1991	51.89
1988	42.4		

The board of trustees for Parnassus includes one woman, who is also a minority, on a three-member board.

The portfolio has included Margaux, Tandem Computers, Raymond Corporation, Mentor Graphics, Inland Steel, Hewlett-Packard, Digital Equipment, Cummins Engine, Baxter International, ASK Computer, and Xerox Corporation. The minimum investment is $2000, and there is a sales charge of 3.5 percent. The fund charges an 0.86 percent management fee and has a total operating expense of 1.77 percent.

Jerry Dodson receives high marks for his candid quarterly and annual reports and his letters to shareholders. His business acumen and start-up experience in the responsible investment community are unequaled.

Dodson's new challenge as a manager will be to continue his contrarian approach at Parnassus while opening up three traditional portfolios as part of the Parnassus Income Fund: a balanced portfolio, a fixed-income portfolio, and a California tax-free portfolio.

The balanced portfolio will be invested in stocks and bonds, will charge a 3.5 percent load and a management fee of 0.75 percent, and will have a total operating expense of 1.25 percent.

The fixed-income portfolio will invest in government agency securities and corporate bonds; it will charge a 3.5 percent load, a management fee of 0.50 percent, and a total operating expense of 1.00 percent.

The California tax-free portfolio will invest in socially responsible California tax-free municipal bonds, and will charge a 3.5 percent load, a management fee of 0.50 percent, and a total operating expense of 1.00 percent.

In the case of both the Balanced Portfolio and the Fixed-Income Portfolio, up to 10 percent of each portfolio may be invested in community development loan funds. The social policy of the Parnassus Income Fund will be to select portfolio companies that treat employees fairly, provide sound environmental protection, provide good equal employment opportunity, provide quality products and services, have a sensitivity to the communities where they operate; and have ethical business practices.

According to the Parnassus Income Fund SEC filing, the trustees are to include Dodson's friends and colleagues Joan Shapiro from Chicago's South Shore Bank and Howard Shapiro, a Social Investment Forum Board member from Portland, Oregon. The new California Tax-Exempt Portfolio will compete head-to-head with Kieschnick's Muir Trust.

Jerry Dodson has been a very active member of the Social Investment Forum and a director since its inception. The Parnassus Fund does not vote its shares at annual corporate shareholders meetings and has yet to introduce a shareholder resolution.

Dodson's portfolio management and research skills are very good. He runs a tight ship at Parnassus and should be able to make money if his investors in the Parnassus Fund don't bail out for safer funds in the family or go elsewhere.

Jerry's marketing material and public relations are the best on the West Coast. Kieschnick's Muir California Investment Trust will have a very tough time against Dodson's marketing acumen. The big question for Jerry will remain his rollercoaster performance history at Parnassus and whether or not he can reduce performance volatility, hold his original investors, and increase fixed-income fund assets now that interest rates are low.

Schield Progressive Environmental Fund

In February 1990 the Progressive Environmental Fund (PEF) was born, thanks to the success of both the environmental movement and Glenn Cutler, the fund's advisor.

Cutler, up until February 1992 the portfolio manager for PEF and the author of *Market Mania* (an investment advisory newsletter), believes that the 1990s will be an unprecedented decade of global environmental expenditures because of the growing public and political demand for legislation and regulation to provide solutions to environmental problems.

Glenn Cutler combined his environmental stock picking ability with PAM's ability to screen companies from a social and environmental standpoint. The fund is a nondiversified environmental sector fund that invests in emerging growth companies for maximum capital growth.

The investment advisor for PEF is Schield Management Company, administer and distributor of the fund. Schield is owned by Marshall L. Schield, its president. In early 1992 Schield and Cutler had a falling out, and Schield took over as portfolio manager.

Progressive Environmental has retained PAM, a full-service, Oakland-based brokerage firm, to screen social and environmental investments.

The fund's minimum investment is $1000. It is a low-load fund with a 4.5 percent sales charge, a management fee of 0.94 percent and a 12 b–1 fee of 0.95 percent. Total operating expenses are 2.50 percent making it one of the most expensive of the responsible investment funds. As of December 31, 1991, assets totaled $3.8 million. No women or minorities are included on PEF's five-member board of trustees.

Progressive Environmental Fund Performance	
Date	**Return**
1990	4.1%*
1991	−1.97

*Partial year

The portfolio of PEF includes the following companies: Advatex Associates, Allwaste, American Waste Services, Applied Extrusion Tech, CRSS, Inc., Farr Company, Groundwater Tech., Harding Associates, ICF International, Kimmins Environmental Services, Martech USA,

Midwesco Filter Resources, Plants for Tomorrow, Sanifill, US Filter, Valley Systems, and Wahlco Environmental Systems.[20]

Cutler had extremely good performance numbers when the fund was launched in 1990, and it was the top mutual fund in the second quarter of 1990. Unfortunately, his performance has slipped somewhat since then, and with Schield taking over portfolio management duties, it's anybody's guess how the fund will perform. If small environmental service companies do well, however, this fund's performance could improve despite its past difficulties.

Merrill Lynch Eco·Logical Trust

The creation of the Merrill Lynch Eco·Logical Trust 1990 and its opening on Earth Day 1990 is a success story for both Stan Craig of Merrill Lynch's defined investment department and Peter Camejo, president and CEO of PAM. It also was the first strong positive investment response from Wall Street to the Exxon Valdez oil spill and the on-going threat to our environment.

A few weeks after the spill, Merrill Lynch sent its brokers a confidential investment alert, suggesting that there were "investment opportunities in pollution control."

"The huge oil spill in Alaska's Prince William Sound may prove to be more than an ecological disaster," the report stated. "It could prove to be the factor that galvanizes public opinion behind calls for far-reaching, coherent government action to alter the way industries deal with the environment . . . increase efforts to protect the environment and provide opportunities for investors."

The report urged brokers to promote the stocks of leading pollution control firms like Browning-Ferris and Waste Management, Inc. "We think the long-term operating outlook for the pollution-control industry is becoming increasingly positive," the report noted.

Shortly afterward, Merrill Lynch established a "unit investment trust which focuses on the environmental sector." It was called the Clean Technical Trust.

In early 1990 the *San Francisco Bay Guardian* asked PAM to evaluate mutual funds that were being offered to the public as environmental. The study, released in March 1990, identified only two of six mutual funds as screening out environmental polluters: the New Alternatives Fund and the Progressive Environmental Fund. Those funds marketing themselves as environmental but actually investing in major polluters included the Fidelity Select Environmental Fund, the Freedom Environmental Fund, the SFT Environmental Awareness Fund, and Merrill Lynch's Clean Technical Trust.

In the fall of 1989 Peter Camejo contacted Bob Basso and Joe Sturdivant, who were in charge of PAM's clearing operations at Merrill Lynch's Broadcort Capital Corp. (They are now with Paine Webber's clearing firm, Correspondent Services.) They put him in touch with Stan Craig at Merrill Lynch. Peter told Stan of his concerns that Merrill's Clean Technical Trust would be perceived by the public as proenvironmental when it was actually investing in some of the worst polluters. Stan, an environmentalist, was upset and asked Peter to fly to New York and meet with him to discuss the matter.

Camejo and Craig met at Merrill Lynch in New York in October. Out of that meeting came the concept for the Eco·Logical Trust. Merrill Lynch not only decided to create a new environmentally and socially screened unit trust but broke new ground by selecting an outside firm, PAM, to screen the trust and by making a commitment to donate a portion of the profits to a national environmental coalition. This was a first for Merrill Lynch on both counts. Progressive Asset Management coordinated the screening of the Eco·Logical Trust along with the Oakland-based Data Center, CEP, and Cambridge-based KLD. A portion of the trust's profits are donated to the Environmental Federation of America's One Fund for the Environment, which supports the programs of 27 national environmental organizations.

Because Eco·Logical is a unit investment trust (UIT), the portfolio, once selected, remains the same and is supervised but not actively managed. Capital appreciation over five years is the goal.

Companies selected for the Eco·Logical Trust include:

1. Allwaste
2. Ametek, Inc.
3. Apple Computer, Inc.
4. Atlanta Gas Light Co.
5. Baldor Electric Co.
6. Bay State Gas Co.
7. Brooklyn Union Gas Co.
9. Burlington Resources, Inc.
10. Calgon Carbon Corp.
11. Chambers Development Co. Inc. Cl. A
12. Citizens Utilities Co. Cl. A
13. Consolidated Natural Gas Co.
14. Corning, Inc.

15. Diversified Energies, Inc.
16. Ecology & Environment, Inc.
17. Equitable Resources, Inc.
18. Groundwater Technology, Inc.
19. Gundle Environmental Systems, Inc.
20. Idaho Power Co.
21. Jacobs Engineering Group, Inc.
22. Metcalf & Eddy Companies, Inc.
23. NICOR, Inc.
24. Peoples Energy Corp.
26. Rubbermaid, Inc.
27. Stewart & Stevenson Services, Inc.
28. WalMart Stores, Inc.
29. Washington Energy Co.

When the trust was initially offered, there was a 4 percent sales charge. The shares of the trust trade on the secondary market and can be purchased and sold the same way stocks can be purchased and sold. Transaction costs will vary depending upon brokerage firm commissions.

According to Merrill Lynch, the Eco·Logical Trust was the second top-performing Merrill Lynch UIT in 1991, increasing in value 31.6 percent.

Working Assets Money Fund

The nine-year history of Working Assets exemplifies the struggle, the conflict, and the tremendous success of socially responsible investing in America. Working Assets was created in 1982 and 1983, a time when banks and savings and loans were being deregulated and were able to offer competitive returns to money market funds. Socially responsible investing was neither proven nor respected in the financial community.

Totally independent of the creation of Silby and Guffey's Calvert Social Funds on the East Coast, several people on the West Coast organized Working Assets. In June 1982, after I had resigned from the Sacramento Investment Board and moved to Napa, California, I received a call from Jerry Dodson, whom I had met when we were members of the governor's public investment task force. I had appointed Jerry to chair the small business committee of the Task Force. Now that we had completed the task force's final report, Jerry and I were both looking for a new project. I had recently joined Drexel Burnham Lambert to manage union and church pension funds, but a move to Los Angeles had been delayed. Jerry convinced me to stay in Northern California and help him organize a socially responsible investment business.

Dodson, who had recently served as president of Continental Savings and Loan in San Francisco, initially brought together six people in the Bay Area to write a business plan and raise capital. One of the first ideas was a bank or venture fund, but those were rejected because of the capital required, California's regulatory restrictions, and risk. We also wanted to create a national financial entity. We believed that the investing public would feel more comfortable investing in a safe, socially screened money market fund than a more risky venture fund or bank.

The six people Jerry organized in San Francisco included his colleague, the founder and president of the Solar Center, Peter Barnes. Together they created a Solar T-Bill, which was a six-month money market certificate, the proceeds of which were used to retrofit rental units with solar panels. Dodson raised about $3 million from about 150 investors in eight months.

Michael Kieschnick and Julia Parzen, his colleague in the California governor's office of economic policy, were also recruited by Dodson, as was David Kim, president of Landtech Development Company (a San Francisco housing developer), and David Olsen, a progressive Bay Area business person and activist (David left to start another business before Working Assets was created). Drummond Pike, a leader in the San Francisco progressive foundation community, was also asked to join Dodson's original team. Pike is presently manager of the Threshold Foundation and founder and president of the San Francisco Tides Foundation, which makes grants to economic, peace, and environmental concerns.

I brought in my state capital colleague, Brian Hatch, from Sacramento. I had met Brian in 1975. He was a lobbyist for the California Federated Firefighters and a well-respected advocate for corporate responsibility. He was instrumental in convincing the California legislature to adopt a policy to encourage local governments to vote their pension-owned stock proxies in a more responsible manner. Today he is a well-respected and powerful voice for firefighters throughout California.

Originally we wanted to call the money fund Working Capital, but the name had already been taken by a bank, so we decided on Working Assets. Other names that we considered were Bottom-Line Plus and Market Rate Plus.

I was to handle institutional marketing, so most of our first business plan reflected my own institutional marketing biases, focusing on labor, pension funds, churches, progressive nonprofit groups, and foundations. Since I had chaired the governor's task force and had the most socially responsible investing experience, I had the greatest influence on the setting of our investment criteria and the selection of our first board of advisors.

It took us over a year to write a business plan and raise over $700,000 to capitalize the management company, which was organized as a limited partnership and a Massachusetts business trust. In September 1983 the fund was opened to investors with $100,000 in assets; by 1988 assets had increased to over $75 million. As of December 31, 1991, assets totaled $236.8 million.

Jerry Dodson was the first president and CEO of Working Assets. The staff included Julia Parzen, Carmen Wyllie, Keith Goodlett, and me. The first registered representatives of the company were Gail Work and Duncan Meaney. In mid-1984 Jerry resigned as president to open the Parnassus Fund. I then took over as president and served until January 1986, while Julia Parzen was CEO.

From 1986 to 1991 Working Assets went through many internal disputes and changes. A new president, Malon Wilkus, was hired on a split vote by the board of directors—only to resign nine months later following his unsuccessful attempt to merge Working Assets with his company, American Capital Strategies, a employee leveraged buy-out and investment banking firm. Several new Working Assets Management Company shareholders and directors were also added, including Frank Tsai, Beth Rosales, and Katie Deamer. In late 1987, primarily because of personality differences on the board of directors, the board voted to split into two separate companies: Working Assets Management Company, responsible for continuing to manage the assets of Working Assets Money Fund, and Working Assets Funding Service, responsible for marketing donation-linked credit cards, long-distance telephone, travel, and other services to help fund progressive social change organizations.

In August 1990 Frank Tsai, who had taken over as president of Working Assets Management Company following the resignation of Wilkus, was removed by the board of directors on a divided vote after he refused to resign. Jerry Dodson then took over as acting president and CEO until Mitch Rofsky was hired as president in mid-1991. In late October 1991 the shareholders of Working Assets Money Fund gave final approval to the sale of Working Assets Management Company to a group of investors led by Sophia Collier, an entrepreneur from the East Coast.

In a relatively short amount of time, Working Assets grew rapidly into the country's largest socially responsible money market fund. It has been the most outspoken national advocate of responsible investing and has articulated its point of view in the most outwardly political manner. Its social investment criteria are the most comprehensive of any responsible investment mutual fund and are both exclusionary and inclusionary.

Working Assets avoids investments in alcohol-, tobacco-, and gambling-related businesses, nuclear power, and weapons manufacturing. It will not knowingly invest in any companies that discriminate on the basis of race, religion, age, disability, or sexual orientation or that violate regulations of the EEOC. Working Assets also does not invest in companies that violate regulations of the National Labor Relations Board, appear on the national AFL–CIO "do not patronize" list, or have a record, according to the AFL–CIO, of hiring union-busting consultants. It also avoids transnational companies that have fewer than half of their employees in the United States unless a majority of their eligible U.S. employees are represented by organized labor.

In addition, Working Assets does not invest in corporations that consistently violate EPA or OSHA regulations. Investments are prohibited in companies that violate Section 8 of the Export Administration Act of 1979 (Arab boycott of Israel), and the money market firm does not invest in Eurodollar instruments that drain capital from productive use in the United States. Treasury securities are also avoided since they "are used primarily to finance a federal deficit caused in part by wasteful defense spending."[21] South African investing is prohibited, as is investing in corporations "that have a substantial presence in or are part of a strategic industry in a foreign nation controlled by a repressive regime (e.g. the Republic of South Africa) or which finance such a repressive regime."[22] Other than South Africa, repressive regimes have never been defined or identified.

Working Assets purchases securities that create jobs and develop the U.S. economy (rather than those that rearrange existing assets through mergers and acquisitions) and invest in financial institutions that reinvest deposits in their local communities. Emphasis is placed on investing in housing, education, family farms, and small business. Working Assets invests in companies involved in alternative energy, companies that have a positive impact on the environment, and companies that are creative and generous in their community charitable contributions.

Working Assets Money Fund yields are slightly below average money market yields because of a high expense ratio. As of December

31, 1991 assets totaled $236.8 million. Almost 69 percent of assets were invested in corporate commercial paper, 13 percent in U.S. government agencies, almost 4 percent in Small Business Administration variable rate notes, and 12 percent in Bankers Acceptances. A variable rate note was held in the Farmers Home Administration and a CD in South Shore Bank.

Corporate debt securities held in the fund include Kern River Co-generation, General Mills, Consolidated Natural Gas, The Limited, Inc., McGraw-Hill, Pitney Bowes, The Times Mirror, Toys 'R' Us, and Dillard Investment Company. The ten-member board of trustees includes six women and four minorities.

The minimum investment in Working Assets is $1000. It is a no-load fund and has a management fee of ½ of 1 percent and a 12 b–1 fee of .22 percent. Total operating expenses are 1.05 percent.[23]

Working Assets is the most progressive voice on the West Coast for socially responsible investing. It has involved itself in pro-active social investing on issues such as South African divestment, labor, the environment, and defense conversion. The company has a very politically active board of advisors, and its research team is the best on the West Coast.

The new owners of Working Assets will probably move the headquarters to New Hampshire but retain an office in San Francisco. They have expanded the board of trustees to include more East Coast representation. Prior to the new owners taking over, the research staff was reduced, and Keith Goodlett left to join the Muir Trust. After the new owners arrived, several key staff members resigned, including founding senior staff member Carmen Wyllie. A founding trustee also announced her resignation. Rumor has it that the research functions and bookkeeping will shift to the East Coast, with research possibly being supplemented by KLD. The strong social investment criteria will remain, but political views and statements from the company will probably be moderated somewhat.

Working Assets has broad appeal on the West Coast and a good reputation among progressive investors across the country. Expect to see more mutual funds including a fixed-income, balanced, and equity fund from Working Assets, an institutional cash management program, and an energized national marketing campaign. The new 60 percent owner of Working Assets, Sophia Collier, will have a great deal to say about socially responsible investing in the future and will, hopefully, exert progressive national leadership.

CHAPTER NINE

The Future of Socially Responsible Investing

South Africa has not been removed from the agenda of responsible investors, but it no longer occupies center stage. As investors look ahead to the rest of the decade, South African criteria may well evolve from exclusionary to inclusionary, from negative to positive.

Following the overwhelming March 17, 1992 white vote to support continued reforms, I'm hopeful that the Afrikaner minority in South Africa will accept a transition to majority rule and will work with the ANC and other nonwhite organizations to totally eliminate apartheid. The responsible investment community will accept no less than majority rule in South Africa. When such change takes place, private sector and non-profit foundation investments will be made in South Africa that will lead to greater economic decentralization and strengthen community economic development. As ICCR's delegation reported in July 1991, much needs to be done to reconcile and reconstruct South African society and the economy.

Efforts are already underway to lure progressive capital into South Africa once majority rule is a reality. ICCR, the American Committee on Africa, the Fund for a Free South Africa, and many in the foundation community are already putting together economic development and job training programs to strengthen black urban and rural community economic development. Discussions are also underway between the Social Investment Forum members and private economic development organizations about the preparation of securities offerings and investment opportunities for investors to directly invest in the re-capitalization of a new South Africa. Pension fund managers and others that currently prohibit South African investments will, in the near future, be asked to invest in South Africa through investment vehicles that have a positive impact on South African society.

Environmental Investing

"I think the environment is clearly the issue of the nineties, and it's going to take more and more of ICCR's time, and it's exciting," said Tim Smith, ICCR's executive director.

"I'm hearing from the marketplace, and what I'm hearing is that the environment is and will be the main issue of the nineties," said Stan Sorrell, president and CEO of the Calvert Group.

"The overwhelming issue of the nineties is going to continue to be the environment. The real challenge for us is, can we institutionalize a code of conduct or criteria for corporate management?" asks Alice Tepper Marlin, founder and executive director of CEP.

"Environmental considerations will be the dominant force of the movement because it appears less political than it is," says John Schultz, president of the Social Investment Forum.

If a vote were taken within the responsible investment community on the most important issue concerning socially conscious investors, it would clearly be the environment. From ozone and rain forest depletion to the cost of cleaning up and disposing of nuclear and hazardous waste, the issues of the environment are overwhelming. According to the U.S. Department of Energy (DoE), over the next 20 years the cost of environmental restoration is estimated at $64 billion, waste management at $23 billion, and routine environmental regulatory compliance at $14 billion, for a total of $101 billion. The Department of Energy's five-year plan to clean up DoE facilities calls for federal expenditures of $34.7 billion. According to the NRDC, however, until the total number of hazardous waste sites can be identified, no upper limit of the total cost of clean-up can be estimated.

Environmentally related problems cannot be limited to hazardous and nuclear waste; they include air and water pollution, wildlife protection, and the threat to health and safety from pesticides, insecticides, herbicides, and other chemicals entering the ecosystem.

Wall Street has been slow to recognize the plight of the environment. It often looks at environmental problems only from the perspective of investing in companies that can take the utmost advantage of increased federal expenditures to clean up the environment. Initially less concern was voiced for recycling, conservation, and protection of the environment. In other words, from an environmental point of view, clean-up is important but prevention and conservation are even more important.

An Environmental Code of Conduct

The Valdez Principles

The corporate and investment communities can no longer ignore environmental conservation and protection issues. A new age of awareness was ushered in on September 7, 1989, with the introduction of the Valdez Principles.

The 10 Valdez Principles address the release of pollutants, the sustainable use of natural resources, reduction and disposal of waste, energy efficiency and conservation, and risk reduction to employees and surrounding communities. They also address the marketing of safe products and services, damage compensation, disclosure of potential hazards, the inclusion of an environmental representative on corporate boards of directors, and annual and independent corporate environmental audits.

The Valdez Principles were drafted by the combined efforts of some of the nation's leading environmental organizations, including the Sierra Club, the National Audubon Society, and the Social Investment Forum, under the committed leadership of Joan Bavaria, president of the FRDC, and CERES. Joan and Dennis Hayes, director of Earth Day 1990, serve as co-chairs. The Coalition for Environmentally Responsible Economics is a consortium of environmentalists and investors who played an important part in the original drafting of the Valdez Principles and who now oversee their implemetation. The name Valdez was chosen to evoke the disastrous oil spill by the Exxon Valdez oil tanker off the Alaskan coast in 1989.

The Valdez Principles were inspired in part by Rev. Sullivan's code of conduct for South Africa, but unlike the Sullivan Principles, the Valdez Principles were drafted by the responsible investment community and environmental advocates without participation by industry. Harrison J. Goldin, former comptroller of New York City, and Gray Davis, California state controller, said the code would be the basis of shareholder pressure on companies to improve their environmental performance. Members of SIF and CERES are convinced that the code can be used as another responsible investing criterion for company selection or rejection. Environmental groups immediately announced that they planned to use the information to praise corporate efforts they endorse and to focus negative publicity or even boycotts on companies with poor records.

THE VALDEZ PRINCIPLES

1. **Protection of the Biosphere**

   We will minimize and strive to eliminate the release of any pollutant that may cause environmental damage to the air, water, or earth or its inhabitants. We will safeguard habitats in rivers, lakes, wetlands, coastal zones and oceans and will minimize contributing to the greenhouse effect, depletion of the ozone layer, acid rain, or smog.

2. **Sustainable Use of Natural Resources**

   We will make sustainable use of renewable natural resources, such as water, soils and forests. We will conserve nonrenewable natural resources through efficient use and careful planning. We will protect wildlife habitat, open spaces and wilderness, while preserving biodiversity.

3. **Reduction and Disposal of Waste**

   We will minimize the creation of waste, especially hazardous waste, and wherever possible recycle materials. We will dispose of all wastes through safe and responsible methods.

4. **Wise Use of Energy**

   We will make every effort to use environmentally safe and sustainable energy sources to meet our needs. We will invest in improved energy efficiency of products we produce and sell.

5. **Risk Reduction**

   We will minimize the environmental, health and safety risks to our employees and the communities in which we operate by employing safe technologies and operating procedures and by being constantly prepared for emergencies.

6. **Marketing of Safe Products and Services**

   We will sell products or services that minimize adverse environmental impacts and that are safe as consumers commonly use them. We will inform consumers of the environmental impact of our products or services.

7. **Damage Compensation**

   We will take responsibility for any harm we cause to the environment by making every effort to fully restore the environment and to compensate those persons who are adversely affected.

8. **Disclosure**

   We will disclose to our employees and to the public incidents relating to our operations that cause environmental harm or pose health or safety hazards. We will disclose potential environmental, health or safety hazards posed by our operations, and we will not take any action against employees who report any condition that creates a danger to the environment or poses health and safety hazards.

9. **Environmental Directors and Managers**

   We will commit management resources to implement the Valdez Principles, to monitor and report upon our implementation efforts, and to sustain a process to ensure that the Board of Directors and Chief Executive Officer are kept informed of and are fully responsible for all environmental matters. We will establish a Committee of the Board of Directors with responsibility for environmental affairs. At least one member of the Board of Directors will be a person qualified to represent environmental interests to come before the company.

10. **Assessment and Annual Audit**

We will conduct and make public an annual self evaluation of our progress in implementing these Principles and in complying with applicable laws and regulations throughout our worldwide operations. We will work toward the timely creation of independent environmental audit procedures which we will complete annually and make available to the public.[1]

In 1991, 28 companies had signed the Valdez Principles. By March 1992 the number signing had increased to 36. In 1991, 52 shareholder resolutions were introduced that requested corporate management to sign the Valdez Principles or release substantially similar environmental corporate information to shareholders and the public.[2] Many of the Valdez shareholder resolutions were withdrawn when companies agreed to disclose environmental information or release environmental data. Many cities and states have introduced ordinances and legislation to pressure corporations to comply with a corporate environmental code of conduct. In California, the California Public Interest Research Group (CALPIRG), a Nader-sponsored public interest nonprofit organization, came very close to circulating a Valdez Initiative for the November 1990 statewide ballot. The reason CALPIRG decided not to proceed was due to an already crowded ballot and competing environmental measures—two competing timber preservation measures were on the ballot, as well as Big Green, an omnibus environmental initiative. All three measures were defeated.

Global Environmental Management Initiative

Industry has not been slow in responding to the Valdez Principles. Business Roundtable initiated a study in late 1989 to assess corporate environmental needs. In responding to environmentalists, the industry group developed a corporate environmental code called the Global Environmental Management Initiative (GEMI). According to George Carpenter, director of environmental energy and safety for Proctor & Gamble and chairman of GEMI, "GEMI's distinction is that it was formed by environmental professionals within the business community according to their hands-on experience in environmental management issues. Critical to GEMI is the vision of how such an organization—and how business as a whole—can work to improve corporate performance on a global scale." The GEMI mission is to "foster environmental excellence by business worldwide."[3]

GEMI is the corporate answer to the Valdez Principles, the same way the adoption of the Sullivan Principles was the corporate answer to the divestment campaign.

Tim Smith, executive director of ICCR, is, however, optimistic about GEMI:

> I think the good thing is that we don't have to throw these out and say they are absolutely worthless. The companies are talking about global environmental responsibilities and it's very important. At the same time, whether or not this is an adequate set of principles is another question, and we'll keep on pushing for more public accountability.

International Chamber of Commerce

The Business Roundtable and GEMI are also being supported by efforts of the International Chamber of Commerce (ICC), which met in Rotterdam in April 1991 to launch its own 16-point, nonbinding Business Charter for Sustainable Development. More than 200 companies signed the nonbinding charter.

According to IRRC, ICC's principle on compliance and reporting is worded to give companies broad discretion in determining what environmental information is appropriate for disclosure to boards of directors, shareholders, employees, government authorities, and the public.[4] Jack Doyle, an analyst with Friends of the Earth and a CERES boardmember, questioned the significance of signing a nonbinding, unmonitored statement of intentions:

> There may be signatures [to the ICC code], but where is the environmental bottom line? We really think a more neutral third party disclosure process is needed, and that is what the Valdez Principles offers. While we're flattered by the imitation, we hope that companies will realize that nonbinding codes sponsored by trade associations are not the real thing and cannot satisfy the public. You can have eight principles or 16, but the real thing is the Valdez Principles.[5]

Individual companies and the chemical industry are responding directly to the Valdez Principles in an effort to deflect its political influence. Although it has rejected Valdez, Waste Management, Inc., already under intense pressure from environmentalists, approved an expanded environmental policy on March 7, 1990. In April 1990 the Chemical Manufacturers Association also released their Guiding Principles.

Environmental Hype

The year 1990 was certainly characterized by environmental hype. "Environmental" mutual funds were popping up left and right. It was so confusing that the *San Francisco Bay Guardian* requested PAM to conduct a study of all the green funds. In the resulting report, investigative reporter Lew Tremaine and PAM broker Tom Van Dyck identified those environmental mutual funds that screened out major polluters and those environmental funds that did not.[6] According to the *Bay Guardian:*

> One of the reports from the Environmental Protection Agency (EPA) and numerous state regulators, as well as reports from several major newspapers and environmental groups showed how the two biggest waste haulers in the United States, Browning-Ferris Industries (the company dropped out of the hazardous-waste business in 1990) and Waste Management, Inc., left a trail of dirty air, poisoned water, scarred lands and angry communities.[7]

Freedom Environmental Fund

The PAM study pinpointed Waste Management and Browning-Ferris because some of the mutual funds that were being sold by brokers as "social" and "environmental" included such companies. One such fund was John Hancock's Freedom Environmental Fund. Peter Camejo, president of PAM, said, "I'm fed up with investment firms that are trying to cash in on the environmental movement and not really caring."[8] Camejo sent letters to the Securities and Exchange Commission (SEC) charging that the Hancock fund was misleading the public by advertising that investors "could make a positive contribution toward cleaning up the Earth" while investing in companies with poor pollution-control records.[9] According to PAM, Waste Management "has been cited for pollution more than 600 times by the U.S. Environmental Protection Agency."[10]

Freedom Environmental Fund portfolio manager David Beckwith responded. "There are no pristine companies," he said, insisting that Waste Management was part of the solution instead of the problem. "They run the cleanest landfill dumps in the business and have received a lot of violations because they're easy to target."[11]

Waste Management has 80 lawyers and 22 Washington staffers who lobby for favorable legislation related to garbage and hazardous waste. The $19 billion company is not afraid of paying large fines. In 1988 the EPA charged Waste Management with failure to monitor emissions and other violations and fined it a record $3.75 million. Waste Management "wrote the check out without blinking an eye," the EPA official said.[12]

In May 1990 John Danello of the Freedom Capital Management Corporation was so upset with the negative publicity their Freedom Environmental Fund was receiving that he fired off a letter to John Schultz, president of SIF, in which he attacked PAM for claiming that the SEC was conducting an investigation of the Freedom Environmental Fund. Danello was referring to a complaint filed with the SEC by an investor, Ruth Dyke of Auburn, California, who had invested $15,000 in the Freedom Environmental Fund because her broker had sold her the fund as socially and environmentally responsible. Dyke wrote the fund on February 28, 1990, asking for her money back and complaining about misrepresentation:

> I am left with the impression that you want to appear as though you are concerned about our environment so that people like myself will invest in your fund. But in reality you will invest in any company in certain industrial sectors, regardless of their environmental record. . . . The fact is that your advertising is misleading and your prospectus clearly states an orientation that you are not following.

Because she received no response, Ruth Dyke also filed a complaint with the SEC, which regulates the nation's stock exchanges and brokers. Her complaint alleged that the fund fraudently presented itself as an investment opportunity that would be limited to environmentally responsible companies.[13]

Peter Camejo responded to Danello's charge; he wrote a letter to Schultz, saying:

> Part of our debate with the Freedom Environmental Fund has been with regard to its assertion that Waste Management's business practices are good for the environment. The Environmental Grant Maker's Association recently voted to disqualify Waste Management, Inc. from making donations to its efforts. According to the April 17, 1990 Chronicle of Philanthropy Report (page 6), Waste Management, Inc. ". . . has engaged in a pattern of abusive corporate conduct involving repeated violations of criminal and civil law." In addition, Waste Management, Inc. was chosen by the Multinational Monitor of December 1989 as one of the ten worse companies for 1989. Waste Management ended 1989 with major convictions for price fixing and 96 EPA location citations pending. No respected group, individual or firm in the SRI community recommends Waste Management, Inc. It is an oddity that Mr. David Beckwith's fund materials titles itself as "socially responsible" given that he has become the most public defender of Waste Management, Inc.[14]

"Environmental" Funds

The controversy over environmental hype has been productive in that public and investor attention is now focusing on the companies that are actually in the portfolio and on environmental fund performance. In 1990, for example, three funds screened to avoid major polluters were the top three of the environmental funds. In 1991 most of the environmentally screened funds, with the exception of Progressive Environmental, out-performed nonscreened environmental funds. Only Kemper Environmental performed as well as the environmentally screened mutual funds.

Mutual Funds	1990	1991
Progressive Environmental★	1.6%	−1.9%
Eco·Logical Trust (Merrill Lynch UIT)★	0.1	31.6
Global Environmental★	0.1	24.1
Fidelity Select Environmental	−4.2	7.6
Oppenheimer Global Environmental	−5.0	−2.5
New Alternatives★	−10.7	25.6
Freedom Environmental	−11.8	8.3
Alliance Global	−12.2	5.9
Kemper Environmental	−13.4	24.1
Enviro-Tech 1 (Merrill Lynch UIT)	−14.7	20.3
Enviro-Tech 2 (Merrill Lynch UIT)	−18.2	15.2
Standard & Poor's 500	−7.0	26.3

Note: Performance figures do not include dividends.
★ Funds that screen out major polluters.

The controversy over green funds led to the creation of three new funds: Merrill Lynch's Eco·Logical Trust, Schield's Progressive Environmental Fund, and the Global Environment Fund.

Global Environment Fund

Global Environment is a California limited partnership founded in 1989. This fund is available only for high-net worth individuals and institutions; for that reason, it is not publicly traded and not in Chapter 8. It was founded by two committed environmentalists: Jeff Leonard, the fund's president, and John Earhart, chairman of the board.

Global Environment Fund charges a fee of 1 percent to its limited partnership for portfolio management. The allocation of its assets in mid-1991 included 18 percent private placement, 35 percent New York and American Stock Exchange equities, 19 percent international securities, and 28 percent over-the-counter traded securities. It is a balanced fund in that 31 percent of the public securities portion of the portfolio is in fixed-income securities (mostly convertible bonds) and 50 percent is in stocks.[15] The market value of Global Environment as of December 31, 1991 was $23.6 million.

Convertible bonds include Ben & Jerry's Ice Cream, CML Corporation, Environmental Systems, Lyonnaise Des Eaux, Northwest Natural Gas, and Ogden Corporation. Stocks include American Water Works, Body Shop PLC, Betz Labs, Eastern Enterprises, Norit, SafetyKleen, and Wahlco. Private placements include IRRC participating note, Aurora Flight Sciences, Buzzworm Inc., and Hambrecht and Quist Environmental Fund.[16] Global Environment has offices in Laguna Beach, California, and Washington, D.C.

Progressive Asset Management's Environmental Screening

Progressive Asset Management acts as the Subadvisor for the Progressive Environmental Fund and initially screened stocks for Merrill Lynch's Eco·Logical Trust. PAM submitted a list of 100 companies to Merrill Lynch for the Eco·Logical Trust. Using its own financial criteria, Merrill pared the list down to 29 companies in which it would invest during the trust's five-year life.

Recently PAM signed a contract with the giant mutual fund and asset manager, California-based Franklin Funds, to environmentally screen companies along with KLD. Franklin's asset management department eagerly sought PAM's assistance when it was approached by two environmental organizations seeking environmentally and socially screened asset management services. PAM now provides environmental and social screen services to high-net-worth individual investors, institutions, and portfolio managers.

Green Mutual Funds

The Massachusetts Public Interest Research Group (MASSPIRG) and the Fund for Public Interest Research have formed a company, Green Century Capital Management, that will offer two no-load environmentally screened mutual funds, a money market fund and a balanced fund. According to *Responsive Investing News,* the Ralph Nader-oriented Public Interest Research Groups (PIRG) in Massachusetts, California, and New Jersey have pledged to invest in the Green mutual funds. The funds will screen out companies operating in South Africa and companies involved in nuclear power and the manufacture of nuclear weapons.[17] Mindy Lubber, president of the new venture, said she hopes it will be profitable within five years since the funds will have to attract $100 million to break even.[18]

Everybody is Green

No financial institution can do enough for the environment. Mutual funds such as Progressive Environmental and Eco·Logical Trust donate a portion of their marketing costs or profits to the Environmental Federation of America (which also operates under the trade name Earth Share). In September 1990 the mutual fund giant, Fidelity Investments, encouraged its clients to contribute funds to the Smithsonian Institution Rainforest Project. This financing concept was first proposed by internationally known conservationist Tom Lovejoy, the Smithsonian's assistant secretary for external affairs. Fidelity client donations are used for debt-for-nature swaps by allowing the Smithsonian to buy small amounts of the foreign debt owed by Latin American countries. The debt is canceled in exchange for an investment in local currency in a host country's conservation and research efforts. Among the projects considered are expanding a national park and wildlife refuge, protecting 1 million acres of park lands, and reforestation and agroforestry programs in buffer zones of existing park lands.[19] Fidelity contributed to the Smithsonian's overhead costs so that 100 percent of contributions would go directly into the program. In early 1991 Fidelity announced that 2,000 of its customers had donated $110,000 to the project.[20]

Small companies are also attempting to widely publicize their commitment to the environment. I recently received an invitation to an open house of 3 Com Corporation (a Santa Clara, California company) to view their new manufacturing process, which represented the company's "commitment to support global efforts to reduce depletion of the earth's ozone layer." The corporation is the world's largest manufacturer of Ethernet adapter boards. According to 3 Com Corporation:

> Our new adapter board manufacturing process represents an investment of more than a half million dollars to support recommendations of the Montreal Protocol on Substances that Deplete the Ozone Layer. We have created a more environmentally sound manufacturing facility by replacing the freon-based solution normally used in printed circuit assembly

with a cleaning solution of water and Axarel, a chemical developed by DuPont Electronics. The Environmental Protection Agency recently named Axarel as one of the chemicals meeting requirements specified in the Montreal Protocol.[21]

First Environmental Bank

The offering of stock of the First Environmental Bank (based in Portsmouth, New Hampshire) began in the spring of 1991 and initially raised $10 million. This year it will begin lending to small and medium-sized companies involved in the restoration and conservation of the environment. Ron Reilly, the bank's founder and an investment banker who specializes in environmental companies, states "Small companies continue to suffer from a lack of capital and small environmental companies aren't faring any better."[22]

First Environmental is the first bank to focus exclusively on the environmental industry. The bank has the technical and environmental expertise to review and conduct due diligence of businesses in such areas as solid waste processing, water and waste water, air pollution control, hazardous waste processing, alternative energy, and new and emerging technologies. The bank intends to contribute up to 2 percent of its annual pretax profits to nonprofit environmental organizations.

Green Publications

Environmental publications and services are cropping up all over the world. The monthly *Green MarketAlert,* published in Bethlehem, Connecticut, reports on corporate environmental initiatives, green consumer surveys, legal and regulatory developments, and market analysis. Published in Ontario, Canada, *EcoSource* is a monthly digest of current trends, ideas, statistics, and opinions on environmental issues, gathered from more than 40 major daily newspapers and 150 environment-related periodicals. The new Environment News Service, published in Vancouver, Canada, is the world's first exclusively environmental news agency, gathering news from a worldwide network of investigative journalists. By mid-1991 Environment News Service anchored an environmental news broadcast on EIS, a new satellite television channel.

An excellent environmental investing publication is *Environmental Investing News* (EIN), published monthly in Newton, Massachusetts. It provides subscribers with comprehensive financial and general information on environmental companies. *Environmental Investing News* also publishes performance information on environmental mutual funds. It has developed its own EIN Index that it provides to subscribers to use as a comparison for environmental mutual fund performance.

Both CEP and ICCR have initiated new environmental research publications. Corporate Environmental Data Clearinghouse, published by CEP presents a comprehensive environmental profile of each individual company, including an overview of the company's business, its environmental policy, lobbying and political issues related to the company's activities, products and consumer issues, environmental impact of the company's technologies or products, and legal and regulatory review relating to the company's activities.

In May 1991 IRRC initiated a new publication, *Investor's Environmental Report,* one component of IRRC's Environmental Information Service, which was developed to provide in-depth coverage of significant environmental issues. *Investor's Environmental Report* provides information about companies' initiatives and efforts in the environmental arena by exploring how companies are responding to environmental pressures and how all of these factors affect the companies' financial performance. In addition, IRRC offers company-by-company environmental profiles and book-length reports on key global environmental issues.

Are Environmental Organizations Investing Green?

As we enter the nineties, the environmental movement is at the top of most people's list of important concerns. The strongest advocates of the environment are nonprofit environmental organizations. How are they investing their money? Have they adopted social and environmental investment criteria similar to that developed by several mutual funds and portfolio managers? Are they on the cutting edge of the environmental investment movement?

To answer this question, I spoke to Kalman Stein, executive director of the Environmental Federation of America (EFA), which is based in Washington, D.C. A coalition of 27 national environmental organizations, EFA promotes public health and recreation by protecting clean air, water, wilderness, rivers, wildlife, and green spaces. Kal suggested that I survey his member organizations to see if they had developed social or environmental investment criteria.

Of the 27 members to which questionnaires were sent, 11 responded. Of those that responded, only two had developed general environmental or social investment criteria. No respondent had developed comprehensive written social or environmental investment criteria, but two organizations were "working on it." One organization responded that it avoided over 100 companies in the S&P 500 in industries incompatible with the organization's mission statement, such as companies involved with energy, chemicals, minerals, or natural resources extraction. Another indicated that it didn't have enough money to carry out an investment program but did buy one share of stock in some major polluters in order to attend the annual shareholder meetings to protest corporate practices. Several indicated that they didn't have money to invest but used all funds for program-related purposes.

Several organizations stated that they only invested in money market funds, treasuries, and short-term securities, while one responded that it did not knowingly invest in companies engaging in activities deleterious to the environment. Another environmental group invested in short-term securities, including treasury notes, corporate commercial paper (Ford, GE, and IT&T), and corporate notes, including General Motors Acceptance Corp. and Ford. In a telephone conversation, one representative of an environmental board said that it was their policy not to respond.

Environmental Criteria

I discussed the results of my survey of EFA members with Kal Stein. He said:

> The difficulty with environmental investment criteria is the complex nature of environmental problems. No one at this point can identify a single perfect environmental product, much less an entirely perfect environmental company. Absolutes in this area don't exist, and what we have to work with are relative judgements. This same problem has made the environmental product certification programs quite difficult to implement.
>
> The problem of establishing environmental investment criteria is solvable, but it is going to take more time and sophisticated study until we are all comfortable with those criteria. We also know that the public is confused and quite interested in learning the answers.
>
> We can say confidently that environmental products and services will continue to expand over the next decade and present investment opportunities. The problems won't just go away, and the companies that develop tangible and responsible solutions will be big winners for their investors.

I've often heard the saying, "While some things change a lot, some things never change." This is certainly the case with responsible investing. In early 1971, when I began investigating how major institutions invested their funds, I was startled to find out that large church organizations invested in defense and weapons contractors. That has changed over the past 20 years. Now you would have to look very hard to find a church investing in weapons, defense, alcohol, tobacco, or the gambling industry. Most church organizations refuse to invest in South Africa. Many have developed comprehensive social investment criteria.

In the early seventies into the eighties, I discovered that many organizations involved in health and safety, such as the American Medical Association and the American Cancer Society, invested in companies that produced or manufactured products that were diametrically opposed to the health and safety mission of the organizations. This has also changed, largely in part to the consciousness raised by the SRI movement over the past two and a half decades.

In 1978 Randy Barber's *The North Will Rise Again* woke up organized labor to the fact that their members' pension funds were not being invested to exclusively benefit them. In fact, these monies were often invested by portfolio managers in such a manner as to actually destroy their economic base and the viability of their pension plan.

Environmental organizations are now where the churches were 20 years ago. It is not surprising that they are only now beginning to develop environmental criteria. Environmental criteria are not simple or straightforward either from an exclusionary or inclusionary standpoint. A major environmental organization that responded indicated that its one sentence policy, adopted in June 1990, had not yet been implemented because after four meetings they were still not able to develop guidelines in a manner satisfactory to the board, finance, and investment committees.

In regard to South Africa, objective data is available from a variety of sources, allowing the portfolio manager to simply exclude companies from the portfolio. This is the reason so many large institutional investors, after carefully reviewing performance studies, divested. The policy was easy, straightforward, and simple to implement. Many portfolio managers even created South Africa-free indexes or composites weighted to the S&P 500 to match index performance.

Environmental investing, however, must be both exclusionary and inclusionary. Investors may wish to avoid major polluters, but they also must search out companies benefiting from expanded government clean-up programs as well as companies that are on the leading edge of recycling, conservation, and alternative energy. This is necessarily a labor-intensive process, but no less important than it was regarding South Africa.

Environmental investing is a process that will evolve as part of the SRI movement. Some environmental criteria have already been included in responsible investment criteria implemented by several mutual funds and many portfolio managers, brokers, and financial planners.

The Hawaiian Case

In September 1991 I was asked to fly to Honolulu to meet the Hawai'i Lā'ieikawai Association Inc., an environmental and native Hawaiian cultural foundation, to help the board draft a socially responsible and environmentally sound policy statement. After meeting with the board and its executive director for many hours, I was impressed not only with their commitment to adopt strong environmental criteria but also with their commitment to setting aside a portion of the foundation's portfolio for Hawaiian program related investments (PRIs). Program related investments are popular with several large foundations on the East Coast and in the Midwest, particularly with Ford and the MacArthur Foundations. Basically, PRIs allow nonprofit organizations to set aside assets to invest for high social impact programs that meet foundation program goals. Such investments may mean higher risk, lower returns, limited liquidity, or all three.

In the case of the Hawai'i Lā'ieikawai Association, the responsible investment criteria includes the following:

> The Foundation's purposes are to protect and preserve the natural environment and enhance Hawaiian cultural development. The Foundation recognizes that all investment decisions have economic, social and often political impacts upon society. To ensure that the Foundation's assets are invested consistent with its environmental objectives, the following policy is hereby established:
>
> Assets of the Foundation shall not be invested in companies that have violated regulations of the U.S. Environmental Protection Agency (EPA), or any environmental regulations of appropriate state and local government environmental regulatory agencies. Funds shall not be invested in companies that have been found to degrade or harm the natural environment and the ecosystem or in any way engage in activities deleterious to the environment. Investment in companies specifically engaged in the production of nuclear power is prohibited.
>
> The Foundation's approach to environmentally responsible investing is to be positive. In this regard the Foundation will seek to invest in companies engaged in activities protecting the biosphere, enhancing the sustainable use of natural resources, reducing and disposing of all forms of waste, companies engaged in the wise use of energy, marketing safe products and services, reducing or minimizing environmental, health and safety risks and restoring the environment and compensating

those persons who are adversely affected by any environmental damage caused by a corporate activity. The Foundation will endeavor to invest in companies that have a clear and concise commitment to the environment evidenced by action as well as policy, paying particular attention to those corporations signing and endorsing the Valdez Principles, fully disclosing environmental information, establishing environmental committees of the Board of Directors, appointing members of the corporation's Board of Directors qualified to represent environmental interests and to those companies conducting and publicizing annual environmental audits made by independent outside sources.

The Foundation will also vote its stock proxies or assign voting power to its portfolio manager to vote shares consistent with the environmental goals and objectives of the organization. The Foundation may also introduce or co-sponsor shareholder resolutions consistent with the environmental and Hawaiian cultural objectives of the Foundation.

The Board of Directors may set aside up to 3 percent of the assets of the Foundation for high social impact, program related investments with preference given to Hawaiian-based business entities or cooperative enterprises, profit or nonprofit. Such high social impact investments shall be made consistent with the objectives of protecting and preserving the natural environment and/or enhancing Hawaiian cultural values. Such investments may involve a high degree of risk, less than market-rate returns and the lack of liquidity in a secondary market.

The Future

In 1980 I drafted legislation to create a California Home Loan Program so that public employees in the state could utilize their pension fund for below-market home mortgages. In a public hearing before the Assembly Public Employees and Retirement Committee, the chairman of the committee looked at me and said, "If it ain't broke, don't fix it." That attitude still haunts me. It is reactionary and unquestionably destroys innovation and vision.

In the case of the environment, for example, we cannot wait until it "breaks," or it will be too late. Our environment is in desperate need of repair *now*. It can't be replaced— it's the only one we have. By investing our money with social and environmental criteria, by being responsible consumers, and by forcing our politicians to do what's right, we may have a chance to save our planet.

Investors are presently being given a chance to change the direction of our economy and society. A potpourri of mutual funds and investment vehicles representing various levels of risk, return, and liquidity are available. These social investments meet different social goals and offer varying degrees of positive social impact. You can now create a personal investment portfolio that enables you to not only feel good about how you're investing, but to do good with your investment.

Environmentally screened funds are proving to be competitive performers. Progressive Environmental Fund was up 36.44 percent for the 12 months ending March 31, 1991, to gain nineteenth place overall on Lipper Analytical's Top 25 Mutual Fund Performers.[23] In that period of time the S&P 500 was up 14.4 percent. For 1990 and 1991, three out of four environmentally screened mutual funds outperformed the nonscreened environmental funds. In 1990 three out of four outperformed the S&P 500 and in 1991, Merrill Lynch's Eco·Logical Trust outperformed the S&P 500. This performance, however, doesn't mean environmentally or socially screened portfolios are always going to outperform nonscreened portfolios. Remember that past performance is no guarantee of future performance.

The performance of socially responsible mutual fund portfolio managers show conclusively that you can do just as well with socially responsible investing as with traditional investing. In fact, in many instances you can do better. If you compare nuclear versus non-nuclear investments, defense versus nondefense company investments, or investments in South Africa versus those that are South Africa–free, you find that the responsible choice also pays as well as—or even better than—the traditional approach.

Remember, however, that financial performance alone is only part of the equation. In the long run, much will depend on the economy as a whole and whether or not we are successful in redirecting capital toward a more politically and economically just society and the protection of the environment of our planet. Companies that take care of their employees, the environment, and the community—as well as producing safe quality products—are tough competitors for those that don't. Such companies will be less likely to run afoul of the law, regulations, and the courts, therefore reducing costs. These companies also have a competitive advantage when it comes to negotiating with unions, working with community and environmental organizations and government, and meeting health, safety, and environmental standards.

Return on your portfolio includes social performance as well as financial performance. You have to be concerned with both. Social and financial performance is interactive, just as an investor is also a consumer, a voter, and a taxpayer. These roles are interactive; each one of them has a direct impact on society, the economy, and the environment. The economic and political issues affecting society also affect a corporation's bottom line. The activity of a corporation will certainly have a tremendous impact on our local and global community. We truly are what we eat, consume, and invest.

Controversial social issues will continue to be raised at annual shareholder meetings. Shareholders, activists, and community groups will focus on corporate charitable contributions, compensation for women and minorities, employee advancement, child care, and other family and workplace issues.

Women's organizations will become more active shareholders, attempt to break the glass ceiling, and demand upward mobility, more women in high-level management positions, and more women on corporate boards of directors.

Responsible mutual funds will break new ground by inserting prospectus language that requires pro-active investing and communication between fund managers and corporate management to advance women's and family issues. This will result in a more equitable work environment and lead to corporations paying serious attention to sexual harassment and similar workplace issues. It will also force corporate management to address gay and lesbian rights and develop guidelines for employee handbooks.

New mutual funds will be developed that advance feminism, environmental standards, global social investing, and domestic and Third World community economic development. Many existing responsible mutual funds will amend prospectus language and become more proactive investors, not only communicating with corporate management but actually participating in or organizing corporate campaigns to affect policy change. Sophisticated corporate campaigns coordinated by church, community, labor, shareholder, taxpayer, and environmental organizations will become the rule, not the exception. In 1992 Ray Rogers' Corporate Campaign, Inc. has been hired by Greenpeace and Fund for a Feminist Majority to cooridinate innovative national corporate campaigns. Increasingly the public realizes that the electoral process continues to produce corporate-purchased politicians whose only solution to any problem is to tax and to borrow.

America is concerned with health, safety, and a clean environment. Shareholder resolutions and more sophisticated corporate campaigns will be leveled against tobacco and alcoholic beverage companies. State and local governments will be urged to take action to restrict advertising of such products. Their employees' pension funds will be asked to vote against corporate management at annual shareholder meetings. Shareholders will urge divestment in an effort to force tobacco and alcohol companies to limit or eliminate advertising. If these products have been proven to adversely affect public health and safety, the companies may be forced to cease conducting business.

Just as companies compete against one another in the public relations arena to convince the public and their shareholders of their commitment to the environment, so too will politicians compete against one another to convince the public of their strong stand against polluters. Similarly, just as every two years Californians get treated to competing statewide ballot initiatives, so too will shareholders be faced with the competing environmental principles of Valdez, GEMI, and the ICC.

Increasingly the distinction between public and private sector issues will blur. Local, state, and federal politicians and bureaucrats, Democrats as well as Republicans, have preached "tax and borrow" to the saturation point. Taxpayers have reached their limit on their willingness to pay. Public interest groups and those organized to affect change in the public sector will therefore shift more and more to the private as well as the nonprofit sectors to affect social change. New coalitions will be built between the responsible investment community, churches, environmental organizations, labor, social activists, shareholders, and the public. Such shareholders will be dominated by the $3 trillion in pension fund assets and $1 trillion in mutual fund assets. The interest of the beneficiaries has already become the interest of the public. They are one and the same because they are all investors and consumers in the private sector.

Represented in part by their loose association in the Council for Institutional Investors, pension funds, by design or fact, will inevitably gravitate toward a more social orientation. Institutional investors will not give up on corporate governance issues. Council members will concentrate on management pay, fringe benefits, and issues considered financial. Beneficiaries of retirement plans and trustees will demand more corporate accountability.

Public sector pension funds already have proven themselves to be active players on social justice issues such as South Africa and the environment as well as instruments for economic change through targeted investing. Pension funds will need to deal with numerous shareholder issues but will also likely be faced with coordinated corporate campaign strategies involving various employee and retiree groups, taxpayer organizations, churches, and social activists—all representing pension fund beneficiaries. Investment targeting will continue, if not increase in scope, as much as for its political expediency as to protect the beneficiaries' economic base and the financial viability of pension funds.

Private sector pension funds and mutual funds in general have been slow to take a more active role on issues considered social, but that is changing. Mutual funds and portfolio managers have already started introducing shareholder resolutions. Responsible investing continues to increase in popularity, as witnessed by its rapid growth in assets over the last six years. Investors have awakened to their diminished ability to control political events and are beginning to exert economic and political influence by the acts of consuming and investing.

The power to control America's political and economic system will inevitably shift from the ballot box to the dollar. In reality, it already has. As citizens awaken to the fact that they have the potential to wield immense power by how they invest and what they consume, they will begin to use it. The power of money, both through investing and consuming, will influence corporate conduct and therefore national and international events. Politicians and political parties will become more irrelevant and will simply represent the financial special interests that pull their strings.

Milton Friedman was correct when he discovered the power employees had through their pension funds, but he didn't envision and certainly could not understand the tremendous power of socially responsible investing. Randy Barber discovered this power but was never able to sell it to organized labor: The concept was difficult to grasp, the timing was wrong, and the evolving legal questions about ERISA (Employee Retirement Income Security Act of 1974) and fiduciary responsibility proved frightening to labor pension fund trustees. Developing a strategy for pension fund capital has been time-consuming, expensive, and low on the list of priorities for labor leadership, especially when compared with more pressing issues.

I vividly remember trying in 1980 to convince convalescent home hospital workers in the San Joaquin Valley to negotiate for increased pension benefits when they were barely earning more than the hourly minimum wage. A defined contribution pension plan seemed esoteric to hourly paid workers who needed cash in their pockets. They couldn't conceive of their own retirement and a pension plan and certainly weren't excited about seeing more money taken out of their checks. Employee pension fund power would not even compute with them.

What has changed in America in the nineties is that socially responsible investing has become a $625 billion growth industry. It has even spread to Europe, Canada, Australia, and New Zealand. The political and economic decisions have shifted from the public to the private sector. In the United States, state and local governments and the federal government can barely support financing the public debt and cannot support the costs of infrastructure, much less cover the increasing demands for health care, welfare, and education. Government, like labor and large corporate business, has become more centralized—large and bureaucratic but much less powerful. The power and role of representative government and labor decrease while the concentration of power in the private sector increases. The only control the public really has is the ability to invest and purchase. Two-thirds of the gross national product is consumption. The private sector must have access to capital and a market to sell its goods and services. This is where you as an investor and consumer have the most strength and influence.

First and foremost, you as an individual investor must take control of your economic destiny and educate yourself about money and the power that investment capital has to change the world. Second, you need to decide whether to manage your own assets or select a socially responsible professional to assist you.

It's not enough to practice avoidance; you also have to become proactive. That may only mean voting your stock proxies, or it could mean introducing a corporate shareholder resolution. It could also mean actively investing in a mutual fund, an environmental company, a cooperative venture, a loan fund, or a social venture fund to have a positive economic and social impact on the world. It could even be as simple as selecting the right bank in your neighborhood.

Finally, you must make sure your investing or savings is consistent with your policy of charitable giving, your tax strategy, how you spend your money, and how you vote. It is all part of the same process; doing one without the other lessens your control of your own environment. It also means others make decisions not only for you, but for your children and grandchildren. You owe it to yourself and to future generations to do more.

A responsible investment agenda for institutional and individual investors is not only appropriate, it is necessary for economic democracy. It is long overdue in this country. Money is power and access. Responsible control of investment capital will determine the kind of society and environment in which we live. A more activist and responsible ownership or stewardship of corporate capital is required if stakeholders are to be adequately rewarded and society served. Pension beneficiaries and other shareholders have the same interests as the public and taxpayers. By the same token, you cannot separate your role as a voter, a consumer, a pension beneficiary, and an environmentalist.

State-of-the-art responsible investing allows you to invest in a variety of investment vehicles (including stocks, bonds, real estate, mutual funds, loan funds, community banks, and venture funds) to have both a direct and indirect positive social, economic, and environmental effect without sacrificing financial reward or return. The agenda for the nineties will require increased investor activism and social consciousness.

Investors influenced America's corporations and banks to disengage from South Africa. The Sullivan Principles had little influence on U.S. corporations in South Africa. U.S. companies did not exert progressive pressure on the South African government. As long as American capital and technology flowed into the country, the white minority was able to resist change, militarily repress the majority nonwhite population, and diversify and strengthen its apartheid economy. The minute the capital was turned off and the domestic political and economic situation worsened, the government began to lose its grip. The ultimate power was, is, and will continue to be capital or money.

This same force can be brought to bear on social, economic, environmental, and political issues in this country. It cannot be accomplished overnight and perhaps not in this decade, but certainly in a generation. Cat Stevens sang a song that asked, "Oh very young, what will you leave us this time?"[24] We can leave our children a world that is environmentally safe and free of war, hunger, and oppression. We can do it peacefully, without firing a shot, throwing a rock, or even refusing to pay our taxes.

All you have to do is take control of your life and invest your money wisely and responsibly. You won't lose any money doing it. In fact, there's a good chance that you will make more money than those that don't do it. As a socially conscious investor, you can indeed change the world.

DIRECTORY OF FINANCIAL TERMS

bear market   A period of declining stock market prices.

beta   A measure of a stock's volatility; how the stock moves in relation to the market as a whole.

blue chip stock   Securities of major companies known nationally for a continuous record of earnings, dividend payments, and price stability.

bond   An interest or noninterest bearing note issued by a corporation, government, government agency, or other entity.

book value   As applied to an asset, the amount at which it is carried on a company's balance sheet. As applied to a company, the amount of stockholder equity, less all debts and liabilities, expressed either on a per-share or total basis.

building a book   The process of a stockbroker adding individuals to his or her book of clients. This book includes name, address, telephone numbers, and financial and trading history of the client.

bull market   A period of advancing stock market prices.

capital   Investment in a company for the purpose of conducting business; normally composed of a mix of debt, preferred and common stock, and retained earnings.

capital asset   An asset that is not bought and sold in the normal course of business and that has a useful life longer than one year.

capital gain (loss)   The difference between the sale price and purchase price of a capital asset or security.

certificate of deposit   A negotiable form of time deposit on which a bank or savings institution pays principal and interest at a stated maturity date.

Chapter 7 bankruptcy   This act of the 1978 Bankruptcy Reform Act deals with liquidation, provides for a court-appointed interim trustee with broad powers and discretion to make management changes, arrange unsecured financing, and generally operates the debtor business in such a way as to prevent loss.

Chapter 11 bankruptcy   This act deals with reorganization and provides that, unless the court rules otherwise, the debtor remains in possession of the business and in control of its operation.

cold calling   A telephone sales solicitation method normally used by brokers to contact prospective clients using a listing of professional association memberships or other computer-printed listings.

commercial paper   Short-term, negotiable, unsecured promissory note issued in relatively large denominations by business concerns. It represents a major short-term investment competing with certificates of deposit, short-term bonds, and the like.

common stock   Securities issued by a corporation that have lowest priority claim to the corporation's assets but share directly in its profits and usually carry voting rights.

credit union   A federally chartered, nonprofit savings and lending institution owned by its member-depositors. Credit unions are organized within and limited to a specific group of people, such as residents of the same county, employees at the same company, and so on.

debt security   Security representing money borrowed that must be repaid and having a fixed amount, a specific maturity, and usually a specific rate of interest or an original purchase discount.

default   The failure of a debtor to make timely payments of interest and/or principal as they come due or to meet some other provision of a bond indenture.

dividend   A payment, either in cash or stock, to the holders of a company's stock. Dividends on preferred stock may be fixed, while dividends on common stock often vary with the company's success.

Donoghue's Money Fund Average   An average of all major money-market fund yields, published weekly for 7- and 30-day yields.

Dow-Jones Industrial Average   A composite average of 30 industrial stocks chosen by Dow-Jones as representative of stock market activity. Composite averages are also computed for transportation and utility stocks and are used to evaluate market trends.

due diligence   A review, research, and evaluation process to determine the quality of information pertaining to an investment offering, including the validity of any market assumptions.

earnings per share (EPS)   The amount a company earns (usually after tax) per share of common stock.

effective annual interest rate   The total amount, expressed as a percentage, that one dollar will earn in one year. The effective annual interest rate is used in calculating interest payments, as in the case where interest is earned and compounded at intervals during the year.

equity   The net worth of a business, found by subtracting liabilities from assets.

fair market value   A price in a competitive market that would induce a willing seller to sell and a willing buyer to buy.

fiduciary   One who holds something or acts in trust for another.

futures   Contracts that require delivery of a commodity of specified quality and quantity at a specified price on a specified date.

general partnership   A partnership in which all partners are responsible, both individually and as a group, for debts and other liabilities of the partnership. General partners have equal power to make commitments on behalf of the partnership, and creditors may collect from partnership assets or the personal assets of any individual partner to offset their claims.

gentrification   Describes the changes communities experience when people of a higher socio-economic status move into a neighborhood or community, rehabilitate existing structures, and force the exodus of the original population.

glamour stocks   Stocks attracting large investor interest. They usually sell at a high price earnings ratio in anticipation of continued or dramatic earnings growth.

growth stock   The stock of a corporation that has, over time, advanced in price at a rate greater than the overall market average and/or has an expectation of an above-average advance over a prolonged period.

hedge   A strategy used to offset investment risk.

interest   Money paid in return for the use of borrowed money.

investment   The purchase of some form of security with the expectation of achieving some relative gain. The form of investment will usually meet a specific objective such as growth, income, speculation, or preservation of capital.

Investment Company Act of 1940   Congressional legislation enacted to regulate investment companies and mutual funds, including SEC registration.

investment grade   A bond with a superior rating of AAA to BBB.

investment vehicles   Investments of all types, including stocks, bonds, commodities, options, real estate, private ventures, partnerships, and so forth.

liability   Any debt or obligation of a company.

limited partner   A member of a partnership who gives up an active role in management and obtains l.mited legal liability for the actions of the management.

limited partnership   An organization made up of a general partner who manages projects and limited partners who invest money but have limited liability, are not involved in day-to-day management, and usually cannot lose more than their capital contribution.

line of credit   An approved level of credit. It is often obtained in anticipation of a seasonal or short-term need of funds or the desire to have an ensured source of funds for unexpected financial needs. Banks may charge a nominal fee for extending the credit line and usually subject it to the condition that there be no material changes in the company's financial status.

liquid assets   Any asset that can readily be converted into cash.

liquidity   The extent to which an asset can be converted into cash without significant loss.

margin calls   A demand for a client to put up money or securities when a purchase is made in a margin account.

market correction   A reverse movement, usually downward, in the price of an individual stock, bond, commodity, or index, or of the market in general.

market value   The price at which something is currently being sold in the market, or the price a company could obtain for an asset it owns.

money market fund   A mutual fund consisting mainly of short-term fixed obligations. Such a fund usually yields a dividend return higher than that offered by commercial banks or savings and loans, yet still allows the investor a high degree of liquidity.

municipal bond   A bond issued by state or governmental subdivision, such as city, town, county, or the like. Although interest rates on municipals are generally low, the interest is usually exempt from income tax, thus making them attractive to investors in high income brackets. The payment of principal and/or interest on municipals may or may not be backed by the issuer's taxation powers.

NASD   The National Association of Securities Dealers is a nonprofit organization formed to comply with the federal Maloney Act. The

Maloney Act was to standardize practices in the securities industry, establish high moral and ethical standards relative to securities trading, and enforce fair and equitable rules of trading.

NASDAQ   The National Association of Securities Dealers Automated Quotation system provides price quotations for securities.

over-the-counter   Stocks traditionally those of smaller companies that do not meet the listing requirements of the New York Stock Exchange or the American Stock Exchange. These OTC stocks are traded through a system of multiple trading by many dealers, which some companies prefer over the centralized trading approach of the New York Stock Exchange.

payout ratio   The percentage of a firm's profits that is paid out to shareholders in the form of dividends.

pink sheets   A daily publication of the National Quotation Bureau that details the bid and ask prices of thousands of OTC stocks.

preferred stock   Generally entitles owner to dividends at a fixed rate that takes preference to payment on common stock. In addition, preferential claim is usually granted with respect to the distribution of assets upon liquidation.

prime rate   The interest rate that commercial banks charge on loans to their most credit-worthy customers.

principal   Face value of original amount on a loan or other such investment. Also the owner or operator of a business who is a party to a contract or agreement, or one who employs another as an agent.

probate   An often costly court certification of a will.

profit-taking   The selling of securities to realize gains.

rate of return   The annual percentage of invested capital that is returned to the investor over and above the amount invested. There are various types of rates of return (such as simple, average, etc.) that are employed depending on the amounts and timing of the associated cash flows and the level of analytical sophistication desired.

SEC   The Securities and Exchange Commission is a federal agency created by the Securities Exchange Act of 1934. The SEC's main purpose is to protect the investing public against malpractice in the securities markets.

secondary market   Markets where securities are bought and sold subsequent to original issuance, which took place in the primary market.

sinking fund Money accumulated on a regular basis in a separate custodial account that is normally used to redeem or retire debt.

Standard & Poor's Index (S&P 500) A broad-based measurement of changes in stock market conditions, based on the average performance of 500 widely held common stocks.

stock option The option to buy or sell a specific number of shares of a stock at a specified price within a specified period of time. Listed options (puts and calls) offer the speculative investor limited risk with the possibility of substantial capital gains.

stocks/equities The ownership of a corporation represented by shares that are a claim to the corporation's earnings and assets.

stock split Declaration by the issuing company whereby shares are divided. It is sometimes used to lower the market price of a stock into a range attractive to more investors. A reverse split can also take place—for example, 1 for 5—to reduce the overall number of shares.

tax-exempt bond See *municipal bond*.

Tax Reform Act of 1986 A landmark federal legislation that made comprehensive changes in the system of U.S. taxation. It affected both businesses and individuals.

trust A formal agreement by which a person or organization holds title to property and administers it and its income according to the terms established by the trust.

trustee A person or organization appointed to manage and execute a trust. A trustee has fiduciary responsibilities for the powers and duties granted under the trust agreement. Such powers and duties may range from those of a mere overseer to those of a manager of an operating business.

venture capital Equity capital invested or available for investment in new or early-stage companies that have potential for significant growth, usually confined to privately held companies. Venture capital may be supplied by corporations, institutions, wealthy families, groups of individuals, and the like.

yield (current) The effective annual rate of return on an investment.

yield (to maturity) The rate of return expressed in the percentage that will be obtained on an investment if that investment is held to maturity. Yield to maturity may be higher or lower than current yield or coupon yield.

DIRECTORY OF RESPONSIBLE INVESTING

Books

The Best Companies for Women, Baiala Zeitz and Lorraine Dusky (Simon & Schuster, New York, 1988).

The Better World Investment Guide. Council on Economic Priorities (Prentice Hall Press, New York, 1991).

Childhood's Future, Richard Louv (Houghton-Mifflin, Boston, 1990).

Ethical Investing, Amy Domini and Peter Kinder (Addison-Wesley, Reading, MA, 1986).

The Ethical Investor, John Simon, Charles Powers, and Jon Gunnemann (Yale University Press, New Haven, CT, 1972).

Everybody's Business, Milton Moskowitz, Robert Levering, and Michael Katz (Doubleday, New York, 1990).

The Field of Social Investment, Severyn T. Brwyn (Cambridge University Press, Cambridge, 1987).

The Global Marketplace, Milton Moskowitz (Macmillan, New York, 1987).

Good Money, Ritchie P. Lowry (W W Norton & Co., New York, 1991).

Hazardous Waste in America, Samuel Epstein (Sierra Club Books, San Francisco, 1982).

The 100 Best Companies to Work for in America, Milton Moskowitz, Robert Levering, and Michael Katz (Doubleday, New York, 1988).

Investing with a Social Conscience, Elizabeth Judd (Pharos Books, New York, 1990).

Lobbying the Corporation: Citizen Challenges to Business Authority, David Vogel (Basic Books, New York, 1978). *Ms. Money Book,* Emily Card, Ph.D. (E P Dutton, New York, 1990).

Ms. Money Book, Emily Card, Ph.D. (E P Dutton, New York, 1990).

The North Will Rise Again: Pensions, Politics and Power in the 1980s, Jeremy Rifkin and Randy Barber (Beacon Press, Boston, 1978).

People/Profits: The Ethics of Investment, Charles W. Powers (Council on Religion and International Affairs, New York, 1972).

Rating America's Corporate Conscience, Council on Economic Priorities (Author, New York, 1987).

Shopping for a Better World, Council on Economic Priorities (Author, New York, 1990).

Socially Responsible Investing, Alan J. Miller, (New York Institute of Finance, 1991).

Socially Responsible Investment: The Impact of Socially Screened Investment in the 1990s, Allen Miller (Financial Times Management Reports, London, 1991).

Social Responsibility and Investments, Charles W. Powers (Abingdon Press, Nashville, TN, 1971).

The Thoughtful Christian's Guide to Investing, Gary Moore (Zondervan Publishing, Grand Rapids, MI, 1990).

The Unseen Revolution, Peter E. Drucker (Harper & Row, New York, 1976).

Warm Hearts and Cold Cash, Marcia Millman (Free Press, New York, 1991).

Newsletters/Magazines

Building Economic Alternatives
Co-op America
2100 M Street, NW,
Suite 20036
Washington, DC 20036
(800-424-COOP)

Business and the Environment
Cutter Information Corp.
37 Broadway
Arlington, MA 02174-5539

Business Ethics Magazine
Mavis Publications
1107 Hazeltine Blvd., Suite 530
Chaska, MN 55318-1035

Business and Society Review
870 7th Avenue
New York, NY 10019
(212-977-7936)

CEP Newsletter
Council on Economic Priorities
30 Irving Place
New York, NY 10003
(212-420-1133)

Clean Yield
The Clean Yield
224 State Street
Portsmouth, NH 03801
(603-436-0820)

Conscious Consumer
New Consumer Institute
P.O. Box 51
Wauconda, IL 60004
(708-526-0522)

The Corporate Examiner
Interfaith Center on Corporate
Responsibility (ICCR)
475 Riverside Dr., Room 566
New York, NY 10115
(212-870-2936)

Defense Monitor
Center for Defense Information
1500 Massachusetts Ave., NW
Washington, DC 20005
(202-862-0700)

EcoSource
Box 1270
Guelpf, Ontario
Canada, N1H6N6
(519-763-8888)

The EGG (An Eco-justice
Quarterly)
Eco-justice Project and Network
Anabel Taylor Hall
Cornell University
Ithaca, NY 14853
(607-255-9240)

Environmental Action
6930 Carroll Ave. #600
Tacoma Park, MD 20912
(301-891-1100)

Environmental Investing News
Robert Mitchell Assoc.
2 Cannon St.
Newton, MA 02161
(617-244-7819)

Environmental News Service
3505 West 15th Ave.
Vancouver, BC V6R 2Z3
Canada (604-732-4000)

The Ethical Investor
The Ethical Investment
Research Service
4.01 Bondway Business Centre
71 Bondway
London SW8 1SQ (71-735-1351)

FORUM
Social Investment Forum (SIF)
430 First Avenue N
Minneapolis, MN 55401
(612-333-8338)

Foundation News
The Council on Foundations
1828 L Street, NW,
Suite 300
Washington, DC 20036
(202-466-6512)

The Good Investor
Vermont National Bank
Socially Responsible Banking
Fund
P.O. Box 804
Brattleboro, VT 05302
(800-544-7108)

*Good Money: The Newsletter for
Social Investing*
Center for Economic
Revitalization
Box 363
Worchester, VT 05682
(802-223-3911)

Green Market Alert
345 Wood Creek Rd.
Bethlehem, CT 06751
(203-266-7209)

INFORM
INFORM, Inc.
381 Park Avenue South #1201
New York, NY 10016
(212-689-4040)

Insight
Franklin Research and
Development Corp.
711 Atlantic Avenue,
5th Floor
Boston, MA 02111
(617-423-6655)

Investor's Environmental Report
IRRC News for Investors
Investor Responsibility Research
Center (IRRC)
1755 Massachusetts Ave. N.W.,
Suite 600
Washington, DC 20036
(202-234-7500)

Labor and Investments
Industrial Union Dept.
AFL-CIO
815 16th Street, NW
Washington, DC 20006
(202-673-5000)

Multinational Monitor
P.O. Box 19405
Washington, DC 20036
(202-387-8030)

Pensions and Investments
740 N Rush St.
Chicago, IL 60611-2590
(312-649-5407)

The Proxy Monitor
Proxy Monitor, Inc.
61 Broadway,
Suite 1901
New York, NY 10006
(212-785-3450)

Responsive Investing News
1 Liberty Square, 12th Floor
Boston, MA 02109
(617-426-5450)

Social Investment Database
Kinder, Lydenberg, Domini &
Co., Inc.
7 Dana St.
Cambridge, MA 02138
(617-547-7479)

Socially Responsive Investor
600 Vine St.,
Suite 2000
Cincinnati, OH 45202
(800-654-5777)

USA Advocate
United Shareholders Association
1667 K Street, NW,
Suite 770
Washington, DC 20006
(202-393-4600)

Professional Associations

Bay Area Socially Responsible
Investment Professionals (BASRIP)
P.O. Box 26277
San Francisco, CA 94126-6277

Businesses for Social
Responsibility
2100 M Street NW
Suite 315
Washington, DC 20037
(202-467-5566)

Investors' Circle
Capital Missions Company
156 Whittington Course
St. Charles, IL 60174
(708-513-8384)

Long Island Social Investment
Forum
1325 Franklin Ave., Suite 250
Garden City, NY 11530
(516-663-1564)

Pacific Northwest Social
Investment Forum
P.O. Box 69625
Portland, OR 97201
(503-224-7828)

Social Investment Forum (SIF)
430 First Avenue N
Minneapolis, MN 55401
(612-333-8338)

Social Venture Network
1388 Sutter St. #1010
San Francisco, CA 94109
(415-971-4308)

Research Organizations

The Africa Fund
198 Broadway
New York, NY 10038
(212-962-1210)

American Committee on Africa
198 Broadway, Room 402
New York, NY 10038
(212-962-1210)

Animal Rights Front (ARF)
P.O. Box 3307
Yale Station
New Haven, CT 06520
(203-776-1928)

Northern California Interfaith
Committee on Corporate
Responsibility (CANICCOR)
220 Golden Gate Avenue, 9th Fl.
San Francisco, CA 94102
(415-885-5102)

Catalyst
250 Park Ave. South, 5th Floor
New York, NY 10003
(212-777-8900)

The Catalyst Group
139 Main St.
Brattleboro, VT 05301
(802-254-8144)

Center for Corporate Public
Involvement
1001 Pennsuylvania Ave. NW
Washington, DC 20004
(202-264-2425)

Center for Defense Information
1500 Massachusetts Ave., NW
Washington, DC 20005
(202-862-0700)

Citizens for a Better Environment
407 S. Dearborn #1775
Chicago, IL 60605
(312-939-1530)

Clergy and Laity Concerned
340 Mead Rd.
Decatur, GA 30030
(404-377-1983)

Coalition for Environmentally
Responsible Economies
(CERES)
711 Atlantic Ave.
Boston, MA 02111
(617-451-0927)

Community Information Exchange
1029 Vermont St. NW, #710
Washington, DC 20005
(202-628-2981)

The Conference Board
845 3rd Ave.
New York, NY 10022
(212-759-0900)

Co-op America
2100 M Street, NW,
Suite 20036
Washington, DC 20036
(800-424-COOP)

Corporate Data Exchange/Locker
Associates
225 Broadway #2625
New York, NY 10007
(212-962-2980)

Council for Community-based
Development
128 East 28th Street
New York, NY 10016

Council on Economic Priorities
30 Irving Place
New York, NY 10003
(212-420-1133)

The Data Center
464 19th Street
Oakland, CA 94612
(510-835-4692)

Eagle Eye Publishers, Inc.
1010 N. Glebe Rd., Suite 890
Arlington, VA 22201
(703-528-0680)

The Ethical Investment Research
Service (EIRIS)
4.01 Bondway Business Centre
71 Bondway
London SW8 1SQ
(71-735-1351)

The Environmental Federation of
America
3007 Tilden St., NW, Suite 4L
Washington, DC
(202-537-7100/800-875-3863)

The Environmental Defense Fund
1875 Connecticut Ave. NW, #1016
Washington, DC 20009
(202-387-3500)

Franklin Research and
Development
711 Atlantic Ave.
Boston, MA 02111
(617-423-6655)

The Funding Exchange
135 East 15th St.
New York, NY 10003
(212-529-5300)

INFACT
256 Hanover St.
Boston, MA 02113
(617-742-4583)

INFORM, Inc.
381 Park Avenue South, #1201
New York, NY 10016
(212-689-4040)

Institutional Shareholder Partners
3333 Water St. NW
Suite 220
Washington, DC 20007
(202-298-6612)

Institutional Shareholder Services
3333 K St. NW, Suite 400
Washington, DC 20007
(202-333-0339)

Interfaith Center on Corporate
Responsibility (ICCR)
475 Riverside Drive, Room 566
New York, NY 10115
(212-870-2936)

Investor Responsibility Research
Center (IRRC)
1755 Massachusetts Ave. N.W.,
Suite 600
Washington, DC 20036
(202-234-7500)

James Vitarello Development
Associates
P.O Box 21177
Washington, DC 20009
(202-332-4455)

National Audubon Society
950 Third Avenue
New York, NY 10022
(212-546-9100)

National Congress for Community
Economic Development
1875 Connecticut Ave. NW, #524
Washington, DC 20009
(202-234-5009)

National Organization for Women
1000 16th St. NW, Suite 700
Washington, DC 20036
(202-331-0066)

National Wildlife Federation
1400 16th St., NW
Washington, D.C. 20036-2266
(800-432-6564)

Natural Resources Defense Council
(NRDC)
40 West 20th St.
New York, NY 10011
(212-727-2700)

Nuclear Free America
325 E. 25th St
Baltimore, MD 21218
(410-235-3575)

People for the Ethical Treatment
of Animals (PETA)
P.O. Box 42516
Washington, DC 20015
(301-770-7444)

Providence Capital, Inc.
527 Madison Ave.
26th Floor
New York, NY 10022
(212-888-3200)

Proxy Monitor, Inc.
61 Broadway,
Suite 1901
New York, NY 10006
(212-785-3450)

Resource Center for Women and
Ministry in the South
P.O. Box 7725
Durham, NC 27708
(919-687-0408)

The Trust for Public Land
116 New Montgomery St.
4th Floor
San Francisco, CA 94105
(415-495-4014)

United Shareholders Association
1667 K Street, NW
Suite 770
Washington, DC 20006
(202-393-4600)

Portfolio Managers/Broker–Dealers

Affirmative Investments Group,
Inc.
129 South Street
Boston, MA 02111
(800-633-2747)

AFL-CIO Housing Investment
Trust
1700 Montgomery St., Suite 225
San Francisco, CA 94111-1079
(415-433-3044)

Christian Brothers Investment
Services, Inc.
675 Third Avenue, #3100
New York, NY 10017
(800-592-8890)

Clean Yield Asset Management
224 State Street
Portsmouth, NH 03801
(603-436-0820)

First Affirmative Financial
Network
1040 S. 8th St., #200
Colorado Springs, CO 80904
(800-422-7284)

Franklin Management Company
217 Lewis Wharf
Boston, MA 02110
(617-367-1270)

Franklin Research and
Development
711 Atlantic Avenue
Boston, MA 02111
(617-423-6655)

Gallegos Institutional Investors
Corp.
235 Montgomery St.,
Suite 600
San Francisco, CA 94104
(415-394-5885/800-347-8355)

Harrington Investments, Inc.
1001 Second St., Suite 325
Napa, CA 94558
(707-252-6166)

Kinder, Lydenberg, Domini &
Co., Inc.
7 Dana St.
Cambridge, MA 02138
(617-547-7479)

Progressive Asset Management
(PAM)
1814 Franklin Street,
7th Floor
Oakland, CA 94612
(510-834-3722/800-786-2998)

The Social Responsibility
Investment Group, Inc.
The Candler Building,
127 Peachtree Street, NE
Atlanta, GA 30303
(404-577-3635)

United States Trust Company
40 Court Street,
Boston, MA 02108
(617-726-7000)

Banks

Community Capital Bank
111 Livingston Street
Brooklyn, NY 11201
(718-802-1212)

Self-Help Credit Union
413 E. Chapel Hill St.
Durham, NC 27701
(800-476-7428)

South Shore Bank
7054 S. Jeffery Blvd.
Chicago, IL 60649
(312-288-1000)

Vermont National Bank Socially
Responsible Banking Fund
P.O. Box 804
Brattleboro, VT 05302
(802-257-7151)

Women's World Banking
8 W. 40th St., 10th Floor
New York, NY 10018
(212-768-8513)

Mutual Funds

Calvert Social Funds
4550 Montgomery
Bethesda, MD 20814
(800-368-2750)

Domini Social Index Trust
437 Madison Ave.
New York, NY 10022
(800-762-6814)

Dreyfus Third Century Fund
200 Park Avenue
New York, NY 10166
(212-922-6000)

Eco·Logical Trust 1990
Merrill Lynch Unit Investment
Trust
P.O. Box 9051
Princeton, NJ 08543-9051
(800-847-4160)

Muir Investment Trust
1 Sansome St., #810
San Francisco, CA 94104
(800-648-3448)

New Alternatives Fund
295 Northern Blvd.
Great Neck, NY 11021
(516-466-0808)

The Parnassus Fund
244 California St.
San Francisco, CA 94111
(415-362-3505)

PAX World Fund
224 State Street
Portsmouth, NH 03801
(603-431-8022)

Progressive Environmental Fund
390 Union Blvd.,
Suite 410
Denver, CO 80228
(303-985-9999/800-826-8154)

Working Assets Money Fund
230 California St.,
5th Floor
San Francisco, CA 94111
(415-989-3200)

Foundations

Appalachian Community Fund
517 Union Ave., #206
Knoxville, TN 37902
(615-523-5783)

Bread and Roses Community
Fund
924 Cherry St.
Philadelphia, PA 19107
(215-928-1880)

Chinook Fund
2412 W. 32nd Ave.
Denver, CO 80211
(303-455-6905)

The Council on Foundations
1828 L Street, NW
Washington, D.C. 20036
(202-466-6512)

Crossroads Fund
3411 W. Diversey #20
Chicago, IL 60647
(312-227-7676)

Ecumenical Development Corp.,
U.S.A.
155 N. Michigan St., Suite 627
Chicago, IL 60601
(312-938-0884)

Fund for Southern Communities
552 Hill St. SE
Atlanta, GA 30312
(404-577-3178)

Haymarket People's Fund
42 Seaverns Ave.
Jamaica Plain, MA 02130
(617-522-7676)

Headwaters Fund
122 W. Franklin Ave.
Minneapolis, MN 55404
(612-879-0602)

Liberty Hill Foundation
1320c Third St. Promenade
Santa Monica, CA 90401
(213-458-1450)

Live Oak Fund
P.O. Box 4601
Austin, TX 78765
(512-476-5714)

McKenzie River Gathering
Foundation
3558 SE Hawthorne
Portland, OR 97214
(503-233-0271)

Morning Star Foundation
403 Tenth St. SE
Washington, DC 20003
(202-547-5531)

Ms. Foundation for Women
141 5th Ave.
New York, NY 10010
(212-353-8580)

National Network of Women's
Funds
1821 University Ave., Suite 409 N
St. Paul, MN 55104
(612-641-0742)

North Star Fund
666 Broadway, #500
New York, NY 10012
(212-460-5511)

The People's Fund
1325 Nuuanu Ave.
Honolulu, HI 96817
(808-526-2441)

Threshold Foundation
1388 Sutter St., 10th Floor
San Francisco, CA 94109
(415-771-4308)

Tides Foundation
1388 Sutter St., 10th Floor
San Francisco, CA 94109
(415-771-4308)

The Vanguard Public Foundation
14 Precita Ave.
San Francisco, CA 94110
(415-285-2005)

Wisconsin Community Fund
122 State St., #508
Madison, WI 53703
(608-251-6834)

The Women's Foundation
3543 18th Street
San Francisco, CA 94110
(415-431-1290)

Venture Funds

Calvert Social Venture Partners
7201 Wisconsin Ave., Suite 310
Bethesda, MD 20814
(301-718-4272)

HFG Expansion Fund
Alterra Financial Group
1030 Massachusetts Ave.
Cambridge, MA 02138
(617-661-4852)

Sand County Securities
c/o Muir Investment Trust 326
1 Sansome St., Suite 810
San Francisco, CA 94104
(415–677–8500)

Loan Funds

ACCION International
130 Prospect St.
Cambridge, MA 02139
(617–492–4930)

ARABLE
715 Lincoln Ave.
Eugene, OR 97401
(503–485–7630)

Community Reinvestment Fund
821 Marquette Ave., #2400
Minneapolis, MN 55402
(612–338–3050)

The Global Fund for Women
2400 Sand Hill Rd.
Menlo Park, CA 94025–6941
(415–854–0420)

Institute for Community
Economics Revolving
Loan Fund
57 School St.
Springfield, MA 01105
(413–746–8660)

Lakota Fund
P.O. Box 340
Kyle, SD 57752
(605–455–2500)

National Association of
Community Development
Loan Funds
(NACLDF)
924 Cherry St.
Philadelphia, PA 19107–2405
(215–923–4754) (contact for a
comprehensive list of loan
funds)

Partners for the Common Good
8035 13th St., #1
Silver Springs, MD 20910
(310–565–0053)

Socially Responsible Films

Mother Lode Productions
305 Montford Ave., Suite 7
Mill Valley, CA 94941
(415–381–3573)

Pacific Film Fund
916 Kearny St., Suite 201
San Francisco, CA 94133
(415–398–1617)

NOTES

Chapter I

1. *People/Profits: The Ethics of Investment,* edited by Charles Powers, 1972, Council on Religion and International Affairs, p. 4.
2. *"Global Perspective,"* a publication of NH Enterprises, edited by Norm Berryessa, April 27, 1987, San Francisco, CA, p. 1.
3. *People/Profits,* p. 6.
4. "Social Responsibility Funds Beat Market . . . Finally." *Mutual Fund Forecaster,* January 11, 1991, Issue # 72, p. 5.
5. The American Medical Association (AMA) pension fund divested from stocks held in R.J. Reynolds and Philip Morris in September 1981.
6. "American Steel Jobs and South Africa: How U.S. Support for South Africa Affects Your Community . . . " Washington Office on Africa Educational Fund, September 1984, New York.
7. Charles W. Powers, *Social Responsibility and Investments,* (Abingdon Press, 1971), Nashville, TN, p. 15.
8. *Social Responsibility and Investments,* pp. 16–17.
9. American Report, May 5, 1972, American Friends Service Committee, Philadelphia, PA.
10. *The Better World Investment Guide,* Prentice Hall Press, New York, 1991, by the Council on Economic Priorities, p. 6.
11. *The Ethical Investor,* John G. Simon, Charles W. Powers, and Jon D. Gunnemann (Yale University Press: 1972), New Haven, CT, pp. 54–56.
12. Irwin L. Gubman, Secretary, Bank of America, letter to Senator John F. Dunlap, September 8, 1977, Sacramento, CA.
13. *Ibid.*
14. "Regents Connections Disclosed," *The California Aggie,* UC Davis, February 3, 1969, p. 7.
15. "South Africa on Campus," *El Gaucho,* UC Santa Barbara, October 24, 1969, p. 2.
16. Appendix B, Office of the Treasurer, September 12, 1973, University of California Regents, *Item For Discussion Regents Agenda.*
17. "The State of California and Southern Africa Racism: California's Economic Involvement With Firms Operating in Southern Africa," Assembly Office of Research, June 1972, Sacramento, CA.
18. Press release, Office of Assemblyman John Burton, State Capital, Sacramento, California, July 23, 1972.

19. Letter to California State Assemblyman Bill Lancaster, dated September 5, 1973, Sacramento, CA.
20. "World Council of Churches Divest," *The San Francisco Chronicle,* August 23, 1972, p. 13.
21. "Vote on 'Apartheid' Stocks," *The San Francisco Chronicle,* Sept. 27, 1972.
22. Rachel Richman, "Divestment: Legacy of Liberation," Africa Resource Center, Oakland, CA, 1990.
23. Carl Irving, "Apartheid Issue Hits UC," *The San Francisco Chronicle,* June 10, 1973, p. 1.
24. "South African Connection," Senate Select Committee on Investment Priorities and Objectives, California Legislature, Aug. 1977, Sacramento, CA.
25. Later I discovered that many large institutional investors and pension fund portfolio managers handled statements in the same way—it was a last priority and they'd only vote the proxies if they eventually got around to it. With a few exceptions, in those days most would "vote with management or sell."
26. Letter from Assemblyman John Dunlap to Stan Fowler, President of CALPERS, July 31, 1974, Sacramento, CA.
27. "Shareholder Voting Condemned," *Woodland Daily Democrat,* February 8, 1975, p. 23.
28. "UC Budget Reviewed," *Sacramento Bee,* April 30, 1975, p. C3.
29. "IRRC Launched," *New York Times,* December 14, 1972, p. 13.
30. Public Law 93-406, ERISA, 1974, Section 404.
31. "Pension Fund Investment Policy, 1979," Hearings before the Sub-Committee on Anti-Trust, Monopoly, and Business Rights, U.S. Senate Judiciary Committee, p. 5, Washington, DC.
32. Don Smart, "Investment Targeting: A Wisconsin Case Study," Wisconsin Center for Public Policy, 1979, Madison, WI.
33. "Up to $5.4 Billion Earmarked," *Responsible Investing News,* July 22, 1991, p. 1.
34. "In Brief...," *Responsible Investing News,* September 2, 1991, p. 5.
35. ULLICO Bulletin, January/February 1979, p. 1.
36. Joann Lublin, "Unions Step Up to Use of Pension Cash to Push 'Social Desirable' Projects." *Wall Street Journal,* July 23, 1980.
37. "Pensions: A Study of Benefit Fund Investment Policies," Industrial Union Department, AFL-CIO, June 1980, Washington, DC.
38. "Final Report," Governor's Public Investment Task Force, State of California, October 1981, pp. 55–56, Sacramento, CA.
39. "Scaife Buys McGoff's Half of Sacramento Union," p. 10, *San Francisco Chronicle Examiner,* July 21, 1979; "Publisher Says Attacks Are Unfair," p. 5, *San Francisco Chronicle Examiner,* March 18, 1980; and "Publisher Must Reveal Ties to Pretoria," *Sacramento Bee,* January 23, 1982. p. 10.
40. "South Africa Divestment Urged," *Sacramento Bee,* October 1, 1979, p. C1.

41. "Board Member Resigns," *Sacramento Union,* February 24, 1980, p. 1.
42. "Automating Apartheid: U.S. Computer Experts to South Africa and the Arms Embargo," NARMIC/American Friends Service Committee, 1982, Philadelphia, PA.
43. "Automating Apartheid," p. 15.
44. "Shareholders Vote on Proposals," Xerox Annual Meeting Report, 1982 p. 12.
45. "Xerox Sees Net Off," *Wall Street Journal,* May 21, 1982, p. 6.
46. Richard Knight, "Unified List of United States Companies Doing Business in South Africa," The Africa Fund, 1990, New York.
47. *The Corporate Examiner,* Vol. 20, No. 3, 1991, p. 5.
48. Letter to the author dated November 11, 1982 from Mary McCarthy, Ph.D., Vice President of Research, BERI, Hyattsville, Maryland.
49. Letter to the author dated June 20, 1985 from Dumisani Kumalo, Project Director, American Committee on Africa, New York.
50. Update, Vol. 9, No. 4, published by the Africa Policy Information Center, African American Institute, April 1985, p. 1.
51. Letter dated June 28, 1977 to Roy T. Brophy, Chairman, Board of Trustees, California State University and Colleges from Carl Noffke, Information Counselor, Embassy of South Africa, Washington, DC.
52. "Sullivan Code Author Calls for Divestment," *Daily Trojan,* University of Southern California, December 2, 1987.
53. "Summary Chart on Public Fund Divestment," American Committee on Africa, June 1985, New York.
54. "Perspective: College Actions as South African Investment," American Council on Education, Washington, DC, May 1985.
55. Survey of California State University and College Auxiliary Organizations, California State Senate Select Committee on Investment Priorities and Objectives, Sacramento, CA, January 1979.
56. "Oregon Shift on South Africa Investment Is Unlikely to Signal Start of Stampede," *Wall Street Journal.*
57. Oregon Prepares to Lift South Africa Sanctions," *Responsible Investing News,* July 22, 1991, p. 1.
58. *American Banker,* October 29, 1985, p. 40.
59. James White, "New York's Regan to Pensions: 'Hands Off'," *Wall Street Journal,* May 3, 1991, p. C1.
60. "Wilson and Pension Fund Dispute," *BusinessWeek,* July 1, 1991, p. 29.
61. "Proxy voting Results, Fiscal Year 1990/1991," CALPERS, Agenda Item 10, August 19, 1991, Sacramento, CA.
62. James White, "Giant California Pension Fund Softens Approach to Influencing Corporations," *Wall Street Journal,* October 7, 1991, p. B3.
63. James White, "Big Pension Fund Plans New Options for Its Participants," *Wall Street Journal,* November 1, 1989.

Chapter 2

1. *Final Report,* California Governor's Pulic Investment Task Force, October 1981, Sacramento, CA, Governor's Office of Planning and Research, p. 22.
2. "Consulting Services Review," Shearson Lehman Hutton, April 1989, pp. 1–2.
3. *Responsible Investing News,* September 2, 1991, p. 1.

Chapter 3

1. *Pension and Investment Age,* October 17, 1983, p. 12.
2. *The North Will Rise Again: Pensions, Politics and Power in the 1980's,* (Beacon Press, 1978), p. 226.
3. "Investing in Our Future: An AFL-CIO Guide to Pension Investment and Proxy Voting," AFL-CIO, May 1991.
4. *The North Will Rise Again,* p. 147.
5. *Ibid.,* p. 50.
6. *Wall Street Journal,* October 21, 1980, p. 3.
7. A. H. Raskin, *New York Times,* October 1, 1980, p. 6.
8. *American Corporations in South Africa,* United Church of Christ, 1991, New York, p. 6.
9. *IRRC News for Investors,* June 1991, Washington, DC, p. 10.

Chapter 4

1. John L. Levy, *Coping with Inherited Wealth,* Copyright 1990, J. L. Levy, June 1990, p. 7.
2. "1991–1992 Bay Area Financial Professionals Referral Directory," The Women's Foundation, San Francisco, 1991.
3. 1990 Annual Report, *Threshold Foundation* March 1991.
4. *Ibid.*

Chapter 5

1. John G. Simon, Charles W. Powers, and Jon P. Gunnemann, *The Ethical Investor,* pp. 15–64.
2. *The Corporate Examiner,* ICCR, Vol. 20, No. 3, 1991, p. 5.
3. The MacBride fair employment principles are named for their author, Sean MacBride, the founder of Amnesty International and winner of the 1974 Nobel Peace Prize. The principles, which apply to companies operating in Northern Ireland, include provisions for the recruitment and training of minority religious groups for advanced and supervisory positions, for layoff and recall procedures that "do not in practice favor" specific religious groups, and for offering minority employees adequate security during travel to and from work as well as on the job.

4. *The Ethical Investor,* p. 171.
5. *Insight,* Equity Brief, December 1990.
6. The Sullivan Principles were developed by the Rev. Leon Sullivan, a black minister who was elected to the General Motors board of directors due to the efforts of Campaign GM. His voluntary corporate principles were adopted by many U.S. companies in South Africa to eliminate apartheid by desegregating the workplace and paying equal pay for equal work. The principles were abandoned by Sullivan in 1987 when he called for total U.S. economic disengagement.
7. Working Assets Management Company briefing, "South African Criteria," January, 1991.
8. *Council on Economic Priorities Research Report,* April 1991.
9. Group Health Medical Associates, Tucson, AZ.
10. *The Better World Investment Guide,* CEP, pp. 275–278.
11. *Wall Street Journal,* May 21, 1991.
12. *San Francisco Chronicle,* May 21, 1991.
13. *News for Investors,* IRRC, Social Issues Service, June 1991, p. 6.
14. Tobacco Divestment Project, Project Overview, Boston, MA, August 12, 1991.
15. *Wall Street Journal,* January 30 and January 31, 1991.
16. *Ibid.*
17. California Public Utilities Commission, Table 2, Pacific Gas & Electric Co., Diablo Canyon Nuclear Power Plant Unit 1 and 2, Decommissioning Cost Summary, March 6, 1987, A.84-06-014, A.86-08-025 ALJ/ACP/FS.
18. *Wall Street Journal,* March 19, 1987, p. 6.
19. *News for Investors,* ICCR, June 1991.
20. The Humane Society of the United States, 2100 L Street, N.W., Washington, D.C. 20037 (telephone: 202-452-1100).
21. William L. Donnelly, Ph.D., and Cynthia A. Erber, private papers, Seattle, Washington, May 1988.
22. *Ibid,* p. 278.
23. *Socially Responsible Investing,* p. 247.
24. *News for Investors,* ICCR, June 1991, p. 8.
25. The Working Assets board of advisors includes representatives from several interest groups, including labor, the environmental movement, social investment research, the American Committee on Africa, ICCR, a cooperative business organization, and a mayor.
26. Working Assets Management Company briefing, "Proposed Animal Rights Criteria," January 1991.
27. *The Better World Investment Guide,* p. 223.
28. *Businessweek,* June 24, 1991, pp. 44–45.
29. *Prudential Securities Strategy Weekly,* April 17, 1991, pp. 13–16.
30. *Business Week,* August 19, 1991, pp. 29.
31. *Shopping for a Better World,* p. 19.

32. *The Better World Investment Guide,* p. 47.
33. "Responsible Investing News," Vol. 1, No. 5, June 24, 1991, p. 6.
34. Memo from the author, who was a member of the board at the time, to the Sacramento board of administration, investment and fisical management, January 21, 1980.
35. *Pension Funds and Ethical Investment: A Study of Investment Practices and Opportunities, State of California Retirement Systems,* CEP, 1980, pp. 62–63.
36. Working Assets Money Fund, *Prospectus,* November 1, 1991, p. 3.
37. Corporate Data Exchange, Inc., *CDE Handbook,* New York, 1979.
38. "Reform in South Africa: The American Angle," Edward M Kerschner, *Investment Policy,* PaineWebber, August 4, 1991, and "U.S. Firms Step Up Non-Equity Links to South Africa: IRRC," *Responsive Inverting News,* Vol. 1, No. 24, March 16, 1992.
39. *Ibid.*
40. *Ibid.*

Chapter 6

1. Richard Saul Wurman, Alan Siegel, and Kenneth M. Morris, New York: Access Press, 1990.
2. Beta, which was derived from what has been termed Modern Portfolio Theory, is a measurement of stock volatility. The Standard and Poor's 500 Stock Index represents a volatility of 1.0, or a change in price valuation of the entire 500 stocks comprising the S&P 500 index.
3. *Wall Street Journal,* May 10, 1991.
4. *Wall Street Journal,* June 27, 1991.
5. Mortage interest is deductible on equity loans up to $100,000.
6. *Wall Street Journal,* June 14, 1991, p. A5A.
7. *Harvard Business Review,* May–June 1991, p. 90.
8. Ronald Grzywinski, "The New Old, Fashioned Banking," *Harvard Business Review,* May–June 1991, p. 6.
9. Community Capital Bank, offering circular, October 20, 1989.

Chapter 7

1. *Wall Street Journal,* April 12, 1991, p. C–1.
2. *Los Angeles Times,* May 15, 1991.
3. *Wall Street Journal,* July 2, 1991, p. C–1.
4. *San Francisco Chronicle,* February 10, 1988.
5. *San Francisco Chronicle,* December 29, 1990.
6. *Wall Street Journal,* May 13, 1991.
7. *Wall Street Journal,* May 29, 1991.
8. "First Affirmative Financial Network: An Overview," 1991, Colorado Springs, CO.

9. "First Affirmative Financial Network," letter from Ed Winslow to author dated August 12, 1991, and *Responsible Investing News,* September 8, 1991, p. 3.

10. U.S. Trust Company, Asset Management Division, "Socially Sensitive Investing," 1991.

11. *Franklin's Insight,* "Social Assessment Ratings Key," January 17, 1992.

12. "Description of Services," Clean Yield Asset Management, Portsmouth, New Hampshire, 1991.

Chapter 8

1. Pax World Fund Inc., Investment Portfolio, June 30, 1991.

2. *BusinessWeek,* February 17, 1992, p. 76.

3. Dreyfus Third Century Fund, State of Investments, May 31, 1991.

4. *Mutual Fund Forecaster,* No. 84, January 1992, p. 1.

5. *The Better World Investment Guide,* p. 473.

6. Calvert Social Investment Fund Prospectus, January 1, 1991, p. 9.

7. *Ibid.,* pp. 9–10.

8. *Ibid.*

9. Calvert Social Investment Fund, Money Market Portfolio Fund, June 31, 1991, p. 104.

10. Calvert Social Investment Fund, Prospectus, January 1, 1991, p. 4.

11. *The Better World Investment Guide,* p. 472.

12. *Calvert Dialogue,* Calvert Group, Vol. 6, No. 7, July 1991, p. 2.

13. New Alternatives Fund Prospectus, March 15, 1991.

14. "NRDC Policy Regarding Geothermal Development on the Island of Hawaii," Press Release, March 15, 1990.

15. Muir California Tax-Free Bond Fund, Prospectus, June 12, 1991, p. 3.

16. News Release, Peter D. Kinder & Co., January 26, 1989.

17. Press Release, Kinder, Lydenberg, Domini & Co., Inc., August 2, 1991.

18. The Parnassus Fund, Prospectus, May 1, 1991, p. 5.

19. *Ibid.*

20. Portfolio Valuation, Progressive Environmental Fund, July 31, 1991.

21. Working Assets Money Fund Prospectus, November 1, 1990.

22. *Ibid.*

23. Working Assets Money Fund Prospectus, November 1, 1991, p. 2.

Chapter 9

1. CERES headquarters, 711 Atlantic Ave., Boston, MA 02111.

2. BASRIP News, Vol. IV, No. 2, June 30, 1991.

3. Scudder Stevens Clark, *The Socially Responsive Investor,* Cincinnati, Ohio, Spring 1991.

4. "Investor's Environmental Report," IRRC, Spring 1991, p. 9.

5. *Ibid.,* p. 11.

6. SFT Environmental Awareness was transferred to Penn Square Mutual on July 19, 1991. SFT is no longer in business.

7. Tim Redmond, "Wall Street's Environment Scam," *The San Francisco Bay Guardian,* March 14, 1990.

8. Earl Gottschalk, Jr., "Investments Promoted As Ecologically Clean Pop Up Like Weeds," *The Wall Street Journal,* April 10, 1990.

9. *Ibid.*

10. Michael Parrish, "Some 'Green' Investments Called Shams," *The Los Angeles Times,* March 15, 1990, p. D7.

11. Gottschalk, April 10, 1990.

12. Jeff Bailey, "Waste Disposal Giant, Often under Attack, Seems to Gain from It," *The Wall Street Journal,* May 1, 1991.

13. Redmond, p. 1.

14. Letter to John Schultz from Peter Camejo, dated June 12, 1990.

15. Global Environment Fund Limited Partnership Annual Report, December 31, 1990.

16. *Ibid.*

17. *Responsive Investing News,* August 19, 1991.

18. *Ibid.*

19. "Smithsonian Institutions News," Press Release, September 7, 1990.

20. "Fidelity Focus," Winter 1991.

21. Letter to author dated March 5, 1991 from Andrew W. Verhalen, vice-president and general manager, network adapter division, 3 Com Corp.

22. Udayan Gupta, "Financing Small Business: Growth Firms Plan to Boost Investments, Survey Finds," *Wall Street Journal,* October 22, 1991, p. B2.

23. Krystyna Strzelec, "Clean Air Act Boosts 'Green' Funds," *The Denver Post,* April 22, 1991, p. 13.

24. ©1974 Cat Music Ltd. Administered worldwide by Westbury Music Consultants, Ltd.

INDEX